D0287721

Writers and Rebels

FROM THE FABIAN BIOGRAPHICAL SERIES

Edited by MICHAEL KATANKA
Introduction by DAME MARGARET COLE

ROWMAN AND LITTLEFIELD
TOTOWA, NEW JERSEY

First published in the United States 1976
by ROWMAN AND LITTLEFIELD, Totowa, N.J.

Copyright © 1976
Charles Knight & Company Limited

ISBN 0 87471 697 7

Printed in Great Britain

FOREWORD

THE FABIAN BIOGRAPHICAL SERIES consisting of short biographies
of pioneer radicals, socialists and social reformers has been in
constant demand since the first tract was published in October,
1912. Some of the early tracts were reprinted again and again,
but for many years the whole of the series has been out of print.
Nor has it been possible, except rarely, to obtain them from
secondhand bookshops where occasional copies, listed in cata-
logues, have fetched high prices as collectors' items. Very few
libraries have sets as this is the first time they are available in
book form.

There were 15 pamphlets in the original series. In this volume
there are studies of Jeremy Bentham, William Cobbett, Richard
Carlile, John Stuart Mill, John Ruskin, Charles Kingsley and
William Morris. The others were published in a previous volume
under the title *Radicals, Reformers and Socialists*.

Eminent writers and historians, including G. D. H. and M. I.
Cole, St. John G. Ervine, Mrs. Barbara Hammond, Kingsley
Martin, C. E. Vulliamy and Edith Morley and others, were
commissioned to write the series and the quality of their work
was such that subsequent full-length works were able to add but
little which had not already been touched upon in these essays.
Indeed, on Place, Lovett, the Webbs and Carlile, there have
been no full length studies published since these pamphlets were
first written.

For greater legibility the originals have been re-set in new
type but apart from the correction of a few misprints and
obvious errors, nothing has been changed. We have retained,
for example, the form of spelling favoured by Mr. George
Standring, the printer of many Fabian publications. We have,
however, added new bibliographies for each essay and notes on
contributors.

In preparing this volume we have been fortunate in having
the advice and co-operation of Dame Margaret Cole, President

of the Fabian Society. Her lively introduction places these essays firmly in their Fabian background. Tom Ponsonby, General Secretary of the Fabian Society has been enthusiastic and helpful from the beginning. Edmund Frow has supplied elusive texts from his vast collection.

M.K.

CONTENTS

Margaret Cole

I INTRODUCTION

It was late in 1912 that the Fabian Society, then 28 years old brought out the first of its new series of *Tracts*—Biographical Tracts—of which 15 appeared between then and 1955 : all but one are reproduced in these volumes. The time needed for the writing and printing of these Tracts meant, obviously, that the decision to launch out in this line must have been taken some time previously; and in fact it was not unconnected with the period of sudden growth and inner turbulence in the Society, of which the first part was described by Edward Pease, its official historian, as 'The Episode of Mr. Wells', and which, in my *Story of Fabian Socialism,* I called 'The Second Blooming'— the first 'blooming' having taken place nearly 20 years before, after the publication of *Fabian Essays.*

The radical revival which was so startlingly manifested in the general election of 1906 brought something like 2,000 or 3,000 new recruits to the Fabian Society—'the *little boom*', as Beatrice Webb correctly if patronisingly described it—but they tended to be recruits of a rather different stamp from those who had been admitted, after careful scrutiny by the Executive, in earlier years. Many of them were young. They were restive and critical, anxious to transform the Society in one way or another, to widen its scope, to force it to take up attitudes and enter upon activities not hitherto contemplated. In the first clash, as all social historians know well, the rebels lined up under the banner of H. G. Wells, whose lively memorandum, *The Faults of the Fabian,* loudly demanded that Fabians should cease to be a grubby collection of coral-insects endeavouring to build a new world unseen, but should learn to think big and talk big, move into large bright offices and produce large bright publications on all the burning issues—in short, modernise and make a splash in the world. Wells lost his battle, defeated, as he himself admitted in later years, largely through his own incapacity to handle a public meeting when self-pitted against such formidably-equipped adversaries as Bernard Shaw and Sidney Webb. After a brief period of recrimination he stormed out of the Society and showered abuse on its Old Gang in the pages of that rather over-lengthy political novel, *The New Machiavelli*. But, as Shaw pointed out to Beatrice Webb in a letter—in which he was later reinforced by the very near victory of those superior and more persistent tacticians the Guild Socialists, only a few years after-wards—the victory of the Old Gang was really only a paper victory, for the membership largely sympathised with what Wells was trying to do, even though it could not honestly support his detailed and wildly impracticable proposals. Realising this, in the years immediately following, the Society, as well as putting into effect one or two minor changes in organisation (and for the first time declaring itself in favour of votes for women), began to widen its scope somewhat; a Fabian Arts Group made its appearance, and several local Fabian dramatic societies—and the Biographical Tracts attesting new interest in the human side of radical history. To mark the occasion as a new departure —and also to draw the sting of a motion that 'the appearance of Fabian publications be made less repellent'—the new series was equipped with covers containing portraits of its subjects, and a penny added to the selling price.

The series started well, with five studies appearing in the first 14 months. But then came the war, and most of the potential Fabian writers both Left and Right were engulfed in it, if not in the armed forces themselves, then as administrators or in course of time as opponents. The two Tracts which appeared while the war was on show a clear falling-off; one, indeed (No. 7) is so slight and has so little relevance to the main purpose of the series that it has been excluded from this reprint. Only when the war and the post-war turmoil were safely over was the series resumed with three more important Tracts. One, however, was not specially written, but was the printed text of a lecture given by G. D. H. Cole which, though its subject, William Cobbett, had little that was Fabian about him, signified the author's reconciliation, after the collapse of the Building Guilds and the eclipse for a very long while of the doctrines of Guild Socialism and workers' control, with his former antagonists of the Old Guard. The two other Tracts of the twenties, on William Lovett and Tom Paine, were excellent value, but there was only a faint revival of the Fabian Society to support them.

With the rise, and subsequent crash, of the Labour Party and the conversion of the Webb Partnership to whole-hearted interest in and devotion to the principles and practice of Soviet Communism, the Society entered the long period of inertia from which it was only rescued, on the verge of a new world war, by amalgamation with the vigorous group of younger men and women which called itself the New Fabian Research Bureau, and from whom sprang so many of the parliamentarians and civil servants of the wartime coalition and of the Labour Government of 1945. The unquestioned leader in the regenerated Society was G. D. H. Cole, for so many years its chairman; so one is not surprised to find that the resumption of the series between 1941 and 1943 consisted of just three Tracts from that prolific pen. Finally, after the war was over, the Webb Partnership safely in Westminster Abbey and the Labour Government already fallen, Margaret Cole contributed *Beatrice and Sidney Webb,* the 15th and last of the Tracts.

There were no more, which is sad, for they sold well, and as a whole were very helpful to the reader, well-written by persons who had troubled to get up their subjects properly if they did not know them well already; they have dated little and contain a good deal which is still apposite, even after the passage of 60 years of violent change in society. This is not, of course, equally true of all of them; a small struggling society with scanty financial resources, as the Fabian Society has always been, cannot carry out a completely ordered plan of publication, but must depend, both for subject and for author, on the willingness and availability of writers to carry out the original design.

In this particular series, the intention was to choose subjects whose life and work would have a particular appeal to Fabian Socialists and those whom they hoped to enrol or to influence; and the first, in which St. John Ervine, the Edwardian dramatist who later published the best, so far, biography of Bernard Shaw, studied that masterly Radical, wire-puller, Francis Place, 'The Tailor of Charing Cross', fulfilled that intention admirably. Place, though he came from a much lower stratum and had

known real degrading poverty, might almost have sat as a model
for Sidney Webb, so far as his political energies were concerned;
and Ervine is at pains to drive this home. 'An Early Victorian
Fabian', he calls him, one of the men who came after the first
pioneers and built upon their faith without ever despising them
for their errors; and he describes him as 'full of rare courage
and rare faith'—sentiments which in his later disillusioned years
Ervine might well have felt like revising. His Tract does not, of
course, go deeply into the vast mass of personal material in
the British Museum which is known as the Place MSS; but the
vividly-told story of the organisational effort which led to the
1824 repeal of the Combination Acts and prevented their reim-
position in the following year might well carry lessons for trade
union leaders of the present day. Technology may have helped
striking miners to produce a much more rapid effect on the
economy, but it does not appear to have had any comparable
effect on the abilities of trade union organisers to plan
campaigns.

The subject of the second of the Tracts, Beatrice Hutchins's
Robert Owen, is a less obvious candidate, whose inclusion some
would actually find surprising. The last 35 years of Owen's long
life, from the settlement of New Harmony in Indiana through
the co-operative and trade union boom and crash at the beginning of the 1830s to the millennial aberrations of its closing years,
suggest anything rather than Fabianism. But those latter years
were not covered by the Fabian Tract at all, which confined
itself, as the sub-title states clearly, to *Robert Owen, Social
Reformer.* (A footnote promised a supplement on Owen's later
life, which did appear as *Robert Owen, Idealist*; but this was so
sketchy and so largely concerned with experiments other than
Owen's, that it has not been included in this collection.) As Social
Reformer, however, Owen's claim is clear. In his brain, and in
part in his practice, he pioneered, almost all the ideas of social
reformers for generations to come; in such diverse spheres as
school education, its purpose, content, and method, state training
of teachers, the proper attitude towards children and criminals,
town planning and garden cities and communal services, high
wages, short hours, factory conditions, the use of leisure, the
reform of the Poor Law and the prevention of unemployment,
his suggestions were so far in advance of his own day that some

are still awaiting implementation even in our own. Beatrice
Hutchins, co-author of the then standard history of factory
legislation, was eminently fitted to describe them; and though
her account of Owen's personal history needs supplementation
from recent research into the finance of his various businesses,
including New Lanark, the main picture stands today.

The inclusion of *John Stuart Mill*, by Julius West, first secretary of the Fabian Research Committee and later one of the
historians of Chartism, as No. 4 in the series, needs no justification. Mill was undoubtedly a Fabian born prematurely,
unfortunate to have died 10 years too early to have been one of
the founding fathers. Some of his observations, such as that the
Combination Laws were 'enacted and maintained for the
declared purpose of keeping wages low', and that 'what is called
morality in these times is a regulated sensuality' have a remarkable modern ring. He was ahead of his Utilitarian friends—and
anticipatory of Bernard Shaw—in finding the problem of poverty
fundamental to his social thought; and the very opposite fact
that the father of Sidney Webb helped in his election campaign
in Westminster only points the moral.

The third Tract, however, on William Morris, shows quite
clearly that in this Second Blooming there were two classes of
Fabian 'heroes'. Mrs. Emily Townshend was not a young Rebel,
but a lady of past middle age, whose daughter was married to a
young manager of one of the Liberal government's newly-created
Labour Exchanges; but she was heart and soul with G. D. H.
Cole and William Mellor in their revolt. The Tract on Morris,
with its eulogistic appraisal of him as 'the greatest Englishman
who has passed out of our ranks', with his *Pilgrims of Hope* as
a magnificent poem which 'will kindle warm interest in our
great-grandchildren', could only have been written by a fervent
Guild Socialist; and it goes so far as to describe Morris's joining
the Fabian Society as 'a kind of death-bed repentance', adding
that if he had lived into the new century he would assuredly
have been a Syndicalist—a remark calculated to give the maximum annoyance to the Fabian elders. (The younger ones enjoyed
it: it ran through five editions.) C. E. Vulliamy's *Charles
Kingsley and Christian Socialism*, which was the last of the first
batch, also derives from the Guild Socialist arguments. Kingsley
was not anything approaching a Fabian, and the Christian

Socialist movement of the mid-nineteenth century was neither
long-lived nor of great importance in its history. But the Anglican
social reformers of the next reign, members of the Church
Socialist League, men like J. N. Figgis, the author of *Church and
State,* or Conrad Noel, the Red Vicar of Thaxted in Essex, found
that the philosophy of Guild Socialism, with its emphasis on
functional autonomy for guilds of producers, chimed in very well
with their own views for the future of the churches. So Kingsley
enters the pantheon. The sixth Tract, in which Professor Edith
Morley wrote on *John Ruskin and Social Ethics,* is also a trifle
eclectic. The Fabians had never got 'on terms' with Ruskin.
They had to admit, because it was a fact, that his ideas, and the
torrent of eloquence in which he expressed them, had played a
great part in the 'climate of thought' of radicals—working-class
as well as middle-class radicals, many of whom went out of their
way to acknowledge a deep debt to Ruskin without being quite
certain what it was; but they did not really see why this should
be so, and were cross about it—and for Ruskin for not being, as
he clearly ought to have been, a socialist, but at best a sociologist,
before sociology became a proud profession. Yet, surely, Ruskin's
conviction that one cannot separate economic man from
emotional man, and his insistence that proper consumption was
a field of legitimate study, and that consumption must be clearly
distinguished from fatal and disgusting 'covetousness', was well
worth the attention of bright young Fabians—as indeed it still is
today. But the Fabians, as a whole, did not take to it—not
because they knew much about the storms of Ruskin's own personal life, which had not in 1916 been disclosed in detail, but
because they resented his general attitude; and this may account
for a slight defensiveness in Professor Morley's treatment of her
subject, a slight over-enthusiasm. She calls him, for example,
'the pioneer of technical education'—an encomium more suited
to Prince Albert; and ascribes to his influence 'almost every
modern measure of social improvement', a staggering assertion
which in time of peace would certainly have been resisted by
critics within the Society. It is a measure of its catholicity, perhaps, that the Tract was published.

   In the twenties, however, orderly progress was resumed. Tract
9, on Cobbett, has already been mentioned, and however explo-
sively Cobbett's ghost would have reacted if it had found itself

in the company of Fabians, whom he would certainly have classed with the 'feelthy philosophers' of the *Edinburgh Review,* there can be no doubt about his status as a radical pioneer. *William Lovett* (No. 8) and *Tom Paine* (No. 10), are both very competent pieces of work, the one written by Barbara Hammond, whose historical reputation as co-author of *The Village Labourer* and *The Town Labourer* was unimpeachable, and the other by the young Kingsley Martin, six years away from becoming the unexpected editor of the *New Statesman,* but already an eager and vivid writer on radical socialism. Modern research has added little to the picture of Lovett, Fabian alike in his tactics and his enthusiasm for education; as to Paine, the man whose journalism upheld one group of successful revolutionaries in the dark days of Valley Forge, who was elected to the directing Committee of another in Paris, and who first demanded that the State should regulate the rights and relationships of property—Paine was so much the epitome of radical social-democracy, its programmes and its hoped-for practice, that it is only surprising that he was not included earlier. Victor Cohen's *Jeremy Bentham* is a slightly more off-beat choice. It may have been partly influenced by the rude remarks which the author of the Mill pamphlet had made about Bentham : but though he would not have been pleased to be called a Socialist, Bentham's mode of thought, his mathematical calculations, his continuous inventiveness of social devices and of neologisms like 'international' which are now deeply embedded in the speech of all countries, clearly foreshadows the coining by the Webbs a century later of the phrase *'Measurement and Publicity'* as a suitable motto for the Labour movement.

The productions of the last phase mirror clearly G. D. H. Cole's leadership in the revived Society : the choice of subjects is his, and the evident erudition his. Here then is Keir Hardie, at the time the unquestioned onlie begetter of the Labour Party itself and of Labour in Parliament, waging a continuous battle with moderate unimaginative trade union leaders on the one hand, and 'no-compromise' socialists of *Tribune* type on the other, and establishing a compromise which according to his biographer here may not have been 'correct' but was assuredly the only course possible at the time. Hardie's language, with its strong reminiscence of his Biblical upbringing dates today—though the descriptions of poverty quoted in Tract 12 still have power to

make the blood boil—and more is known today about his
tactical (and practical) discussions with prominent Liberals; but
the picture of the man the very mention of whose name, many
years after his death, had the emotional power to make a Labour
meeting to rise to its feet in homage or protest against attempts at
innovation in the Labour Party, remains effectively unimpaired.

There follows Richard Carlile—the bookseller and publisher
who claimed with some but not complete truth that with his
printing of Tom Paine's work he had single-handed won the
battle for the free press, and whom we might well celebrate today
for his dictum that the common law in reality is 'judge-made
abuse'—and John Burns. John Burns, the 'lost leader', the first
man who had worked with his hands (at Price's Candle Factory
in Battersea) to become a cabinet minister, the man who earned
working-class hatred by 'dishing the Webbs' over poor law
reform, the only character of the 15 to have a really hostile biography written by a member of his own side (Joseph Burgess of
the *Workman's Times*); John Burns the red-faced white-hatted
traitor who for so many years after he had abandoned national
politics out of principle in August, 1914, maintained that he
might soon come back to lead a working-class party 'without
any of Hyndman's nonsense'. Yes John Burns was a real leader,
in politics as well as in industry, not just a waxwork in Madame
Tussaud's, but the first trade union leader since the days of
Owen who had performed the indispensable task of catching the
public eye, with the 'silver gleam of the docker's tanner'; and
his life, inexcusably neglected by later historians, could be an
important subject of study.

The Webbs were the last to be chronicled. The fifteenth of the
Tracts is rather different from the rest in that it was written and
appeared only a few years after Bernard Shaw's insistent propaganda and the existence of the first Labour government with
a clear majority had laid the Partnership to rest under the flags
of Westminster Abbey—where Ernest Bevin was so soon to be
laid beside them. Beatrice had died President of the revived
Fabian Society : there was therefore no need to remind the membership of the Webbs' existence or even to argue their importance.
They were still living forces, whereas Burns, though he died in the
same year as Beatrice, had been for nearly 30 years, as G. D. H.
Cole had written 'an historical monument rather than a man';

the job of their author then was rather to sort out and present in handy and significant form the main items of their multifarious works and days. This, since their scope was so wide and their energy so shattering, inevitably involved compression and omission; but Beatrice's Diaries, opened after her death, provided so great a mass of contemporary information that the only really fresh story which has come to light since the Tract was published is the magnificently machiavellian—and Fabian to the nth degree—Saga of the Hutchinson Trust, of the way in which Sidney clandestinely converted Hutchinson's legacy to the setting up of a School of Economics and Political Science—an idea of which the testator could hardly have dreamed—and of the host of pump-priming and camouflaging devices whereby he fed and nourished the struggling infant until it became the formidable institution which is called the L.S.E.

With this Tract the series once more comes to an end—a misfortune, to my mind. For taking account the intention of the series, there are a good number of other characters whose names cry out for inclusion : Robert Blatchford of the *Clarion,* Feargus O'Connor, H. G. Wells, George Lansbury, a founding Co-operator less idiosyncratic than Owen, Arthur Henderson, Ernest Bevin, Tom Mann, to take only a few examples. Even granting that Shaw has been over-written and that Ramsay MacDonald may still be too dangerous a proposition, short studies of these men and any of half-a-dozen others who could be mentioned would be welcomed by embryo Socialists. But they will have to wait a long while and pay a good deal more for their construction. For the reason for the stop was not, as some have conjectured, that the Society could not go beyond its founders : rather it was that the proliferation, just beginning in the fifties, of university departments of social history with their courses, degrees and diplomas, and even more, as time went on, of research theses financially grant-aided and painstakingly compiled with the object of obtaining doctorates and therewith advancement in the profession, has radically changed the pattern of publication. To-day, the brief narrative and characterising biography has all too often given place to the learned monograph, weighed down with detailed library and museum references and swelled out with huge footnotes and lengthy quotations from tape-recordings or contemporary newspapers or other documents recently unearthed

—the whole gritty mass costing three or four pounds to buy. It seems a pity.

It was the end, however; and all that remains for one re-reading the whole at the present time, is to add one or two general comments. What must strike everyone at first reading is—how little these apostles of brotherly love loved one another. Were there a Valhalla for Radicals, they would hardly have fraternised happily in its halls—nor would many of the others who might have been included. Burns and Hardie, when both were M.P.s, despised and disliked each other; Robert Owen thought the Benthamites, including Place, poor misguided fellows who based the whole of their philosophic system upon a misapprehension; Place found Owen an amiable impossibilist, Lovett found him overbearing, and Cobbett called him 'a beastly writer'. Few of his contemporaries could put up with Cobbett for long, and he poured abuse on Tom Paine until, having abruptly changed his own political views, in rather flamboyant repentance he brought Paine's bones back to his native land—where they were lost. Carlile had an obscure but fierce quarrel with William Hetherington; H. G. Wells thought the Webbs wicked intriguing old spoilsports, and they found him an irresponsible ill-mannered libertine. And so it goes on. Those who to-day deplore the seeming desire of Socialist propagandists to prove to the world at large that the vast majority of Labour and trade union politicians are fools or liars or traitors or all three, should look back on the records; it has happened before.

Yet it was not quite the same—at least, reading the story again, I do not feel that it was. Through all the recriminations of the past one seems to catch a sense of common purpose commonly felt, a consciousness that we are all really driving to one end, and that the aberrationists, by whatever names it was necessary (and desirable!) to call them, were in the last resort mistaken rather than damned, and might easily be—as often they were—reconciled with their antagonists when the scene changed. This is what camp-followers and rank-and-file workers meant when they spoke of 'the Movement'. The word is not popular with recent historians, some of whom have been busy pecking at it, Namier-wise, until they have proved that, as it lacks definition, it must have lacked existence also—that it was a sentimental fantasy as much as *News from Nowhere*. But it was not; there was no fantasy in the way in which Arthur Henderson, a tough Trade Union politician if ever there was one, used to refer to 'our great movement', which he served with faith and conviction until his death. Much of what has been written recently on the history of the Labour Party and other working-class organisations seems to suggest that the writers (unlike John Ruskin) have no grasp of the emotional content of the word—it may be that one of the results of technological development is to destroy it altogether, which would also be a pity. Meantime, these short lives remain readably attestant to it.

MARGARET COLE

Victor Cohen

2 JEREMY BENTHAM 1748–1832

THE WAY TO BE HAPPY is to make others happy, the way to make others happy is to appear to love them, the way to appear to love them is to love them really.' So wrote the chief exponent of the utilitarian creed, Jeremy Bentham.

He was born in the year 1748 in Red Lion Street, Hounsditch. In his boyhood he displayed unusual zest for learning, and his precocity offered his father hope of seeing his son on the woolsack. Later in life he delighted to recall how before he was breeched he had run home from an aimless walk and installed himself in a huge chair to read Rapin's History of England. But he found that it was a history of throat cutting on the largest scale for the sake of plunder, the throat cutting and plundering being placed at the summit of virtues. He recalled his early 'pain of sympathy'. He began at the age of three to learn French under the tutorship of M. La Combe d'Avigon, with whom he read Fenelon's Télémaque. His father had carefully kept from him any diverting book. His study list was excessively dull; Télémaque consequently had an early and strong influence on his receptive mind.

When he was seven years old he was sent to a typical 18th century scholastic penitentiary, Westminster School. He found little happiness here. 'The instruction was wretched; the fagging system was a horrid despotism; the games he found beyond his strength.' In spite of his diminutive size, his ability inspired respect and enabled him to escape the birch. Already young Jeremy was known as the 'Philosopher', and his delighted father pompously indicated to him the path to greatness : 'If you mean to rise catch hold of the skirts of those above you and care nothing for those who are beneath you.'

At the age of 12, he left Westminster, and following the

routine canalised by ease he entered as commoner in one of the most exclusive and consequently one of the idlest colleges at Oxford—Queens. His strictures on Oxford but corroborate the accounts of Wesley, Adam Smith, and Gibbon. 'The mornings, he noted, were spent in useless routine, the evenings in playing cards.' He found the streets of Oxford 'paved with perjury', for although he was excused the oaths to the Church of England University on account of his youth, he felt the insincerity bitterly, and his whole mental outlook was seared by the sight of several Methodists being expelled their colleges for the crime of heresy. He took his degree in 1763, and in the same year he began to eat his dinners at Lincoln's Inn. But his repugnance to the legal profession was soon apparent, and the boy of 15 returned to Oxford to listen to Blackstone, the holder of the newly created Venerian Professorship of Law, as he was dilating on the glory of the British Constitution. He obtained his M.A. in 1767, and then left for London to begin his triumphal march to the Woolsack. His career at Oxford had been remarkably devoid of incident. As a lawyer his failure was even more glaring. His ambitious and hectoring father heard with bitter annoyance that he had converted his chambers into a laboratory, that he was studying chemistry with Dr. Fordyce, and that he was courting 'Prœtus' Priestley, the discoverer of oxygen. It was nevertheless to this combination of such apparent opposites as Physical Science and Law, that Bentham owes his place in the niche of Law Reformers. It was his interpretation of Politics in terms of Newtonian Physics that supplied him with a method which proved so fatal to the blundering optimism of the 18th Century Governors of England.

Till well in the seventies Jeremy but reflected the leisured and wealthy class into which he was born. The '45 was still a romantic and loyal memory. In his babyhood, amidst Jacobite surroundings, he had learnt to worship at the shrine of Charles the Martyr, and to regard loyalty and virtue as interchangeable terms. He wrote a sonnet on the death of George II which was praised by the Tory oracle of the period, Dr. Johnson. He espoused the cause of royalty against the attack of Junius; he hounded down Wilkes, and when a darker cloud appeared on the horizon, the truculent and rebellious attitude of the American Colonies, Jeremy Bentham, with his friend John Lind, again took up the cause of royalty and authority in a 'Review of the Acts of the thirteenth Parliament in 1775'. Nevertheless the Tory ne'er do well was not an idle dilettante. By judicious study he became the intellectual legatee of the 18th century; for he focused in himself its philosophy, its scientific optimism, its individualism and its anti-clericalism. Instead of carving for himself a brilliant legal career he began questioning the very assumptions of political life, and his despairing father found in him not a prop and a potential pillar of society but a hardy and dangerous innovator. He received his son's appeal with paternal resignation. 'In the track I am in I march with alacrity and hope; in any other I should crawl on with despondence and reluctance', and so Jeremy quitted the profession he hated, to add lustre to it by his zealous reform.

18TH CENTURY POLICIES

The 18th Century has a numbing sense of void after the vitality of the 17th, for its tolerance was the result of apathy and not of conviction, and even its sympathy had to seek a selfish veneer. It began with an assertion of the contractual nature of Government, and it ended with struggle to assert natural rights. Yet never were the logical consequences of these assumptions more openly violated. 'Everything for the people, and nothing by them' was the maxim of Frederick the Great and Bishop Horsley echoed : 'The people have nothing to do with the laws but to obey them.' The English as pioneers in tyrannicide were aggressively proud of their 'Matchless Constitution' created by a 'Glorious Rebellion', and its praise by Montesquieu and De Lolme confirmed them in the self righteous optimism which made any reform hopeless. For in theory the English constitution was the only legitimate one in existence. It alone was based on a sacred contract of King and People; it made provision for the Separation of Powers which was the only true guarantee of liberty; it gave sanction to the Natural Rights of Life, Liberty and Property, which were the *raison d'etre* of every true government. Criticism both sound and cynical had already begun to undermine this elaborate structure. De Lolme had pointed out the ease with which interested apologists confused the actual with the ideal. The cynical and corrupt Fox had sneeringly remarked how the Right to Rebellion, the very basis of the Constitution, had to be presented as potentially possible to the Governors alone, for to the governed it had to be made impossible. Above all the sceptical and corrosive mind of Hume had taken an unnatural delight in destroying what was at once an intellectual error and a Whig fetish.

But the Century of Individual Rights was also the Century of Enlightened Despotism. Bolingbroke's Patriot King, stripped of the selfish motive which inspired its author, was the pale and attenuated replica of the Philosophic Autocrats of the age.

Government was for and not by the people, but Englishmen in no way accepted the political creed of Tyranny. If the tradition of Locke and its new version by Rousseau showed, in Acton's words, that 'not the devil but St. Thomas Aquinas was the first Whig' an indigenous English historical school, led by Cartwright and Benjamin Vaughan, Hollis and Sawbridge, opposed the Divine Right of Kings with the Divine Right of the Individual and appealed to historical precedent to justify the concrete liberties of Englishmen as opposed to the Natural Liberty of Man. But a long period of office had converted even the Whig Party to an unquestioned acceptance of the *status quo* and, by a swing of the party pendulum, George III had brought to power their rivals, who, if they had given up their idol, had not abandoned their idolatry.

In the background of these conflicting theories the Industrial and Agrarian Revolutions were changing the face of England, and these gave force to the mechanical and optimistic outlook which pervaded the Age. Man was at last controlling nature; he could measure its forces, and subordinate it to his purpose. Why should he not extend the same mental attitude to the Social Sciences? The legislator would then be akin to the inventor, for he could control the individual through his egoism, he could mould Society through its self seeking. Benthamism consists in the application of mechanical formulae to the solution of the problems of Ethics and Politics.

If these were the main forces acting on Bentham, his wide reading supplied him with the mental equipment, which enabled him to translate a vague influence into a dynamic force. For he was above all a synchronistic thinker, a genius in method, rather than an innovator in ideas. From Helvetius he adopted the conception that Man as a moral being was the product of the social

atmosphere of the society to which he belonged. But, insisted
Bentham, Who created this social atmosphere? Was it not the
Legislator? By rewards and punishments he could evoke such
conduct as he desired. The Lawgiver moulded human behaviour
and harmonised human passions for the public good. With Law
so potent, Bentham early aspired to create good laws in order to
make good men.

The growing humanity of the 'Brutal Century' no less
influenced him. The sympathy which sought expression in the
anti-slavery agitation and in the growing care of the poor, in
the desire to reform the prisons and to soften the rigours of the
criminal law, he felt intensely. But his creed opposed any structure based on so subjective a foundation as pity. Beccaria
supplied him with the requisite test. The reason for the cruelty
of criminal legislation was that it was based on the principle of
sympathy and antipathy. Men were punished according to no
logical scale of values, but simply because their crimes were
hated. But each man hated different crimes with a different
intensity. If public welfare were taken as the aim and standard
of punishment then barbarity would disappear from law, and
crime would be punished with mathematical accuracy according
as it retarded much or little the social good.

Priestley and Hume taught him that the aim of government
was the greatest good of the greatest number. This gave him the
clue to the labyrinth of law. No longer was it to be 'learning'
painfully acquired. It was to become a Science, having a few
rigid axioms on which government could be easily constructed.
Thoroughly secular in outlook, he threw overboard every theological assumption as to the origin and destiny of society. Hating
complexity as the ally of confused thinking, he at once discarded
the English dispensations of a Mixed Constitution and a Division
of Powers. Obsessed with the Ideal of Utility, he swept away the
Theory of Contract, as being untenable historically and useless
philosophically. Government ought to be built on the foundation, the greatest good of the greatest number.

His acute mind had at once seen through Blackstone's pene-
gyric, but only after a long delay did there appear in 1776 his
'Fragment on Government', a penetrating criticism of the
'Commentaries'. Blackstone, he contended, had carried the
ingenuity of the hireling advocate into the chair of a Professor.

That his criticisms were forceful was universally recognised, and rumour at once ascribed the book to the greatest legal intellects of the time, to Camden, to Mansfield. But his father, glad beyond control that the erudition of his son was at last receiving public recognition, proclaimed his authorship. Immediately the author and the book sank back to obscurity, and Bentham again busied himself with his reading and experiments till, five years later, Lord Shelbourne called upon the author of the 'Fragments' to invite him to Bowood, a great and historic centre of English political life.

Patronage was dying, mortally wounded by the courageous letter of Dr. Johnson to Lord Chesterfield. Bentham, moreover, had little need of the patronage of wealth. There was, therefore, little of servility in the relationship between these two men. He was nevertheless deeply grateful. At Bowood he met the great political figures of the age—Camden, Mansfield, Dunning, Pitt, Price, Romilly, a powerful group whom he hoped to indoctrinate with the creed of utility. He was surprised, however, to meet with such vehement opposition. A Tory, he thought that he had only to tell the governors the good they could do, for them to carry it out. But his doctrine, in the words of Leslie Stephen, 'seemed to some a barren truism, to others, a mere epigram, and to some a dangerous falsehood', and feeling helpless to break the complacency of his countrymen, in 1783, he left for Russia, where his brother Samuel was working on the estates of Prince Potemkin at Critchoff. A failure as he apparently was, he nevertheless dreamed of himself as the founder of Scientific Legislation. 'What Bacon was to the physical world, Helvetius was to the Moral; the Moral world has therefore had its Bacon, but its Newton was yet to come.' Bentham aspired to fill the gap. He spent two years in Russia elaborating his ideas. Under the spur of Pitt's revenue schemes, he sent home his 'Defence of Usury', which extorted the high encomium of his master Adam Smith. It was only on the earnest appeal of one of his early disciples, George Wilson, stating that a Churchman and Dean of Carlyle (Paley) had plagiarised his ideas in his 'Principles of Moral and Political Philosophy' that Bentham returned, and in 1789, on the very eve of the Revolution, there appeared his Magnum Opus, 'An Introduction to the Principles of Morals and Legislation'.

BENTHAM AND THE FRENCH REVOLUTION

The French Revolution has been treated either as a hysterical outburst of passion or as an organised conspiracy against Society. Yet the passion and faith of France in travail sent sympathetic thrills through Europe and traditional English party life was submerged in the emotions it raised. The Whigs, now a party without a creed, joined the Tories in defence of the past, and when an infectious logic reared in Britain and Edinburgh and a London Convention, Whigs and Tories became allies in defence of present wrongs. Burke became the prophet of reaction, and England the prop of monarchy and obscurantism. Pitt and Panic governed the realm. Bentham had no love for the past. With Voltaire he agreed that history was but a record of human folly and human wrong; with Raynal that no people can be free, if it respected the memory of its chains. He believed intensely in new beginnings. He saw in Revolution no sin against organic continuity. Tory although he was, he sympathised with the French. But to the calm calculator of human weakness, the impassioned oratory of the New Assembly was itself offensive. In vain he pointed out the difficulty of building a social structure on Natural Rights; the example of America and the teaching of Rousseau had made this the political orthodoxy of the period, and Bentham was disregarded. Above all, his legal training, his Tory sympathies and the teaching of Hume, had instilled into him a reverent respect for Security. Bentham saw the distinctive index of civilisation in order. The French found the cry of order and security, the swan song of threatened privilege and wrong. Bentham turned away in despair from his new hope, and opened his house as a hospice for French refugees. But in spite of his passive hostility he yet saw in France the most opportune field for his social experiments. England had been an encouraging culture for mechanical invention in search of wealth, but the 'deep slumber of a decided opinion' had rendered social invention impossible. Politics have even ceased to be, in the words of Maine, 'an eternal cricket match between blue and yellow', for the frenzy of Burke had infected both party teams, and coercive acts made slumber a patriotic duty.

To France, Bentham turned in hope. To La Rochefaucauld, to Mirabeau, to Brissot, he sent tract after tract. His 'Essay on Representation' was followed by one on 'Political Tactics'.

This was succeeded by a 'Project of a Code for the organisation of the Judicial System of France'. This again by a 'Project on the Panopticon', and lastly an appeal, 'Emancipate your Colonies'. The young Benthamite circle under Romilly drew up an 'Essay on Procedure for the use of the National Assembly'. But the reply of awakened Nationalism was decisive. 'Nous ne sommes pas des Anglais, et nous n'avons besoin des Anglais.' With the amiable simplicity of the recluse he offered to become the unpaid gaoler of France during the Reign of Terror if only he could experiment with his new pet prison, the Panopticon; but Madam La Guillotine beat him in open competition. The star of Rousseau outshone that of Bentham. Natural Rights still overshadowed utility. But the French were not ungrateful. Having thrown the head of a King as a challenge to European kingship, they were thankful for any helpful gesture, and in 1792 they accorded to Bentham, 'the benefactor of the human race', the title of French Citizen.

He had now reached middle age, and except to a small legal circle he was almost unknown. The wave of Revolution had engulfed his doctrine. Chief Justices Braxfield and Eyre had declared it treasonable to question the divine perfection of the English Constitution; the French had responded to the warm rays of justice and equity, and had been unmoved by the cold although luminous appeal of egoism and utility. Most men would have been content to enjoy passively the mundane delights of good health and financial ease. But Bentham's inventive faculty gave him no peace. He turned again to the English Government with wonderful schemes of domestic utility and legal simplification. In 1795 he sent to the Ministry his 'Protest against the Law Taxes'. To the boast that the English Law Courts were open to all, Horne Tooke had retorted that like the tavern they were open to all who could pay. Bentham desired to remove this stain from English justice and to prevent lawyers becoming merely fee gatherers. In the same year he propounded a scheme of Death Duties in his pamphlet, 'Escheat versus Taxation'. In 1797 he sent to Arthur Young's Annals of Agriculture a solution of the Poor Law Problem which later found expression in the Poor Law of 1834. In 1798 he was busy with Colquhoun drafting a scheme for the reform of the London Police. In 1799 he came out with a scheme, which he submitted

to Cobbett's Peter Porcupine, on the Population Bill, the suggestions of which were adopted in the following year in taking
the first Census. An astonishing fertility in mechanical and social
invention on the basis of the 'greatest happiness principle' was
his inexhaustible gift and peculiar contribution to society. In
1830, two years before his death, Talleyrand paid the com-
pliment to his intellectual resources, 'Though all the world has
stolen from him he remains still rich'.

HIS PHILOSOPHY

Bentham's philosophy possesses the symmetry and narrowness
of simplicity. In the common man he found the source of all
social action, and for the common man he erected the social
structure of the State. He dismissed as mysticism the idea that
society was anything but a collection of individuals. It possessed
no entity of its own, no purpose of its own, no idea of its own,
apart from the individuals who composed it. The ultimate unit
was always the individual, to whom tradition or social purpose
was remote in comparison with his desire for pleasure and his
avoidance of pain. Seeing in the individual the source of all
endeavour and the hope of all improvement, Bentham was led
to an analysis of his mentality. Upon this psychological assumption he erected his ethical and legal edifice. He begins, in his
'Introduction to Morals and Legislation', 'Nature has placed
mankind under the governance of two sovereign masters, pain
and pleasure. It is for them alone to point out what we ought
to do as well as to determine what we shall do. . . .' Consequently he deduced, 'Those acts are good which cause pleasure,
those acts are bad which cause pain. . . . No motive is in itself
either moral or immoral; all human instincts are equally natural.'
The different valuations placed on loyalty and treachery, greed
and charity, love and hate, are based on no common objective
standard. Men are by nature egoists, therefore on egoism is
society to be built. There is a positive and objective science of
mind, and on this government is to be erected. There was
equally a Science of Law, the aim of which was the greatest
happiness of the greatest number. The *raison d'etre* of every
legislative act is its utility. By careful mathematical calculation
the Sovereign could, by the use of sanctions (physical, political,
moral, religious), harmonise the clashing passions of his subjects.

The Sovereign therefore created the Moral Order of the State; it was he who made possible the Equilibrium of Interests demanded by human association. Society was the artificial creation of his labour. The 18th century enlightened Despot is still visible in the School of Utility. Bentham, the true descendant of Hobbes, still saw in the Sovereign 'The common power to keep them in awe'.

The reasoned calculus of the Law Maker could best be secured by following, during this voyage of discovery in search of the greatest happiness of his subjects, four brilliant stars of descending magnitude. Security, Subsistence, Abundance, Equality. That Bentham's Tory philosophy saw in security the chief road to happiness is no matter for surprise. Subsistence and Abundance were Bentham's tribute to the population discussion then raging. Equality was not the least worth striving for; it was the least attainable; all that could be done was to diminish inequality. The Sovereign might secure fraternity but not equality. The doctrine of utility was as yet no egalitarian creed.

The full revolutionary implication of Bentham's creed became apparent only when new social conditions synchronised with a demand for a new theory. Bentham and his disciples did no more than direct the diffused contemporary thought along well defined logical lines. They worked out a small stock of leading ideas in their minutest applications.

The year 1808 saw the rise of a new dawn. Reaction itself was wearying. The famous Westminster Election of 1807—in Bentham's constituency—returned to Parliament Burdett and Cochrane. The Cevallos article having made the Edinburgh Review Whig, the Tories started in opposition the Quarterly Review. Byron, Shelley, and Keats took up freedom's lyre which had fallen from the hands of Wordsworth, Southey and Coleridge. Above all, by a turn of the war tide, England became the ally both of the cherished Nationalism and of the threatened liberty of Europe against the Napoleonic despotism. In the same year Bentham met James Mill, and Utilitarianism passed from a legal aspiration to a political dogma. For 'if Bentham gave to Mill a doctrine, Mill gave to Bentham a school'.

UTILITY AND DEMOCRACY

An old man of 60 now became the Patriarch of English
Radicalism. As a Tory, Bentham had failed to convince the
Tory rulers. Applying his philosophy to the political situation,
he was amazed at the simple solution he found. The governmental clique simply sought its own happiness and not that of
the community. In the very nature of things every group, like
every individual, sought its own pleasure. Consequently the legal
corporation, the clerical corporation, the aristocratic corporation
were 'sinister interests' with selfish desires which were inimical
to Society. In law, in politics, in religion, the final test of goodness was the promotion of the greatest happiness of the greatest
number, the final court of appeal was the public good. How then
was it possible to reconcile the apparently conflicting interests of
Government and Society?

The utilitarian answer to this vital question is hazy. It was
useless to reply with Bentham that 'in me somehow selfishness
has taken the form of benevolence', for no Benthamite could
logically accept a subjective solution. Here Benthamism remains
inherently a self contradictory creed. It postulated an individual
with appetites and aversions; the problem remained how to
organise him in Society. Two solutions presented themselves.
Mandeville in his 'Fable of the Bees', with his brilliant paradox
that 'Private vices are public virtues', has suggested one. Each
man by following his own selfish desires, somehow without any
external co-ordinating body, contributed to the well being of the
Commonweal. This solution was carried to its logical conclusion
by the economists and applied ruthlessly to an Industrial Society.
Adam Smith had shown how each person by close specialisation
and constant search for private gain contributed to and created
thereby an industrial harmony. *Laissez Faire* became the cry
of the economists, and relying on the self-acting automaton of
greed, they excluded government from their society. Ricardo,
Mill, McCulloch, all good Benthamites, could so draw a distinction between Government and People and agree with the
mediaevalism of Paine that Society exists for our needs, Government because of our vices. Shelbourne with the curious English
trait of finding a religious basis for commercial motive saw this
period as the 'Era of Protestantism' in the realm of commerce.
As late as the sixties, Cobden could therefore interpret Free Trade

as the 'International Law of the Almighty', and 'Government as a standing conspiracy to rob and bamboozle'.

But another solution presented itself, that of the Tory Bentham. He, too, saw in the individual the font of all fruitful progress, his egoism the source of all hope; but if egoisms clashed, chaos not harmony, would result. He therefore sought to create a despotic sovereign power, who by sanctions would harmonise opposing egoisms in the interests of the greatest happiness of the greatest number. But now the law maker himself was a sinister interest, intent on his own pleasure. Somehow Government was essential to Society, and yet it was its danger. In the sphere of law and politics, Bentham found the ultimate solution in Representative Democracy; in the sphere of Economics no solution presented itself to him. Maine's criticism of his master is fundamentally just, he injured his creed in proportion as he went beyond legal reform.

Bentham had also suffered personally from the Tory Government. Howard, 'who lived as an apostle and died a martyr', had in vain urged the reform of our prisons. The appeal found a sympathetic response in Bentham, and sympathy, utility and mechanical genius combined to produce the Panopticon. This prison was to be a miniature society, with the gaoler as lawgiver, and the prisoners his subjects. With complete detail he presented his scheme to Pitt and Dundas. But in England, as in France, Bentham was cruelly disappointed. The Ministry was too busy with the war; difficulties arose over the site. At length, when he had spent his fortune, the whole scheme was cancelled. Public opinion rightly objected to the enormous power given to the gaoler, even if it was to his self interest to use it beneficently. Bentham was brokenhearted.

THE PROPHET OF DEMOCRACY

Chiefly as the 'Panopticon man' was he known to the public till 1808. Like so many Englishmen of the period, he appeared to his contemporaries obsessed with one idea, as Spence was with his Agrarian Communism, as Owen was with his scheme of Moral Regeneration in Square Villages. Now he accepted the logical conclusions of his creed, and became the Prophet of Democratic Citizenship, attacking privileged incapacity in every quarter, claiming that Institutions exist for man, not man for

Institutions. In 1809 there appeared his 'Catechism of Parliamentary Reform'. Representative Democracy was to be the bridge between the Sovereign and the People; it was the link between the interests of the Governor and the governed; it was the machinery whereby Government, in the interest of the greatest number, could be applied to modern states. Bentham thus joined hands with Cartwright, his old opponent and a relic of 18th century radicalism, in the demand for universal suffrage. Through Mill he made the acquaintance of Francis Place, and the ex-tailor became the political agent of the new sect. There gravitated to his school all the bolder spirits of the age, Hume, Brougham, Ricardo, O'Connell; Bickersteth brought together Bentham and Burdett, and the latter's demand for Reform in the House from 1818 onward was the political expression of Bentham's creed. The doctrine spread, sown broadcast through Wooler's 'Black Dwarf', and Hone's 'Reformists' Register', and the old man of 70 watched with glee his life work at last bearing fruit.

For not only was Bentham becoming a force at home, but abroad his fame had spread far. He had early sought a translator of his works. At Bowood he had found Dumon, a man of wide experience, as Protestant Pastor at Geneva and St. Petersburg, and he had secured his services. Their joint success was beyond all expectation. In 1802 there had appeared 'Traite's de Legislation Civile et Penale', and the reputation of Bentham spread from Moscow to Madrid. The Czar, Alexander I, solicited his help to codify Russian Law. The liberators of South America, Miranda, Jose del Valle, Bolivar, Santadar, all courted the world's law-maker for utilitarian constitutions. His house became the rendezvous of the world's freedom seekers, and Bentham toiled all day creating utilitarian codes for peoples struggling to be free.

BENTHAM AS EDUCATION AND POOR LAW REFORMER

British problems again claimed his attention. Pious and saintly souls had attributed the world upheaval to the ungodly teaching of Voltaire and Paine, and there grew up a pietistic movement to defend the *status quo* in the name of the Church. The clergy bartered their souls in becoming the moral police force of the State; having a vested interest in the Establishment they now became a sinister interest to an aggressive party. The struggle focused itself round education, and in Bell's National Schools the faithful were to be taught Christian resignation as the subjects of a secular State. But English nonconformity was too deeply rooted to be thus ignored, and the Lancastrian Schools opposed the orthodox teaching in the name of Christian truth. The Benthamites entered into the fray. They recognised the potency of education in the formation of character; in their hands it was to be an instrument to drill the nation in utilitarian politics and economics. Mill, Place, Wakefield, Brougham joined in founding the British and Foreign School Society, while Mill had launched the attack on his 'Schools for all, not for Churchmen only'. Bentham heartily co-operated, and he elaborated a new educational programme in his 'Chrestomathia'. The curriculum embraced all 'useful' subjects. The classics could not be included, and thus there began the controversy as to the merits of a Classical as compared with a Modern education. Bentham helped to frame Brougham's resolutions for Universal Secular State Education in the House in 1820, and he inspired his disciple Roebuck, so effectively that during the clash of measures in 1833 the Benthamite appeal for instruction in citizenship was still heard.

The utilitarian interest in education was however not anticlerical in origin. It sprang from a deeper and older source. The roots of English state education are embedded in the Poor Law, and the State care of the poor had then become the object of grave enquiry. All hope of improvement, every vista of escape for the labouring poor, had been choked up by the Malthusian Law of Population. Competition appeared as much a law of biological necessity as of industrial well-being. If vice and misery were the consequence of the Biblical ordinance to replenish the earth, humanity demanded that the labourers should be taught dignity and continence. The School of Bentham incorporated the teaching of Malthus, and demanded State education as part of the machinery of utility in order to teach the workers of England sobriety and self help. Moreover, a philosophy based on a calculus of pleasure and pain assumed that each man knew his own interests. The social fabric was only possible on this assumption. The Benthamites aimed by state education at teaching citizens what their true interests were.

BENTHAM AND POST WAR BRITAIN

In 1815 the war passed away, but prosperity did not arrive. Thwarted hopes and appalling social distress found vent in riots which threatened the foundation of the State. A stringent coercive policy appeared to be the only bulwark of society. Bentham, a landed proprietor and an ex-Tory, appealed to the Tory governors to mitigate their ferocity. 'Radicalism not Dangerous', in 1820 completed his political apostacy and captured the country. For the former opponent of Natural Rights had by a circuitous route alighted in their camp, and was now advocating their own conclusions.

Bentham, however, demanded universal suffrage and representative democracy, not as the superstructure to a society based in the Rights of Man, but as the machinery by which to identify the interests of people and government. He saw the close relation that existed between Law and the interests of a dominant class; by majority rule he sought to harmonise the conflicting interests in the body politic in the interests of all. Utility demanded that every human being should be considered as of equal legal value, that legislative power should depend not on property but on humanity, that a public office was a public trust. Rousseau and Bentham, so antagonistic in their basic ideas, joined hands in their conclusions.

For the next 12 years Bentham was the outstanding International figure in the realm of law and politics. Every struggling Liberal cause found in him a sympathetic guide. Spanish nationalists and Portuguese constitutionalists appealed to him for advice. He became one of the foremost members of the Greek Committee. He made codes for Morocco and Egypt. To President Madison he sent his Panomion a Code of universal validity. In 1823 he made a world-wide appeal to any nation desiring a Code, and he proclaimed his own credentials as a law-maker, for publicity was the soul of utility.

In England, if he was more than ever a recluse, he was becoming more than ever a force. He began what was to be his *chef d'œuvre*, his Constitutional Code, and his vision of a future society is portrayed in this uncompleted work. His conclusions were startling. For the representation of interests of property he substituted representation of Man. . . . He abolished Monarchy as being incompatible with the identity of interests between governor and governed. He abolished the House of Lords because it was an aristocratic corporation. He appealed for a uni-cameral legislature based on universal suffrage, on equality of voting power, on the secret ballot, and on annual elections. He organised responsibility by the publication of debates and division lists, and by a constant appeal to the tribunal of public opinion. He created new government departments of Internal Communication, Indigence and Relief, Education and Health. He demanded a Public Defender. He instituted competitive examinations for the recruitment of the civil service. He proposed centralised control over local administration. Above all, he insisted that law should be made only by the recognised public organs and not by Judge & Co. in their own interests, for Law was made for society, not for lawyers. His code was thus a charter of emancipation from lawyercraft and kingcraft, and his unfailing optimism saw it as the force to heal the world of the future.

Bentham had been gifted from youth with a capacity for intellectual domination. He now achieved the intellectual conquest of England. But as in all faiths, each priest soon interpreted the Master's teaching in a different light. The economists emphasised the harmony arrived at through self-seeking without any social control; the early English socialists insisted on Government carrying out its function of securing the greatest happiness of the greatest number. The rift within the creed was, however, not at once apparent. The orthodox Benthamites saw in Government only a sinister interest, interpreted freedom only as removal of legal restraint. It was against the advocacy of a barren freedom and an unequal individualism that the finer minds of the 19th century railed. In Carlyle's scathing words: 'it was a scavenger age, appealing for Horse Hood and Dog Hood Suffrage', while 'Sir Jabesh Windbags was being elected to power by the temporary hallelujahs of flunkeys'. To Ruskin the ennobling of greed as an essential element in the state made for Illth, not Wealth.

But in Bentham's lifetime, the divergence was neither so apparent nor so wide, and a growing apostolate spread his doctrine. In 1821, James Mill founded the Political Economy Club. In 1823, the Younger Mill, in nurture the finest offspring of the

new creed, founded the Utilitarian Society for the junior disciples.
It included amongst its numbers, Prescott, Wm. Eyton Tooke,
Wm. Ellis, Graham, Roebuck, Grote, Austin. They met in the
Master's house, they studied his works and confronted the
Owenites and Spenceans with ruthless logic, and achieved their
own political education and graduated as the future leaders of
public opinion, under the guidance of Bentham himself. In
1823 Bentham appealed to a wider circle by starting the Westminster Review. His disciples enthusiastically answered the call
of Campbell and became the founders of the new secular University of London. They supported the struggling Mechanics Insti-
tutes. Of disciples there was now no end—Chadwick, Southwood
Smith, Charles Hay Cameron, James Deacon Hume, Wakefield,
Buller, Hodgskin, and even O'Connell. In vain the Tories, now
by the swing of events transformed into a doctrinaire party,
inveighed against the Professors of the Arts Babbletive and
Scribbletive. Bentham effectively replied in his Book of Fallacies.
This effected by sarcasm what reason could not accomplish, and
he followed up his attack by a trenchant onslaught on the ally
of Toryism, the Established Church. 'Not Paul but Jesus' was a
counterblast to the whole clerical hierarchy, and, working with
George Grote, they together produced under the pseudonym
of Philip Beauchamp the 'Analysis of the influence of Natural
Religion on the temporal happiness of mankind'. Using
Benthamite language they attacked God as a sinister interest,
His Power as an unconstitutional despotism, and the whole
clerical hierarchy as a corporation opposed by interest to truth.
The Tory mind saw the Church as the spiritual facet of Society
slowly adapting itself to human needs, the Benthamites saw it
as only a creation of Priestcraft, and they demanded the complete disestablishment and disendowment of the Church. But
in his attack on this tradition, Bentham did not carry all his
school with him. Wm. Allen, the whole Clapham sect, even
his own secretary Bowring, held aloof, while by the irony of
history the Neo-Catholic movement was just then being founded
in Bentham's old university as a protest against the mechanical
and rational outlook of the age. His prestige nevertheless
coloured the whole of the democratic movement, and it gave
force to the tradition, long maintained, and hardly yet eradi-

cated, of the necessary alliance between irreligion and democracy, anti-clericalism and Radical thought.

More effective was his influence on the new Colonial life of
Greater Britain, and the former author of 'Emancipate your
Colonies' made public recantation as the need for social control
and scientific law-making became urgent in England's depen-
dencies. In India his influence was exceptionally profound.
James Mill was at the India Office. Silk Buckingham and Col.
Young, two ardent disciples, were in India. Macaulay, a
Utilitarian *malgre lui*, and Charles Hay Cameron, his colleague,
a militant Benthamite, were soon to apply his legal and educa-
tion principles on an alien soil. Bentinck on his appointment
as Governor-General wrote with due humility, 'I am going to
British India, but I shall not be Governor-General. It is you
will be Governor-General'. Bentham with less modesty agreed.
'One day I shall be the legislative power in India, 20 years after
my death I shall reign there as despot.' It was to Bentham that
Edward Gibbon Wakefield came for aid to draw up his scheme
for scientific colonisation, and the former author of 'The
Panopticon versus New South Wales' wrote as he saw the success of his plans, 'I am reconciled to the loss of the Panopticon
when I think of the mass of happiness that is being created
there.' The Magna Carta of Colonial Self-Government, the
Durham Report, had for its chief author two Benthamites,
Wakefield and Buller.

English Socialism also owes an inestimable debt of gratitude
to the almost mythical exponent of stern individualism. With
Owen, he possessed the bond of a common philanthropy, but
Hodgskin was his secretary, and in his 'Labour Defended',
Hodgskin attacked, not Bentham, but Mill and Ricardo, with
Utilitarian arguments based on the assumption that the very
goal of government was the greatest happiness of its citizens.
The political and economic strands began to diverge, but
although patent enough in John Stuart Mill, the divergence was
as yet dimly perceived. Wm. Thompson, his disciple, condemned
the existing system of distribution on Utilitarian ethics, and
claimed the teaching of Bentham as its effective reproof.
Charles Hall advocated Progressive Taxation from Benthamite
axioms. In J. S. Mill the struggle between traditional individualism and logical state action became painfully apparent,

and he ended by advocating compulsory state education, and
the social control over socially created values from Benthamite
premises. The curious paradox that individual freedom, in the
realm of labour as in the realm of law, could only be obtained
by increased social control, ultimately made Mill declare himself a Socialist.

In his extreme old age, Bentham was the venerated head of
a brilliant body of disciples; he still lived in his 'hermitage' at
Queen Square Place; he still toiled away at his Constitutional
Code. His life had been singularly happy; he had never endured
pain he had never suffered want. In his veneration of precision
he had invented a new jargon, but he has been as felicitous in
some of his verbal inventions as in his social inventions; and the
terms maximise, minimise, codification, international, have been
of inestimable value to clear political thinking.

In 1832, two days before the passing of the Reform Bill, to
which he had contributed so much, he died in his 'hermitage'.
To avoid giving them grief, he sent his younger disciples away;
he only asked to minimise pain. He bequeathed his body
to science. Dr. Southwood Smith pronounced the funeral
oration.

Of Bentham, it can faithfully be said, that his best monument is the record of social effort in the 19th Century. His
ministry of love embraced every sentient creature. He had
opposed all brutal sports, cockfighting, bull baiting, fox hunting.
'The question is not,' said he, 'can they talk, can they reason,
but can they suffer?' He had espoused the cause of every suffering class; he had advocated freedom for every struggling
people, he had fought for every persecuted sect. But his scientific
mind saw in pity a force which did not lend itself to calculation
and legislation; he attempted therefore to cement a psychological
hedonism with utilitarian altruism. If his psychology was premature, he nevertheless made potent a method of submitting
every institution and every belief to the pitiless searchlight of
utility. Before the question, 'What was the good of it?' incapacity,
jobbery, nepotism slunk away.

If he was irreverent, it was because holy things had become
corrupt, if he became a rebel, it was because authority had
become irresponsible. His vision of society as a group of rational
political equals cut athwart every conception of a social

hierarchy. He shattered the theory that Kingcraft was government, that Priestcraft was the church. By substituting a teleological for a merely analytical conception of political obligation, he created a basis for judging the value of any government in its effects on the happiness of the ordinary man.

G. D. H. Cole

3 WILLIAM COBBETT 1763–1835

THE SIGN WHICH appears above these words is a Gridiron—the sign chosen by Cobbett in his later years as the symbol of his methods of political controversy. In earlier years he had described himself as a 'porcupine', and 'Peter Porcupine' had become, in the United States of America, by far the most redoubtable of anti-Jacobin pamphleteers. Carlyle compared him to a rhinoceros, and Heine to a hound. And Carlyle again called him 'the pattern John Bull of his century'.

A suggestive crop of metaphor—suggestive at least of the man in his public dealings, and as he appeared to the outside world. He was forever grilling his enemies on the gridiron of his invective, or sticking them with his quills of ridicule and contempt; trampling them down like a rhinoceros, and as insensitive to the blows they dealt him back; swift on the scent as a hound, and as tenacious of the chase; and, above all, the John Bull in the china shop of Tory, Whig and Radical alike.

Not merely the bull, observe, but the John Bull! Everyone who has written of Cobbett with sympathy has recognised in him an essence peculiarly English, something typical of England itself. He is not merely English; in a real sense he stands for England. He is 'the pattern John Bull of his century'; but his century is not the nineteenth, in which the best part of his work was done. It is more the eighteenth, still more the seventeenth, yet more again the sixteenth. His roots are deep in the historic past of England; the further back one goes, the nearer one seems to come to the age in which he belongs. Yet one never reaches it;

for the England Cobbett typifies is not the England of any one century, but a deep-seated tradition—a tradition whose swift destruction in his own day called forth his most righteous anger.

Cobbett was a peasant. He came of a peasant stock, and was reared as a peasant, in the heart of a people of peasants. Despite all his experiences, as lawyer's clerk, soldier, teacher, journalist, agitator, Member of Parliament, to the end of his life he thought and felt as a peasant. He did not need to sympathise with the people and their wrongs; he was one of the people, and their wrongs were his. Every blow struck in his day at Old England —and not a minute passed without a blow—was a buffet of which he personally felt the impact. In fighting for the people, and returning blow for blow, he was all the time fighting for himself and for his own people.

He was a peasant in this as well—he made no abstract theories. His judgments were all based directly on what he saw and felt and knew from personal experience. The appeal to first principles never moved him one iota, and he seldom even employed it as a weapon in controversy. 'Liberty, Equality, and Fraternity' left him cold. Robert Owen's Utopian Socialism provoked only his contempt. He became a militant Radical, not because he had any love for Radical principles, but because he saw around him positive abuses and crimes against the people which called for radical remedies. The 'feelosofical' Radicalism of Bentham and Brougham he hated far more than the Toryism of Eldon or Wellington. He could not abide Francis Place.

All too seldom in history has the peasant been able to speak his mind with an eloquence to command the world's attention. Occasionally, he has made himself known by burning villas or *chateaux,* by some blazing terror that has swept swiftly over the countryside. Far more often he has had to leave others to speak for him; and those others have woefully misinterpreted his meaning. It is the peasant's tragedy that, when at last he found his voice in Cobbett's plain and forcible prose, his defeat at the hands of plutocracy was already assured. England had chosen the path of industrialism before Cobbett began to speak; and his was a voice crying in the great wilderness that was soon to be called 'the workshop of the world'.

William Cobbett was born in 1763, and died in 1835. He was born just when the forces of economic change, active for some time before, were gathering that swift momentum which, in a single generation, destroyed the villages of England and created the noisome factory towns. Enclosures and the rise in the cost of living were then just beginning their swift expropriation and pauperisation of the peasantry; and the dispossessed peasants and the pauper 'apprentices' were being made the basis for the concoction of the modern factory proletariat. Most of the phases of this great degradation of the people passed before his own eyes. He saw the peasantry being driven from the land, and the ugly towns rising in the North and Midlands. And as the peasants declined, the new rich rose to power and place. Country seats passed into the hands of bankers, stockjobbers, merchants; and, when at length Reform came, it only enthroned the new lords of the people in the seats of the old. Cobbett's last years were spent in a criticism of the Reformed Parliament fully as sweeping and vigorous as any he had pronounced against the Rotten Boroughs of pre-Reform days. His last articles were written to denounce the new Poor Law of 1834, the measure in which the Reformed Parliament applied its Malthusian faith to the solution of the social problem. He died before, in the Chartist Movement, the factory workers gathered up their forces for a mass protest against the new order—a last protest preceding the triumphant march of Victorian Capitalism towards a goal still undefined.

Cobbett's life thus covers the most critical period in modern history. He saw the two revolutions in industry and agriculture transform the whole social structure of English life, creating at once a new rich and a new poor—the 'Two Nations' of Disraeli's *Sybil*. He heard from afar the thunder of the Revolution in France, which brought the old European State system crashing down in ruins. He lived through the Revolutionary and Napoleonic Wars, and through 20 years of the social struggles which followed them. For 35 years he was a powerful, for 20 years by far the most powerful, journalist in England, unrivalled as a writer of strong simple English, unrivalled too in his knowledge of the mind of the English people. He was arrogant, egoistic, intolerant, quarrelsome, in public affairs; he was often inaccurate in matters of fact, and often wrong in his minor conclusions. But in the big things he was right, the more right because he judged not by principles, but by the direct evidence of his senses, always ready to call a spade a spade, and to give tyrants and hypocrites the names of their vices. Above all, he could always talk in a language the people knew. This was the secret of his power; he talked and wrote like the people, because he felt and thought like the people.

Cobbett was born at 'The Jolly Farmer', Farnham, Surrey, in the heart of the prosperous hop country. It was an appropriate birthplace for a man who, all his life, looked and felt like the jolly farmer who is the traditional John Bull. He was 70 years old when J. S. Buckingham describes him as having 'a ruddy countenance, a small laughing eye, and the figure of a respectable farmer'. To Hazlitt, he recalled 'a gentleman farmer of the last century'.

Cobbett's father was indeed a small farmer, who combined farming with the business of an innkeeper. His earliest memories were of life and work in the fields—crow-scaring, hoeing, ploughing, gardening for the Bishop at Farnham Castle, and contriving to find time for country sports such as coursing as well. He loved gardens, and at 14 he gave a hint of his taste for adventure by running away to London in order to get a job at Kew Gardens, of whose beauty he had heard. He got his job; but before long he returned home and resumed his work on the farm. His next adventure occurred when he was 19. On a visit to relations near Portsmouth he first saw the sea, and conceived at once the desire to be a sailor. His wish was thwarted, only because a kindly captain, who supposed him to be running away for fear of a bastard, persuaded him to return home.

'I returned once more to the plough,' Cobbett wrote, 'but I was spoiled for a farmer.' Within a few months another sudden impulse caused him to leave home for ever. He was going to Guildford Fair, and was on his way to meet two or three girls who were going with him, when he met the London coach coming up the turnpike road. In a moment he made up his mind, mounted the coach, and, without a word to his friends, was off to London, arriving there with but half a crown in his pocket. He was just 20 years old.

In the coach he was lucky enough to meet a business friend of his father's, a hop merchant, who after vainly trying to persuade him to go back home, at length found him a job in a lawyer's office. There, without friends or companions, Cobbett slaved for some months, learning to be an efficient clerk, but pining for green fields and adventure and acquiring a healthy distaste for the law and all its works. His longing for the sea returned upon him. At length, he could bear his office no longer. He went to Chatham, and enlisted, as he thought, in the marines, only to find that he had joined the infantry by mistake. He was now 21.

Cobbett's books are full of memories of his life in the army. For a year he remained at the Chatham depot, and became a corporal. Then, in the spring of 1785, he was ordered to join his regiment in Nova Scotia. Almost at once the regiment was transferred to New Brunswick, and there Cobbett remained, rising to be regimental sergeant-major, until the autumn of 1791.

He was, to the end of his life, very proud of his doings as a soldier. At Chatham he had joined a circulating library, and read everything he could lay hands on. His experience as a clerk caused him to be made copyist to the Commandant, and he began to realise the deficiencies of his education. He set to work, under the extreme difficulties of barrack life, to teach himself what he called 'grammar'—by which he meant the power to speak and write correct and vigorous English. He got Lowth's Grammar, wrote it all out several times, learnt it by heart, and repeated it when on sentry-go, saved up out of his twopence a day in order to buy pens, ink and paper, and pay his library subscription, and even went without food in his search after knowledge. In New Brunswick he continued this work, but found time also to amuse himself hunting and walking, and to make friends both among his fellow-soldiers and among the settlers. At the same time, he was absolutely punctual in his attendance to duty, never a minute late, never in fault with his superiors or his equals.

'There is no situation,' he wrote, 'where merit is so sure to meet with regard as in a well-disciplined army.' Be this as it may, Cobbett was rewarded. As sergeant-major, if we may trust his own accounts, he soon ran the regiment, the officers, intent on amusing themselves, readily resigning the administrative control into his hands. He liked authority, and his army experiences early accustomed him to its exercise.

But he found time for love affairs. In New Brunswick he met

Ann Reid, who later became his wife. She was the daughter of an artillery sergeant, and he fell in love with her at first sight when he saw her scrubbing out a tub at early morning in the snow. 'That's the girl for me,' said he to his companions, before he had ever exchanged a word with her. They became engaged; but soon after the artillery regiment was moved back to England. Cobbett handed over his savings, 150 guineas, to Ann Reid's keeping, and they parted.

Cobbett remained in New Brunswick for some years longer, and once almost got married to someone else. But he remembered Ann Reid, and escaped in time. When his regiment at length returned home he at once sought her out and married her. 'I found my little girl *a servant of all work* (and hard work it was) at *five pounds a year*; and, without hardly saying a word about the matter, she put into my hands *the whole of my 150 guineas unbroken*!' This though he had told her to use it, if necessary, for her maintenance till his return.

Arrived in England, Cobbett at once procured his discharge from the army, and set about a dangerous enterprise that had been long in his mind. He had become aware in New Brunswick that the officers of his regiment systematically pillaged the men, holding back part of the pay, and making all sorts of illicit gains in connection with the supply of provisions and stores. Aided by a corporal, he had made copious excerpts from the regimental books in proof of his case, and had made up his mind to leave the army and devote himself to an exposure of the frauds. He now demanded a court-martial, to be held in London, as in Portsmouth, where the regiment was, he feared intimidation of witnesses. He further claimed the discharge from the army of certain vital witnesses.

Away in New Brunswick, Cobbett had supposed that the corruption he saw was an isolated thing, proceeding from the special depravity of his own officers. Gradually, in face of the obstructions put by the War Office in his way, he realised that he was attacking a spoils system that was common to the whole army, and generally recognised in official quarters. For a time he persisted; but at length he understood he had no chance of success, and that he would in all probability be crushed himself unless he gave way. When the court-martial was at last held, no prosecutor appeared. Cobbett had thought discretion the

better part, and fled to France, then in the throes of the Revolution. This was in March 1792—the Girondins were still in
power; the Terror had not begun.

Cobbett was at this time no politician, and it is doubtful if he
had any political views. He took no part in French affairs, living
quietly with his wife at Tilques, a village near St. Omer, and
using the time to make himself thoroughly master of the French
language. Here he stayed until August, when he set off on a visit
to Paris. On the way, he heard the news of the attack on the
Tuileries and the deposition of Louis XVI. Realising that this
meant war, he made for Havre, and took a boat for the United
States.

For nearly eight years from 1792 Cobbett lived in the United
States, maintaining himself first as a teacher of English to the
stream of émigrés who were arriving from France, and then as
the leading journalist and pamphleteer in the British interest.
He settled first at Wilmington, on the Delaware, but soon moved
up to Philadelphia—a stronghold of Democratic opinion, which
was keenly pro-French. Gradually Cobbett was drawn into
politics, at first by disputing with his French pupils, who were
mostly moderate republicans, and then by the rising tide of anti-
British feeling which developed after the outbreak of the Revolutionary war. At length, his resentful patriotism made him take
up the cudgels publicly for his country. He had taught himself
how to write; indignation caused him to use his talent.

In 1794 Dr. Priestley, the great Radical Unitarian, whose
house had been burnt down by the Birmingham mob in 1791,
came to settle in the United States. The Democratic Club
received him with fervent addresses, denouncing British persecution and acclaiming the principles of Liberty, Equality and
Fraternity. Roused to fury by what he regarded as Priestley's
betrayal of his own people, Cobbett wrote a violently abusive
pamphlet about him, entitled *Observations on Dr. Priestley's
Emigration*.

The pamphlet was a success. It sold largely, and attracted
widespread attention and controversy. Cobbett, having found
the thing he could really do well, enjoyed himself hugely. In
pamphlet after pamphlet he smote hard at the French Revolution and its American supporters, receiving shrewd knocks, but
administering shrewder. Before long, he had become virtually

the unofficial agent of British propaganda in the United States. Pitt's Government offered to take him into its pay; but then, as always, he preferred his independence.

The titles of these American pamphlets give a clear enough indication of their character. *A Bone to Gnaw for the Democrats, A Little Plain English, A Kick for a Bite, The Bloody Buoy, The Scare-Crow, A Letter to the Infamous Tom Paine, The Cannibal's Progress,* and a dozen more vigorous pamphlets soon followed the first. And in 1796 Cobbett began, with the *Political Censor,* the first of his many ventures into controversial journalism. In 1797 *Porcupine's Gazette,* a daily newspaper, replaced the *Censor,* and continued to appear as long as Cobbett remained in Philadelphia.

There is a curious irony in the fact that the greatest of English Radicals thus began his career as a loyalist writer in hot denunciation of the French Revolution and all its works. There was nothing too vile for Cobbett to attribute to the Revolution and its upholders. He wrote a *Life of Paine,* in which he collected all the scurrilous stories he could find. He published pamphlets about the events in France, which were as good examples of horror-mongering as anything lately issued from Riga or Helsingfors about events in Russia. And he libelled the American partisans of France as unmercifully as he dealt with Paine or Robespierre.

Yet a reading of these pamphlets makes the truth plain. There is in them no trace of thinking on political questions, and no considered view of Cobbett's own. They are simply joyous tirades of a naturally combative spirit, loving his own country the more for his absence from it, feeling his countrymen and his own late profession of arms insulted by the friends of France who surrounded him, forgetting in his instinctive patriotism the abuses and the reaction at home, which had driven him forth when he attempted their exposure, and idealising an England which was represented in his mind by the pleasant memories of his childhood at Farnham. Opposition, moreover, always roused him. 'I was never in my life,' he wrote, 'of an accommodating disposition.' Once he was plunged into the controversy about France, everything written in reply to his tirades served to increase the vigour of his own denunciations.

Before long this indiscriminate lashing out brought him into

trouble. Among the 'Democratic' politicians of Philadelphia was
Dr. Benjamin Rush, the leading advocate of the 'bleeding treatment' for combating the prevalent yellow fever. Cobbett nicknamed him 'Doctor Sangrado', out of *Gil Blas,* and pursued him
and his treatment with a curious mixture of medical and
political denunciation. Rush treated George Washington, who
died. Cobbett accused him of murder. But before this Rush had
found matter enough in Cobbett's strictures for a libel action.
After long delays, he won his case, and Cobbett was heavily
fined. He wrote a violent pamphlet attacking the judge, and
actually started a new paper, the *Rushlight,* to pursue his campaign against the Democratic doctor. But America had become
too hot to hold him. At length, in 1800, he gave up the battle,
and set sail for England.

Cobbett was 37 years old at the time of his return. His reputation as a pamphleteer ensured him a welcome from the Government at home. He met Pitt and William Windham, and was
offered the editorship of a Government newspaper, with a certain prospect of good pickings. He refused, and started an independent paper of his own, *The Porcupine,* which, having no
capital behind it, speedily failed. Then, with money supplied by
William Windham and other friends belonging to the extreme
anti-Jacobin group, he started the weekly newspaper with which,
for the rest of his life, his name was associated in the public
mind.

The first number of the *Political Register* appeared in 1802,
at a time when England was just concluding with Napoleon that
Peace which neither side meant as more than a breathing-space
to be used in getting ready for a renewal of the long war.
Windham and his group were violently opposed to the Peace,
and the *Political Register* began its career as an extreme loyalist
and anti-Jacobin journal. The stop-gap Prime Minister, Henry
Addington, later Lord Sidmouth, who had been put into power
by Pitt in order to conclude the Peace of Amiens, incurred
Cobbett's special hostility. To Pitt he gave for the time a qualified
support, but Windham was his real leader and patron.

In 1803 the war was renewed; and in 1804 Pitt again became
Prime Minister, forming a Government largely composed of
the same elements as Addington's. Fox was excluded because the
King would not have him; and Windham and the Grenvilles

would not take office without Fox. Cobbett found his political
associations changing. With Napoleon Emperor of the French,
Anti-Jacobinism was no longer a live issue. Fox, who had upheld the French Revolution, and Windham who, following
Burke, had most bitterly opposed it, had joined hands against
Pitt and Addington. Cobbett, who had denounced Fox up hill
and down dale, found himself in the same political camp.

About this time began that change in Cobbett's political
opinions which caused him, a few years later, to break completely with Whigs and Tories alike, and to pass over definitely
to Radicalism. His new attitude to Pitt seems to have been the
beginning of this change. The more Cobbett surveyed Pitt's
policy with critical eyes, the more he saw in it to disapprove.
Hitherto, he had written, and thought, almost wholly about
foreign affairs. But now that all the political groups were united
in support of the war against Napoleon, Cobbett began to think
and write about home affairs as well. He awoke, with a start,
to a sense of the abuses which were everywhere prevalent. The
rapid increase of the National Debt and the no less rapid growth
of pauperism in the countryside, the multiplication of pensions
and sinecures by the Governments of Addington and Pitt, the
squandering of public money, the enrichment of Government
contractors and stockjobbers, the peculation and inhumanity
prevalent in the army—of these he became consciously aware
for the first time. He began to write about them, and to apply
his power of invective to things and persons nearer home.

This does not mean that Cobbett became at once a Radical.
For some time longer he continued to denounce all proposals
for the reform of Parliament, and to demand the vigorous prosecution of the war. The real turning-point came in 1806, when
Pitt died, and Cobbett's closest political associate, Windham,
joined Fox and Grenville to form the Ministry of All the
Talents. Cobbett at once presented to the new Ministers a
drastic programme of reforms; he expected Windham, as Secretary for War, to clear corruption out of the army, and the
Government as a whole to put a stop to the enormous abuses
which he denounced as the 'Pitt system'. Naturally, he was disappointed; the new Ministers merely carried on in these respects
the traditions of the old. Within a few weeks, he had quarrelled
with Windham, and shaken the dust of the orthodox parties

for ever from his feet. Speedily he moved on to acceptance of
the whole Radical programme, and became an advocate of
Manhood Suffrage as well as of 'economical reform'.

This rapid conversion was not, however, wholly due to
political disillusionment. During the years following his return
Cobbett was gradually rediscovering England. From the time
when he left Farnham in 1783 to his return in 1800 he had
seen practically nothing of the English countryside. He had
lived in New Brunswick, in France, and in the United States,
with only one brief and busy sojourn in England when he got
married and sought unsuccessfully to expose the peculations of
his officers. Even after his return in 1800, he lived in London,
and paid for some years only a few short visits to the country.
But he had not lost his love for the countryside, and at length,
in 1805, he felt well enough established to settle down out of
London, and combine his journalistic work with a little farming.
He bought at Botley, near Southampton, a charming farmhouse
and some land, both of which he set to work vigorously to
improve. His return to the country brought him again into touch
with the life of the people, and opened his eyes to much that he
had failed to realise before.

For the country round Southampton, as he now saw it in
1805, was very different from the memories of his boyhood at
Farnham. The huge rise in prices due to war inflation had
reduced the mass of the rural workers to destitution. Enclosures
were being actively made, usually with little regard to their
effect on the poorer commoners. The rural labourers, a class
swollen by the peasants who had lost their lands or rights of
common, were largely subsisting on poor relief, doled out under
the Speenhamland system in aid of wages on which no family
could live. Even the scale of this relief was being steadily cut
down, as the poor rates and taxes together became an intolerable burden. The farmers, who had profited by war prices, aped
the manners and expense of gentlefolk, and ground down the
labourers in order to retain the means to luxury for themselves.
The stockjobbers, contractors and placemen were busy buying
up estates, or carving new great properties out of holdings taken
from the peasants by enclosure.

All this Cobbett began to realise only when he returned to
the countryside. It roused his indignation as nothing else could

have done. All through his years in America he had comforted himself with an idealised picture of England, based on the pleasant memories of his own boyhood. With this in mind he had flayed the enemies of his country, who appeared to him the would-be destroyers of this rural paradise. Now, at length, he saw the reality, and his anger was proportionate to the contrast with the picture he had cherished.

Thus, Cobbett's Radicalism, as it developed from 1805 onwards, was in its essence a defence of the peasantry against the oppression under which they suffered. He saw the cause of their misery in the prevalent economic abuses—inflation, the growth of the National Debt, heavy taxation, money frittered away in pensions, sinecures, and inefficient and corrupt administration. Since the orthodox parties upheld these things, on which, indeed, their power and wealth were based, there must be a thorough Reform of Parliament, which would replace these by men prepared to pluck up abuses by the root. This involved, in Cobbett's view, no attack on monarchy, or even on the old nobility. The enemies of the people were the new classes which were now dominating society by the power of wealth—the financiers, the cotton lords, the contractors, on whom Pitt and his successors relied for the means to finance the European struggle against France. It is significant that, in the zeal of his new Radicalism, Cobbett turned his invective mainly upon two things—the swiftly growing National Debt, and the transformation of Great Britain from an agricultural to an industrial and commercial country. Exports, he said, harmed the nation; an agricultural country would never have produced such a monstrosity as modern Manchester; the 'commercial system' and the 'funding system' were inseparable; as commerce grew, pauperism and the National Debt grew by corresponding stages.

Rapidly, Cobbett became a power among the Radicals. He developed close associations with Sir Francis Burdett, Lord Cochrane, Major Cartwright, Henry Hunt and other Radical leaders. The *Political Register* became by far the most influential of Radical journals. Naturally, he also incurred the strong hostility of the governing classes; and before long those in power were seeking eagerly for ways of suppressing him. He had, moreover, by this time become also a fluent and popular speaker. He had tried his power on the Radical side in several election campaigns,

and had begun that series of 'rustic harangues' which made him
the greatest agitator as well as the greatest journalist of his day.
This was an additional reason for his suppression.

The Tory Government's chance came in 1809. A small mutiny
over unfair deductions from the soldiers' pay broke out among
the local militia at Ely, and was quelled by the arrival of four
squadrons of the mercenary German Legion. The ringleaders
were tried by court-martial, and sentenced to 500 lashes.
Cobbett wrote a furious article denouncing the floggings; the
Government promptly prosecuted him for sedition. After some
negotiations, during which he hoped at one time that the
charge would be withdrawn on condition of the *Register* ceasing
publication, he stood his trial, and was sentenced to a fine of
£1,000, two years' imprisonment in Newgate, and to give bail
in £3,000, and find two sureties at £1,000 each, at the end of
his term.

From 1810 to 1812, therefore, Cobbett was confined in Newgate gaol. But, according to modern notions, the terms of his
imprisonment were quite extraordinarily lenient. He was allowed
to hire comfortable rooms in the prison, where his children took
turns to come and stay with him, and hampers and provisions
were sent regularly from Botley. He could receive, and entertain
to steak and porter, as many visitors as he liked. And, above all,
he could go on writing and issuing the *Register* as freely as if
he had been at large. For all this he had to pay, and pay heavily;
but he suffered from no other disability than confinement within the walls of the prison.

The *Register,* then, was published regularly during his confinement, and under his editorial control. In it appeared his
Paper against Gold, his most considerable work up to this time,
in which he stated at length his case against inflation, the growth
of the National Debt, and the 'Pitt system' of finance, regarded
as the source of the prevailing pauperism and distress. Inspired
largely by Tom Paine's famous tract, *The Decline and Fall of
the English System of Finance,* Cobbett treated the flood of
paper money, let loose during the war and the Industrial Revolution, as the sign of national decay and the source of the great
rise in prices which had made the few unprecedentally rich and
the many intolerably poor. His book is a queer mixture of true
and false. It was right enough in its account of the effects of

the war-time finance; but it took no account of the needs for more currency and credit in order to finance the swift expansion of industry under the influence of machinery. With all its faults, it became immensely popular, and confirmed Cobbett's position as leader of the Radicals outside Parliament.

Cobbett's life in prison was comfortable and productive; but it was also very expensive. When he came out of Newgate in 1812, he was a ruined man. Even before his imprisonment, his affairs were in a tangle, though he only discovered when he was in gaol the extent of his embarrassments. Never a good business man, he had allowed the business side of the *Register* and his other enterprises to slip into the hands of his assistant, Wright, who had made a thorough mess of them. The *Register* Cobbett saved from the wreck of his fortunes; but he had to sell his house at Botley, and two of his most considerable enterprises, the *Parliamentary History of England,* a great compilation of historical records, and *Cobbett's Parliamentary Debates,* which bought by his printer, Hansard, has become the familiar *Hansard* of our own day. Despite these sales, his financial difficulties continued until 1820, when, by becoming a bankrupt, he got a fresh start.

During the intervening years, a great deal had happened. The long war at last ended in 1815, after the episode of the Hundred Days; and, after the first rejoicings, the country settled down to count the cost. Prices fell, indeed; but the burden of the War Debt rose in proportion. Unemployment was everywhere; and the blow fell with especial severity in the country districts, where the collapse of war prices fell on a labouring population already living on a bare margin of subsistence. With hunger came unrest. The Luddite disturbances of a few years before had shown the depth of discontent in the industrial districts. Now, the troubles became more general; and the governing classes lived in fear of revolution. The first mood, in which ineffectual attempts were made to relieve the distress, soon gave way, under the influence of fear, to a mood of repression. In 1817 the Habeas Corpus Act was suspended, and the Government passed a series of 'Gagging Acts' directed especially against the popular press and the right of public meeting.

These measures had a direct reference to Cobbett's doings. Hitherto, the *Register* had been an expensive weekly, costing 10d.

or 1/-, and therefore bought only by fairly well-to-do persons and a few clubs and public houses patronised by the Radical workers. But in 1816, at the height of the unrest, Cobbett produced a special *Register* at 2d., containing an *Address to the Journeymen and Labourers,* in which he backed up their claims, and urged Radical Reform as the sole remedy for the distress. Intended as an isolated issue, the cheap *Register* had an instant success and Cobbett at once decided to issue it regularly. For some time he sold 50,000 copies weekly—for those days a quite unprecedented circulation. Within a few weeks, he had put himself definitely at the head of the Radical working-class agitation.

Undoubtedly, the success of the cheap *Register* and the growth of Cobbett's influence were among the chief reasons for the repressive laws of 1817. Cobbett at once realised that, if he stayed in England, arrest was certain, and that the conditions of his second imprisonment would be quite unlike those of seven years before. He made up his mind to fly, and, leaving England in secret, returned to the United States of America, where he remained for more than two years, sending copy regularly for publication in the *Register,* which was kept going by his agents during his absence.

Cobbett has been much criticised for running away at this critical time. His own answer to his critics was that he was better occupied writing in America than gaoled in England, and that he could have accomplished nothing by staying. But some of his Radical colleagues who stayed behind and went to gaol were naturally not content with his explanation. Posterity, whether it holds him right or wrong, can at any rate be grateful for the results of his going.

For this two years' sojourn in America begins what is, for posterity, the most fruitful period of Cobbett's life—the period of his greatest writings. At the farm which he rented in North Hempstead, he not only wrote his *Journal of a Year's Residence in America* and his *Grammar of the English Language,* but also planned out many of the books written during the last crowded 15 years of his life. Escape from direct political contacts and the daily struggle set free a part of his mind which had been repressed. He began to write, not merely great political journalism, but great books, greater because he put into them more of himself, a broader view of life, a more abounding sympathy

and virtue. His withdrawal was necessary, not only to save him
from gaol, but still more to enable him to find out more fully his
own powers.

Cobbett returned to England in 1819. The danger was not
over. Indeed, unrest had grown, and the Government, on the
morrow of the Peterloo massacre, was just pushing through
the Six Acts, which went considerably further in repression than
the measures of 1817. He came back, not because it was safe to
come, but because he knew now what he wanted to do.

From 1819 to 1832 Cobbett's life is, in one aspect, the history
of the Reform agitation. But it is also a great deal more. In
1820 he began that series of rural rides which, part pleasure
trips, part missionary tours, part journeys of investigation, are
imperishably associated with his name through his greatest
work. There never was such a work as *Rural Rides*; for there
never was so eloquent a countryman as Cobbett. In it he left
behind not only an unrivalled description of the English countryside, its beauty and wealth and the misery of its people, but also
as plain a revelation of himself as man ever wrote by way of
formal autobiography.

In these years, too, he published in swift succession a series
of books any one of which would give him an honoured place
in our national literature. *Cottage Economy* and *Cobbett's
Sermons* in 1822, *The History of the Protestant Reformation* in
1824-26, *The Woodlands* in 1825, *Advice to Young Men,* and
The English Gardener in 1829, the collected *Rural Rides* in
1830, are only a few of his works of this period, apart from the
steady stream of his periodical writing and a long list of political
pamphlets. He had rediscovered, above all, his capacity to teach
and to give sound, homely advice. His *English Grammar* is still
the best book for the young worker who wants to learn the habit
of writing good English. The simple wisdom of *Advice to Young
Men* still stands, for the most part as good as when it was
written.

On his return in 1819, Cobbett had first, by bankruptcy, to
clear himself of his financial worries. Then he plunged again
headlong into the political fray. Through 1820 and 1821 all
England was being stirred by the case of Queen Caroline.
Popular opinion everywhere backed the Queen against the
reprobate King and his unpopular ministers, and the Radicals

enthusiastically took up the Queen's cause as a stick wherewith
to beat the Government. Cobbett was swept off his feet, and
became the Queen's most determined partisan. He wrote her
famous open letter to the King, and took the lead in organising
the flood of loyal petitions from town meetings, political societies,
and working-class bodies. Queen Caroline, by no action of her
own, had a great influence in furthering Radical and working-
class organisation. In Cobbett's hands, she became a powerful
instrument of the Reformers. Her death, after the withdrawal
of the proceedings against her had been triumphantly secured,
caused a momentary set back to the Radicals. But soon the
movement for Reform went forward more vigorously than ever.

By this time there had been some recovery from the economic
prostration which had followed the conclusion of the war. The
condition of the workers in the countryside remained as bad as
ever; but they were helpless. In the towns, trade was better, and
unemployment had decreased. Distress was still severe; but the
spontaneous hunger riots of the years after the Peace were
already giving place to more sympathetic working-class organisation. Permanent Trade Unions were being formed; and in 1824
and 1825 the repeal of the Combination Acts enabled them to
come out in the open. Under the influence of Owenite doctrines, the workers were beginning to create Co-operative
Societies; and working-class political societies were springing up
in most of the larger towns. In short, the working-class movement was beginning to take shape as an organised protest against
exploitation.

All this time Cobbett was incessantly writing and lecturing.
He was now in close association with the chief bodies of working-class Radicals, and had come to appreciate much more fully
the situation and the aspirations of the industrial workers. His
Tours and Rides took him into the factory districts as well as
the villages; he was a greater power in Lancashire than in
Hampshire or in Sussex. For it seemed as if the rural workers
had been pressed down too far to have any power of resistance
left. Radicalism had its strongholds, not in the villages, but in
Lancashire and Yorkshire, the industrial Midlands, and the
South of Scotland. But these industrial workers too were peasants
—countrymen rooted up from the soil, and planted in the un-
congenial atmosphere of the new factory towns. When Cobbett

spoke to them he spoke as peasant to peasant—and he was understood.

This is not to say that Cobbett had any clearly thought-out policy for coping with the new conditions. Industrialism he hated, and did not pretend to understand. His cry was all for the removal of abuses and oppressions, and he staked his faith in the reform of Parliament as the means to that end. He was for ever saying that he and the people of England wanted 'nothing new', that they sought only a restoration of what had been filched from them by financial jugglery, by enclosures, by the power of the new rich, and by governmental oppression. He was looking back to the Old England that was gone past recall, not forward to the control of the new forces of mechanical industrialism. This disabled him from becoming the leader of the younger working-class Radicals who accepted the industrial Revolution, and were feeling their way towards a Socialist solution of its problems. Cobbett was no Socialist. But the very fact that he was not was a symptom of his unity with the main body of the workers. For these dispossessed peasants were no more Socialists than he. They heeded him, because he felt and thought as one of themselves.

So Cobbett played his part in the great agitation which led up to the Reform of Parliament in 1832. More than any other man, he held the agitation together. And in its final phases he played once more an outstanding part. In 1830, when the towns were shouting for Reform, the labourers of the South-Eastern counties, driven beyond endurance by the lowering of their standard of life, broke out into what has been called 'the last labourers' revolt' in English history. For a time, whole districts were in the hands of the labourers, who marched from place to place demanding higher wages, the abolition of tithes, and other reforms. The Whigs, newly come to power and eager to show their zeal for law and order, suppressed the revolt with military force, followed by savage judicial murders and transportations. Cobbett, while opposing violence, wrote defending the labourers and attacking their oppressors, including the Whig Government. The Government retaliated by prosecuting him. He defended himself in a masterly speech, in which he rather constituted himself the Government's accuser. The jury disagreed, and he was discharged, the Whigs not venturing on another trial. He

had scored a triumph, both for himself and for the cause of
free speech and the rights of agitation.

1831 was the year of the Bristol Riots—a year of happenings
which made reform inevitable. In 1832 the King and the Lords
yielded, and the Reform Act became law. Cobbett, who had
stood unsuccessfully in earlier years for Coventry and Preston,
was returned to Parliament for Oldham, as the colleague of
John Fielden, the Radical employer, prominent as a friend of
Owen and a leader in the agitation for factory reform.

Cobbett was 68 years old when he was returned to the House
of Commons. But his energy was undiminished. From the outset
he made himself the leader of a small group of extreme Radicals,
opening his parliamentary career by opposing the re-election of
the Speaker, and his maiden speech with the words 'It appears
to me that since I have been sitting here I have heard a great
deal of unprofitable discussion'. He supported the Factory Act
of 1833, and spoke and voted regularly against all measures of
coercion in Ireland. Again and again, he led his little band of
followers into the lobby against the dominant Whig majority.

The Whigs he had always hated at least as much as the
Tories; and, though he had been ready to act with them in
securing the passing of the Reform Act, he was under no illusions
about the policy they were likely to pursue. Before the election
of 1832, he had done his best to get together a strong body of
Radical candidates, who would be prepared to take an independent line. He realised that, in putting the middle-classes into
power, the workers were only changing their masters. His worst
fears were realised when, in 1834, the Whig Government produced its Poor Law Amendment Bill.

The last year of Cobbett's life was spent in an unavailing
struggle against the great Whig menace—the systematic application of the principles of orthodox political economy to the
problem of poverty. Ever since his first awakening to the state
of the country 30 years before, Cobbett had been ceaselessly
upholding the right of the poor, not merely to relief, but to
adequate maintenance out of the abounding national wealth.
To demonstrate this right had been the main purpose of his
History of the Protestant Reformation, and he had driven home
his argument in a score of pamphlets, and in hundreds of articles
in the *Register.* Now, the economists and 'feelosofers' of the

Whig party, so far from improving on the niggardly relief granted under the old system, proposed to sweep even this away, and to apply the workhouse test and the principles of 'deterrence' and 'less eligibility' to all claimants for relief. Cobbett divided the House of Commons against every proposal in the Bill, meeting always with overwhelming defeat. He also urged the starting of a national organisation to combat the Bill, not merely in the House of Commons, but when it came to be actually applied.

All through this time Cobbett, in addition to assiduous attention in Parliament, kept the *Register* going and wrote a good part of it, continued to write fresh books and pamphlets, spent his parliamentary vacations in lecturing tours as far afield as Ireland, and conducted the farm near Farnham to which he had moved, from a smaller farm at Kensington, a few years before. The strain was too great, even for his fine physique. For the first time in his life, illness beset him. Hacking coughs, an attack of influenza, prostrated him. In May, 1835, he insisted on sitting through a debate in the House on agricultural distress. He was then taken seriously ill; but he persisted on carrying on his journalistic work. On June 18th, 1835, after a few days in bed, he died peacefully. At his earnest wish, he was carried round his farm the afternoon before his death. On 20 June the *Register* appeared black-bordered, with an article by John Morgan Cobbett announcing that his father was dead.

Cobbett died, then, in harness, after an extraordinarily full life of 72 years. He retained all his powers to the end; his *Legacy to Labourers* and *Legacy to Parsons,* which contain some of his best writing, were written when he was over 70. His most enduring work, *Rural Rides,* were nearly all written when he was over 60. The years beween 60 and 70 were his most fruitful literary period. All his life he lived hard, and had a most extraordinary power of work. And into all that he did he put an abounding vitality, which remains alive to-day in every line of his writing. He had, in a sense, no message or gospel to proclaim. He is not, like his contemporary Robert Owen, the father or founder of many of the movements of our own time. He was not a theorist; he could never form judgments that went beyond the lessons of his own immediate experience. Yet, in another sense, he is all the more alive for that very reason. He translates

for us, into strong, expressive language, the actual feelings and
thoughts of the common people of his day, showing us their perplexities and bewilderments in face of the swift movement of
social change, speaking across the century with Old England's
authentic voice. Against Whiggism and Toryism, against enclos-
ing landlords and exploiting factory owners, against Hannah
More and Wilberforce, Sidmouth and Castlereagh, Melbourne
and Peel, against Scottish 'feelosofers' and disciples of Parson
Malthus, against every reactionary and crazy 'reformer' who
sought to take away the people's right to pleasure, Cobbett's
great protest stands. He may be wrong here, and unfair there.
Many of his 'remedies' may seem to us, in the light of after
days, no remedies at all. But he was right about the main thing,
that he saw the people oppressed and degraded, and that he
fought every oppressor with all his might, and with a deep
sagacity that struck down beneath the facile optimism of the
political economists and the rising middle-class. He was a great
egotist, and a hard man to stomach in his own day. But much
of his egotism was really a personification. As Walt Whitman
identified himself with Young America, Cobbett identified himself with his own people. Every blow struck at him was a blow
at them; every blow at them was a blow at him. All blows were
returned with interest.

It is a curious, and a revealing fact that this egotist, who had
so many quarrels in his own day, is in ours almost universally
popular and beloved. When I published my *Life of Cobbett*,
reviewers of all shades of political opinion united to speak well
of him; and even to claim him as belonging, in some sort, to
their own sects. They did this because they all felt in him something peculiarly typical—something representative of England
as only a few of the greatest writers, such as Dickens, are representative. Cobbett is, indeed, the one British working-class leader
who has in him also the makings of a national hero. Would
there were more!

G. D. H. Cole

4 RICHARD CARLILE 1790-1843

RICHARD CARLILE died in 1843 at the age of 52, and of his adult life nearly 10 years were spent in prison. He was jailed for blasphemy, jailed again for sedition, and jailed yet again as a consequence of his stand against paying Church rates. He was for the greater part of his active life the leader of the struggle for free speech on religious questions and the most hated of all the 'blasphemers' against whom the Vice Society directed its efforts: yet he lived to describe himself as the Reverend Richard Carlile and to publish a periodical with the title of the *Christian Warrior*. He accomplished this seeming *volte-face*, moreover, without any conscious change in his fundamental opinions, albeit with a great change in his ways of expressing them. In matters political he changed much more—from an intransigent Radicalism to an entire disbelief in the value of Radical political methods. But even here the change was more of method than of fundamental aim. Carlile ceased long before the end of his days to believe in Radicalism; but that did not mean that he turned into a Tory or a Whig. It was politics on which he turned his back, in the conviction that political reform would come when men were ready for it, and could not come sooner.

The episode of Carlile's life that is best remembered, and that gives him his assured place in the history of both Radicalism and Freethought, is his re-publication of the writings of Tom Paine. Paine's *Rights of Man* had been a proscribed book ever since 1792, when the author was condemned on its account for seditious libel, but could not be jailed because he had gone to France. Paine's *Age of Reason,* in which he attacked the notion of the Bible as an inspired book and affirmed his own Deism, was also a proscribed book. Thomas Williams had been

61

imprisoned for publishing a part of it in 1797, and Daniel Isaac
Eaton for reprinting it in 1812. Carlile reissued both books in
1818, together with the rest of Paine's political and theological
works. He sold these works both in expensive bound volumes
and in cheap parts, at prices which poor people could afford to
pay; and he continued to publish and sell them in spite of all the
law and the Government could do to stop him. Aided by a long
sequence of volunteer shopmen, who went to jail one after
another for the cause of free speech, he defied the law and the
Government until it was at last thought best to let him alone,
and the persecution collapsed. No one thereafter prevented
Paine's works from being sold; and both 'sedition' and 'blasphemy' were less widely interpreted by the courts of law.
Carlile claimed that this stand made by himself and his followers
had achieved the freedom of the press, which he regarded as
the final guarantee of human progress. In this he claimed too
much. The great battle of the 'unstamped' had to be renewed
by others, such as Henry Hetherington, after Carlile had won his
initial victory; and the struggle against the Blasphemy Laws is
not finished yet. Nevertheless, Carlile's triumph was notable,
and could not have been won without exceptional courage and
singleness of purpose.

HALF-EMPLOYED MECHANIC
Richard Carlile was born at Ashburton, in Devonshire, on
8 December, 1790. His father, in turn cobbler, exciseman,
schoolmaster and soldier, died at the age of 34, when Richard
was four years old. That his father was given to drink may have
had something to do with the son's ardent dislike of alcohol;
but there were other good reasons for such a dislike in days
when gin was dirt-cheap. Carlile's mother was left with Richard
and two elder sisters to bring up on very slender resources; but
Richard, after some years of very rudimentary schooling, was
sent to Ashburton Free School, where he remained until he was
12 and picked up a little Latin. He was then apprenticed to an
Exeter druggist, with whom he stayed only a few months, and
then, after a short interval, to a tinplate worker, with whom he
served out his time—not without certain disputes concerning the
rights of apprentices, but without being influenced by the
Republican ideas which, he tells us, were common among his

workmates. In 1811 he first came to London in search of a job, but spent most of the next two years wandering from job to job about the country. Early in 1813 he was working at Gosport; and there, at the age of 22, he wooed and married a wife some years older than himself, with whom he settled down in London later in the year.

For the next two years and more Carlile worked at his trade as a tinplate-worker in various parts of London, playing no part in politics or other public affairs. But the end of the Napoleonic Wars and the severe economic distress which ensued caused a ferment which brought him, as well as very many others, to a different mood. Carlile reacted at once towards the extremest form of Radicalism and began writing letters, which were not published on account of their violence, to the Radical press. 'A half-employed mechanic is too violent', commented the *News,* in refusing to print one of his contributions. He became convinced, he tells us, that if he could but get a half-sheet pamphlet of his own printed, it would be a novelty in politics, and his fortune would be made. He little knew how soon much more than that chance was to come his way.

1816 was the year of the first great outpouring of cheap Radical journalism addressed directly to the common people. Cobbett's famous *Political Register* had been appearing for 14 years, but at a price which made it prohibitive to the masses. In 1816, because of the stamp duty on newspapers, it cost 1s 0½d an issue. Then Cobbett, moved by the post-war excitement to attempt a more direct appeal than could be got by the reading aloud of his paper in inns and coffee-houses which dared to take it in, conceived the idea of offprinting his own long leading articles and selling them, in unfolded sheets, apart from the rest of the paper. By this method, excluding news as such, he removed his articles from the category of newspapers subject to tax, and was able to get a circulation many times as large as any periodical had ever previously enjoyed. Very soon, he improved on this by making up his articles into weekly pamphlets which, on paying the very much smaller tax imposed on such publications, he was able to sell cheaply without breaking the law. These cheap pamphlets, in which Cobbett published his memorable *Addresses to the Journeymen and Labourers,* were

nicknamed *Twopenny Trash*; and Cobbett seized on the name
with glee, and made it his own.

Very soon, there were others in the field. William Hone, the
famous parodist, started his *Reformists' Register* in 1816; and
in 1817 there followed Jonathan Wooler's *Black Dwarf,* supported by Major Cartwright, and in 1818 John Wade's *Gorgon,*
for which Francis Place wrote and round which rallied the
Trade Unions, so that it deserves to be called the first Trade
Union newspaper. In 1817 appeared also William Sherwin's
Republican, which after a few issues changed its name to
Sherwin's Political Register, because *Republican* was deemed
too dangerous a title.

Carlile, the 'half-employed mechanic', had no use for Cobbett,
whom he regarded as much too moderate. But the *Black Dwarf*
and the *Republican* appealed to him; and in March 1817 he
borrowed a sovereign from his employer and invested it in a stock
of *Black Dwarfs,* which he went round London vending to
retailers whom he could persuade to sell them. Within a week or
two he was selling *Republicans* and other journals as well, but
was refusing, despite many requests from newsvendors, to supply
Cobbett's *Register* or other more popular journals which were
less to his taste. The legality of these Radical papers was doubtful, on more than one account. Pitt's Newspaper Act of 1798
had required all newspapers to be registered, and had imposed
upon them high duties which so raised their prices as to confine
their circulation to the well-to-do; and the same Act had
imposed severe penalties on the printers or publishers of unstamped newspapers, and even on anyone who was found with
such a paper in his possession. Radical journals designed for
poor readers could not pay these taxes; and their doubtful
legality rested on their being regarded, not as newspapers, but
as periodical pamphlets in which opinion rather than news
played the leading part. As pamphlets they needed to pay only
a small tax; and in practice most of them paid nothing at all.
But there was always the danger that the courts might hold a
periodical pamphlet to be a newspaper, and therefore subject
to the full provisions of the Act of 1798.

Moreover, the Radical publishers of 1817 were subject to an
additional danger. In March 1817 Lord Sidmouth, as Home
Secretary, had got through Parliament the first of his 'Gagging'

Acts, under which Habeas Corpus was suspended on plea that there existed 'a traitorous conspiracy for the purpose of over-throwing by means of a general insurrection the established Government, Laws and Constitution of this Kingdom', and Sidmouth had promptly followed up this Act with a circular to magistrates and other officers throughout the country urging them to take active measures for the arrest and conviction of dangerous libellers and seditious persons. Further Acts were speedily passed—a re-enactment with some changes of the Treason Act of 1795 and a new and rigorous Act directed against Seditious Meetings and Assemblies, suppressing by name some of the best-known Radical societies, and threatening with deprivation of their licences owners of public houses who allowed seditious meetings to take place on their premises.

These 'Gagging' Acts, with the exception of the first, did not strike directly at the press. But the suspension of Habeas Corpus and the invitation to the authorities to take strong measures against libellers under the common law were enough to set prosecutions on foot all over the country, and to make Radical journalism an exceptionally perilous trade.

In 1817, in fact, the Tory Government, dominated by such men as Lord Eldon and Lord Sidmouth, and seeing everywhere around it the deep economic distress which had followed upon the end of the long war, was living in daily fear of popular insurrection. Whether the fear was justified is another matter; for there is a long distance between hunger-marching and actual rebellion, and there is no evidence that any organised conspiracy existed to link together the local forces of unrest. The panic of the Government, however is certain; and no moment could have been more perilous for entry upon the trade of Radical publisher. William Cobbett, by far the most influential of the tribe, fled to the United States almost as soon as Habeas Corpus was suspended, and for the next two years edited his *Political Register* from the other side of the Atlantic. His going created a void, which others, bolder or with less at stake, were prompt to fill. Cobbett was roundly abused for running away in the hour of crisis; but he had had his dose of prison already, and it must be added in extenuation that creditors, fully as much as the Government's agents, were pursuing him at home.

It was this danger that gave Carlile his chance. Sherwin got

married, and did not want to take more risks than he need.
He had a printing press; but he was looking for someone to act
as agent for the sale of his *Register*, and thus stand to some extent
between him and the danger of prosecution. He approached
Carlile, who leapt at the chance of taking over Sherwin's shop
in Fleet Street, and there selling his paper for him, with freedom
to embark on what other ventures he might please.

THE FIRST PROSECUTION

Accordingly, in April 1817, Carlile opened shop, and all went
on smoothly until August. But from then events moved swiftly.
Early in the year William Hone had published his parodies on
the Lord's Prayer and on other sacred writings, but had withdrawn them from circulation on being threatened with prosecution. Carlile, with some difficulty, got hold of copies, and reissued
the parodies without Hone's consent, thus bringing upon Hone,
as well as upon himself, prosecution for 'blasphemous libel'. It
is well known how in three successive trials Hone was acquitted
by London juries which laughed immoderately at his wit and
were unmoved by the shocked admonitions of judge and counsel.
Carlile was less fortunate. He was never brought to trial; but he
was kept in prison for 18 weeks before being released as a result
of Hone's acquittal.

In the meantime his wife, Jane Carlile, soon reopened the
shop in Fleet Street, selling not only Sherwin's *Political Register*
but also other dangerous works, including a pirated edition of
Southey's play, *Wat Tyler*, written in his rebellious youth.
Southey, like Shelley in the case of *Queen Mab* and Byron later
in the cases of *Cain, Don Juan,* and the *Vision of Judgment,* had
no power to stop the sale, because the law refused to recognise
any copyright in publications which it regarded as either blasphemous or seditious, and thereby actually helped their circulation, as long as there were printers or booksellers ready to take
the risk.

Carlile, imprisoned in August 1817, was released in December,
after Hone's acquittal. He had employed a part of his time in
prison in writing some parodies of his own, on much the same
lines as Hone's, but much more Radical and very much more
offensive to religious sentiment. These were promptly published;
and he also set about reissuing Tom Paine's works, beginning

with *Rights of Man* and other political writings, which were issued with Sherwin's *Register* and also sold separately in cheap parts, and were later bound up in volume form. From these Carlile proceeded, near the end of the year, to begin the publication of the *Age of Reason* and Paine's other theological writings. He also, during 1818, joined with Sherwin and others in running Henry Hunt—'Orator' Hunt—as Radical candidate for Westminster against Sir Francis Burdett and Sir Samuel Romilly, of whose moderation he disapproved.

It is difficult for those who read Paine's *Rights of Man* nowadays to understand how it remained up to 1818 a book which it was dangerous to publish. It is easier to understand the ban on the *Age of Reason,* though its deistical arguments went no further than a host of writers before Paine had gone with impunity. The difficulty, however, vanishes as soon as one reads the trials for sedition and blasphemy which were held in plenty during the years after 1815; for it at once appears that the judges drew a sharp line between works which were written for the educated classes and works designed to appeal to the 'ignorant masses', and that they treated as criminal all writings of the latter class which either might bring the Christian religion, or even the Established Church, into discredit or contempt, or might bring into similar discredit any part of the British Constitution as it then stood, or even the Government of the day. It was plainly the view of the judges that, whereas gentlemen might wrangle among themselves about religion or politics without risking legal penalties unless they went very far, any attempt to put 'subversive' notions before the 'lower orders' was sedition or blasphemy and punishable under the Common Law, even when it did not offend against any specific statute. Indeed, the judges were apt sometimes to get the offences of 'sedition' and 'blasphemy' so confused as to denounce a prisoner as 'blaspheming' when his offence was only that of questioning the wisdom and impartiality of the judicial bench. The theory on which the judges acted—and juries, being carefully selected from the respectable classes, usually supported them—was that the poor had no business to concern themselves with politics or with religious disputes, and had an unqualified duty of loyal devotion to the established constitution of Church and State.

This was the attitude which Carlile was determined to

challenge, not by half-measures, but out and out. It was his view, which he continued to assert by word and deed for the rest of his life, that no limits at all should be set to the right of free discussion for any section of the people, and that upon this freedom to face all questions in a spirit of untrammelled inquiry the entire hope of human progress was bound to depend. If he talked 'sedition', or published it, this was the cause in which he worked : if he 'blasphemed', this was his final reason for uttering 'blasphemy'.

—AND THE SECOND

In January 1819 his second struggle with the law began. In that month he was indicted for blasphemy, but admitted to bail. In the same month he issued further parts of Paine's *Theological Works,* and opened a new and larger shop in Fleet Street for the display of his own and other Radical and 'blasphemous' publications. These ventures brought William Wilberforce's Vice Society (the Society for the Suppression of Vice, which had been founded in 1802) into the field against him, and he was again arrested and spent four days in prison before he was admitted to bail. He published an *Open Letter to the Vice Society,* defending his conduct and retorting vigorously, and continued to sell in his shop all the offending works. Further charges poured in; and, in accordance with the legal practice of the time, there was a great bandying of technicalities, with the effect of delaying the actual trials. In June the original indictment came on, but the trial was postponed, and Carlile remained at large.

So far, Carlile had been merely Sherwin's agent for the sale of the *Register,* and Sherwin had remained as both printer and publisher, with his name duly recorded in both capacities. Carlile had contributed articles under a pseudonym; but the *Register* had been in no sense his, though he had doubtless played a large part in influencing Sherwin's attitude. In August 1819, however, Sherwin gave up the *Register* entirely to Carlile, who thereupon became both publisher and editor, and defiantly changed the name back to that which Sherwin had abandoned as too provocative in 1817. The *Register,* on 27 August, became again the *Republican*; and Carlile also began to issue the *Deist,* which he announced as a 'collection of all scarce and valuable Deistical Tracts, from both ancient and modern writers'. Among these tracts was *The Principles of Nature,* a work by Elihu Palmer, a blind American Deist; and this publication at once became the basis for further prosecutions instituted by the Society for the Suppression of Vice.

It will be remembered that 1819 was the year in which the troubles which followed the close of the Napoleonic Wars reached their height—the year of the Peterloo Massacre and the Six Acts. In August Carlile, at the invitation of the Manchester Reformers, headed by John Knight, was in attendance at Henry Hunt's great meeting in St. Peter's Fields, when the yeomanry cavalry rode down the unarmed demonstrators and earned for the occasion the name of the 'Peterloo Massacre'. Stationed near Hunt, Carlile escaped from the Fields, and made speed back to London, where he wrote and published in the *Republican* a full account of the massacre and therewith an angry attack on the Government which was responsible for it. His article, in the form of a *Letter to Lord Sidmouth,* led to his prompt arrest on a charge of sedition; but yet again, this time after six days in prison, he was let out on bail.

Carlile's trial came on in October; but he was tried, not for his Peterloo article, but on various charges of 'blasphemy' in connection with Paine's *Age of Reason* and Palmer's *Principles of Nature.* He always referred to the affair as his 'Mock Trial', on the double ground that he refused to recognise the validity of any law which suppressed free discussion, and above all of the Common Law, which he regarded as a judge-made abuse, and that the judges who tried him held that no argument which impugned the truth of the Christian religion could be allowed in court, on the ground that Christianity was the law of the land and any attempt to question its truth therefore criminal. Carlile defended himself. He insisted on reading the whole of Paine's *Age of Reason* in the course of the first trial; and on the second day he attempted by reading and commenting upon many passages of Scripture to prove the inherent contradictions of the Bible story, as well as the immoral tendency of much that the book contained. This procedure led to many disputes with the judge, Abbott, who was reputed to be in private life an unbeliever. In the second trial, held at the instance of the Vice Society, Carlile attempted to repeat the same tactics by reading Palmer's *Principles of Nature,* but was stopped by the

jury. He was convicted on both occasions; but the third accusation against him, on the basis of his Peterloo article, was then
allowed to drop.

SOLITARY CONFINEMENT

In November, Carlile moved for a new trial, partly on technical
grounds but mainly on the ground that the judge's rulings had
prevented him from making his defence. His motion was refused,
and a few days later he was brought up for sentence. For publishing the *Age of Reason* he was fined £1,000 and sent to prison
for two years; and for publishing *Principles of Nature* he was
fined £500 and sent to prison for a year. In addition, he was
called upon, as a condition of release at the expiry of his sentence, to give security in £1,000 and two others in £100 each to
keep the peace and be of good behaviour for the rest of his life.

So severe a sentence would have been felt by most men as
crushing; for where was Carlile to find £2,500 or sureties for
his future good behaviour? Moreover, this was not all. His shop
was seized by the authorities, and his stock of books and papers
taken away; and for a month after his sentence the police
remained in possession. He, meanwhile, was hurried away to
Dorchester Gaol, and there placed in solitary confinement.

Carlile, however, was by no means crushed in spirit. He had
the endurance and the persistence of the fanatical believer; and
he fully intended to go on with the good work. He had begun,
immediately after his trial, to print and put on sale in cheap
parts a full report of the proceedings, embodying the prohibited
text of Paine's *Age of Reason,* which he had read out in full in
court, in order to have a new excuse for publishing it lawfully
as part of the account of his trial. This publication was interrupted when the police seized his premises, and the full report
of the first day's trial was not issued until 1822. But as soon as
the police vacated his premises the shop was reopened, with
Carlile's wife in charge. As the authorities had seized all the
stock they could lay hands on, and would not return it, Jane
Carlile had to reopen with what stock she could scrape together
from the printers, and with such further scraps as she could
afford to print. It has often been said that Jane Carlile did this
having no sympathy with her husband's opinions, but feeling the
call to stand by him in resistance to oppression. But this is

definitely incorrect. There are writings of her own in the
Republican and elsewhere, which decisively confute it. Jane
Carlile did fully agree with her husband's views, though not
so fully with his intransigence in standing up for them. At this
critical juncture she stood by him, and, being an excellent
woman of business, ran the shop with considerable success,
profiting by the large demand which the trials had produced
for a type of publication which the Government and the Vice
Society were uniting their best efforts to suppress.

Probably the notion that Jane Carlile was not in sympathy
with her husband's views arose because they differed about
tactics. Carlile wished to go to all lengths in defying the law, by
putting on sale again as quickly as possible all the works which
had been condemned or seized by the authorities. Jane Carlile,
or those on whose advice she acted, refrained from selling any
work which had been explicitly condemned by a jury, while
continuing to sell and issue other works of precisely the same
character, as fast as printers could be got to produce them. The
printers, however, were not unnaturally somewhat shy; and
though sales were good, cash was always short, because, as
Carlile said later, he put every penny he could lay hands on into
print and paper. Jane Carlile had therefore plenty to do; but
Carlile, from prison, protested publicly at her pusillanimity, and
also the expurgation which the *Republican* suffered weekly
at the printer's hands. But he was powerless; and indeed it soon
appeared that even his wife's partial defiance of the law was
dangerous enough. If she had gone further, there would almost
certainly have been an immediate raid on the shop, and a
seizure of the offending works; whereas, by selling only works
which had not yet been explicitly condemned, she was able to
keep the shop open, and to force the Vice Society to embark
continually on fresh prosecutions.

THE 'GAG' ACTS

Carlile was not the only Radical who suffered condemnation in
1819. There were many victims, who ventured to criticise too
boldly the Government's congratulations to the victors of
Peterloo, or fell foul of the Vice Society or the Government on
other counts of blasphemy or sedition. Even so respectable a
Radical as Sir Francis Burdett, M.P. for Wesminster, went to

jail for six months for attacking the Government's handling of the Peterloo affair; and when, towards the end of the year, the Government, following up Sidmouth's 'Gagging' Acts of 1817, rushed through Parliament the notorious Six Acts, everything appeared to be set for a period of extreme repression. In particular, the outlook for the Radical press was gloomy to the last degree, as it seemed clear that the Government meant to spare no effort in stopping the sale of unstamped periodicals and in intimidating printers by the fear of having their deposits forfeited and their presses shut down.

Of the notorious Six Acts, there were two which struck directly at the Radical press. The Blasphemous and Seditious Libels Act, in its preamble, included in the category of libels not only attempts to alter the constitution of Church or State by other than lawful means, but also any publication tending to bring into hatred or contempt the King or the Government or the Constitution as by law established. The Act itself increased the power of the authorities to search for and to seize libellous publications; and it went to the extreme length of empowering the courts to banish from the British Empire any person convicted under it of a second offence. This was an immensely powerful deterrent to Radical publishers and writers; for it virtually meant that anyone who was not prepared to face the risk of banishment had to retire from action permanently after a single conviction. That was why the struggle for press freedom had to be waged by continuous relays of volunteers, as long as there was any prospect of the extreme penalty being enacted. It is astonishing that, under these circumstances, the Radical press managed to survive at all: yet survive it did.

Nor was this all; for the Government passed also a Publications Act designed to strike directly at the unstamped periodicals which had hitherto been immune from the heavy tax imposed on regular newspapers. Periodicals which were primarily vehicles of opinion rather than news had hitherto paid only a light tax imposed on pamphlets, or no tax at all. But in future they were all to be deemed to be newspapers if they contained either news, or observations on any matters in Church or State, were published oftener than once a month, and cost less than sixpence. Over and above all this, every printer or publisher of a newspaper, as now defined, was to be compelled to enter into a bond of £300 (£200 outside London) as an assurance of payment of any fines or penalties that might be imposed for violation of the law; and justices of the peace were given powers to bind over those accused of offences, or to convict by summary jurisdiction.

Nevertheless, the output of Radical journalism was not stopped, though circulations were seriously curtailed, and Cobbett's *Register* could no longer be produced in its cheap form. Such cheap papers as did survive had to be produced and sold in open defiance of a law which was now both more rigorous and more rigorously enforced. These were the circumstances in which Carlile determined to go on producing his *Republican* despite his incarceration in Dorchester Jail, with Mrs. Carlile as his publisher and help from the friends who had rallied round him.

Nowadays, a convicted prisoner would be given no chance of editing a newspaper and sending out regular articles for publication from his prison cell. But the jails of the early nineteenth century were very different from modern prisons—in some ways much worse, but in others very much better, for the prisoner who had money at his command. It was a regular practice for such prisoners to be allowed to pay for special accommodation and food, and to be allowed their own books and writing materials and a freedom in receiving and sending letters which was practically unlimited. In most prisons, the prisoner who could afford to pay his jailer handsomely was allowed freely to entertain his friends and even to have members of his family to stay with him in the prison. These privileges were expensive; and the lot of the poor prisoner was usually very bad indeed. But even he was not shut up as a rule in solitary confinement; and those who were not appalled by the social and moral atmosphere were probably a good deal less unhappy than the prisoners of today—though they also stood a much greater chance of dying of jail-fever or some other infection before their sentences ran out.

PRISONER'S PRINT

At the time when Carlile was sent to Dorchester Jail the movement for prison reform was in full swing; and Dorchester, unlike the Giltspur Street Compter in London, where Carlile had served his earlier term, was regarded as a reformed prison. Moreover, the Government sent down special instructions that he should be isolated from other prisoners, lest he should contaminate them by his evil influence. The captive therefore found himself condemned to solitary confinement and subject to severe restrictions on his right to exercise in the open air—so severe that he retaliated characteristically by refusing to leave his room at all over a prolonged period. But prison reform had not advanced so far at Dorchester as to prevent him from having free communication with the outside world by means of writing, though his visitors were to some extent restricted. He was therefore able, despite his confinement, to continue bringing out the *Republican*; but inevitably much of the work had to be done by others, and the distance of Dorchester from London presented an additional problem. Carlile, as we have seen, regarded his wife and her helpers as much too timid in their conduct of his affairs.

The *Republican* continued to appear during 1820; and the rest of Carlile's publications were kept on sale. Soon a further crop of prosecutions was pending; but there were the usual delays, and it was not until October that any case actually came into court. In that month Mrs. Carlile was tried and convicted; but the conviction was upset on a pure technicality, and she was never sentenced. The barrister who saved her was Matthew Davenport Hill, later Recorder of Birmingham, and in 1820 a member of the circle of Radical lawyers who had gathered round Jeremy Bentham. This group, including John Austin, the author of *Principles of Jurisprudence,* Henry Cooper, and a number of other rising young barristers, was of great help throughout the struggle to such of Carlile's followers as were prepared to act on legal advice. Most of the victims, however, were less intent on getting acquitted than on using their trials as a means of testifying to their faith and securing publicity for the doctrines which the law was seeking to suppress. By defying the judges, reading out passages which were regarded as blasphemous or seditious, and challenging the right of any court to convict in matters of opinion, they were able to get reported in the newspapers, and in some cases to get the proceedings at their trials reprinted in full in pamphlet form.

The first of these more intransigent victims was Thomas Davison, who was sentenced to two years' imprisonment, and ordered to find sureties to be of good behaviour for a period of five years. This happened in October 1820, on charges based on Carlile's *Life of Paine* and on articles in the *Republican* and the *Deists' Magazine*. Davison, who defended himself, had a tremendous passage of arms with Mr. Justice Best, the most savage of the judges dealing with offences against the laws of blasphemy and sedition. Davison was himself an active journalist as extreme as Carlile, the producer of a number of short-lived journals such as *Medusa* and *The Cap of Liberty*.

In the prosecution of 1820 blasphemy, rather than sedition, was the offence pursued by the law. The Vice Society was active in laying informations and stirring up the Government to prosecute offenders in this field; but there was no parallel unofficial body to deal with the cases of 'sedition'. Towards the end of the year a number of 'loyal' persons, including many who had been connected with the Vice Society and reinforced by the Duke of Wellington and other leading Tories, were induced by a firm of solicitors, who doubtless saw good prospects of profit in the job, to found a Constitutional Association for the express purpose of suppressing seditious publications. This body for the next two years played an active part in the searching out of political offenders; but it was disliked by many of the judges and by many persons in the Government, who preferred not to have this unofficial gadfly on their tails. The group of Radical lawyers of whom I spoke earlier took up arms against the Constitutional Association and, by making the fullest use of legal technicalities, compelled it to spend a great deal of money without very much result. The Association soon found itself in difficulties; and during 1823 it vanished from the scene.

This did not mean that prosecutions ceased, but that they were mostly left to be brought by the Government, which preferred an occasional severe sentence to a continual crop of minor convictions. The struggle of which Carlile's shop was the centre lasted continuously up to 1825; and over the whole of this period shopman succeeded shopman, only to be arrested and convicted for selling one or another of the banned works. The next victim after Davison was Jane Carlile, who was convicted in January 1821 on a political charge arising out of an article in the *Republican* of 16 June, 1820. In this article Carlile, quoting historical precedents, had defended the right of personal

assassination of tyrants. He had argued against conspiracy to
kill, but had urged that a virtuous citizen acting without con-
federates and in the strength of his own conviction had a right
to slay an oppressor. Such a doctrine, in the troubled circumstances of the time, was not likely to be suffered to pass unnoticed; and Jane Carlile, with a young baby, was sent to join
her husband in Dorchester Jail for a period of two years. Her
place in the Fleet Street shop was at once taken by Carlile's
sister, Mary Anne, who had been for some time preparing for
the event. Promptly, both the Vice Society and the Constitutional Society laid information against her; and in July she
joined her brother and her sister-in-law at Dorchester on her
conviction on the blasphemy charge, though with the aid of the
Radical lawyers she succeeded in beating off the assault of the
Constitutional Society.

SCIENCE AND RELIGION

Meanwhile, the *Republican* had ceased to appear at the end of
1820, presumably because Carlile could not find funds to keep
it in existence. He replaced it, for the time, by a series of occasional pamphlets, mostly in the form of a series of *Addresses to
the Reformers,* in which he put his case for root-and-branch
reformation of both Church and State. Hitherto, following
Paine, he had described himself as a Deist; but the fruit of his
prison reflections was a conversion to thorough-going Atheism,
based on a materialistic view of the universe. 'I advocate the
abolition of all religions, without setting up anything new of the
kind,' he wrote in 1821, with evident reference to the various
preachers of 'rational' or 'allegorical' religions who were plentiful
at the time, and whose views he was later to turn to his own
purpose.

This developed irreligion of Carlile's full manhood was based
on a tremendous faith in the cleansing power of knowledge. The
essence of what he taught is best expressed in the *Address to the
Men of Science,* which he published in May 1821. Science, he
believed, was rapidly opening men's eyes to the absurdities of
revealed religion, making clear the material foundations of man's
nature, and affording the basis for a universal enlightenment
which would speedily make an end of persecution, bigotry, war,
exploitation, and all the evils of contemporary society. The

science he had particularly in mind was that of chemistry, which had been making prodigious strides on the foundations laid by Dalton's atomic theory. What Darwin and biology were to the generation which read *The Origin of Species* chemistry was to the materialists of Carlile's day, who found in the light of its discoveries a fresh wisdom in Diderot, Helvetius, and d'Holbach. It is often not realised to what extent there was a scientific ferment based on chemical advance a full generation before Darwin and well before Lyell's *Principles of Geology* (1830) had set the theologians and their critics grappling with the new knowledge about the age of the earth. Biology also played a minor part at this earlier stage; for there were rationalists who had read Erasmus Darwin and invoked his authority against the belief in the immutability of species. But biology was then a side-line : chemistry was in the central position when science was invoked against the dogmas of revealed religion. Apart from that, the main contest was in terms of Biblical criticism : the familiar sport of exposing inconsistencies and historical absurdities in the Scriptures was being widely practised.

Carlile played his full part in this type of criticism, categorically denying that any such person as Christ could be shown to have existed, and that there was any historical warrant at all for the story set out in the books of the New Testament. His difference from most of the critics who took this line was that he was never content with a negative. He set out to preach a positive doctrine of perfectibility through absolutely free speech and discussion, which would not only banish error but also set free the immense powers of scientific discovery to work for the benefit of mankind. The *Address to the Men of Science* is Carlile's best work. Although there is much in it that is outmoded, it puts finely the constructive case for freedom over the whole wide field of human knowledge and intellectual power.

At the beginning of 1822, after a year's intermission, the *Republican* reappeared, and was thereafter kept going until Carlile let it drop at the end of 1826. Its reappearance was the signal for a fresh attack by the Government. In February Carlile's shop was raided by the police and closed, the entire stock being seized as an aid towards the payment of the fines which had been incurred. But this did not stop Carlile's followers.

Six weeks later, a new shop was opened in Water Lane, and the full Report of the 'Mock Trial' of 1819, which had been dropped in consequence of Jane Carlile's prosecution, was gone on with, and the whole issued in volume form with a defiant preface giving an account of the affair. Further prosecutions of Carlile's shopmen speedily followed; and among those convicted during 1822 was a woman, Susannah Wright, a lace-worker and wife of a bookseller, who had offered her services in the cause. Her trial was one of the most effective of the series, from Carlile's standpoint, and reports of it were widely circulated.

JAIL BABY

At the time of the renewed attack on Carlile's shopmen in the early months of 1822, there were yet other worries besetting him. Jane, his fellow-prisoner at Dorchester, was in an advanced state of pregnancy, and he memorialised Peel, the Home Secretary, with a petition for her release. Peel refused to make any concession, merely saying that the jailers would doubtless afford her such conveniences as were consistent with the nature of the place. Accordingly, the child was born in the jail, where Carlile, his wife and his sister were locked up all day in one room, kept apart from all the other prisoners. The *Republican* for this period is full of complaints and petitions from all three of them about their treatment in jail; but it does not appear that any alleviation was granted.

Hitherto, Carlile's following had been largely in London, though he had found since his imprisonment an increasing number of supporters in the industrial districts. In 1822 the *Republican* began a definite campaign to enlist nation-wide backing; and Carlile's followers formed groups in a number of towns, often under the name of Zetetic Societies. By this time, Radical politics were definitely receding into the background, and Carlile was concentrating more and more of his attention on freedom of religious discussion, which he regarded as the test issue, involving the wider matter of free speech in all its varied applications. He had finally broken with Henry Hunt, and had expressed his regret at having promoted his Westminster candidature in 1818. Hunt, in the course of his defence after Peterloo, had publicly dissociated himself from Carlile, and had spoken as if he had had no connection at all with him, although they had in fact ridden to the Peterloo meeting in the same vehicle, and Hunt had been a frequent visitor to Carlile's shop and had expressed strong sympathy with him in his persecution, albeit not with his religious views. There followed a dispute between Hunt and Mrs. Carlile over the sale in her shop of Hunt's Breakfast Beverage—a Radical coffee-substitute which the *Orator* was pushing as part of the campaign against use of excisable commodities. This small affair broadened out into a violent quarrel. In 1822 Hunt delivered a savage attack on Carlile in the *Memoirs* which he was issuing in parts from Ilchester Jail; and thereafter the two prisoners bombarded each other in their rival periodicals and in the Radical press generally. Hunt attacked Carlile's religious views, questioned his title to be regarded as a Radical Reformer, and accused him of being actuated solely by the motive of reaping profit from the sale of his blasphemous publications. Carlile retorted on Hunt with charges of cowardice at Peterloo, of not paying his debts, of letting down his Radical followers when they got into trouble, and of business dishonesty over the sale of his Breakfast Powder. It was altogether an unseemly affair; but the fault was Hunt's, for the form of his attack on Carlile was entirely indefensible.

CRUSADE FOR ENLIGHTENMENT

Hunt was, however, in the right in saying that Carlile could no longer be regarded as a Radical Reformer in the ordinary sense of the term. The fight for free speech, Carlile had decided, was all in all : political reform would be useless without intellectual enlightenment. He expressed his opposition to every kind of society or association, except those formed for purposes of free discussion. Political societies, he held, were useless as long as men remained unenlightened, and would become unnecessary as the scales of error and superstition dropped away from men's eyes. In this mood, he issued in 1823, side by side with the *Republican,* a new periodical, the *Moralist,* in which he appealed to reformers to observe a high standard of personal conduct, expressing sentiments to most of which not even his most inveterate opponents could have taken any exception. In particular, he urged upon his followers abstention from all excisable articles for the double purpose of promoting temperance and

self-discipline among Reformers and of striking the hardest blow
that could be struck at the corruptions of the State. His chief
political demand at this period was that all schools of Reformers
should unite in demanding a reduction of the Government's total
budget from nearly £60 millions to £10 millions; for this, he
said, would of itself suffice to bring the power of the tyrants to
an end.

1823 saw the release of Jane Carlile in February, and of
Mary Anne towards the end of the year. But the arrests of
Carlile's shopmen continued, one of the most famous, James
Watson, being jailed in April. The following year saw the persecution intensified, in a still more determined effort to close
Carlile's shop, which had by this time moved back to Fleet
Street. No less than 11 shopmen were arrested and sentenced
during the early months of 1824; but there was still no dearth of
volunteers, mostly now from the provinces, to take the place
of those who were jailed. Presently there was quite a concourse
of them in Newgate; and in September 1824 they began to edit
collectively the *Newgate Monthly Magazine,* which was published at Carlile's shop and lasted for two years. This year yet
another misfortune visited Carlile, a fire in Fleet Street spreading to his shop, which was thereafter pulled down. This, however, proved to be a disguised blessing, for he was able to sell
his damaged premises on advantageous terms for a street
improvement, and thus to meet the more pressing obligations
which had been crowding in upon him since his imprisonment.
His followers promptly opened up again, at another Fleet Street
address.

PRIEST OF REASON
At this point, the Government and the Vice Society at last
wearied of the struggle. In November 1825 Carlile was released
unconditionally from Dorchester Jail, though his fines had never
been paid and he refused to enter into any sort of recognisances
in respect of his future behaviour. Immediately on his release
he took a bigger shop in Fleet Street, and opened it as the
'Temple of Reason', forming at the same time a Joint Stock
Book Company to finance the publication of the types of work
for which he had been persecuted so long. One of his first issues
from this concern was Shelley's *Queen Mab*; and he also issued

Byron's *Don Juan, Cain,* and *The Vision of Judgment,* as well as Meslier's *Bon Sens* (originally published by Voltaire), Paine's *Works,* Palmer's *Principles,* and a host of other books which had been condemned by the courts. He was left unmolested; and from that time the *Age of Reason* and other works long proscribed were allowed to circulate freely.

This was a notable victory, which could not have been won but for Carlile's own leadership and the devotion with which one follower after another threw himself into the fight. There were many vicissitudes in the course of the long struggle; and many devices were resorted to on both sides. The common practice of the Government and the prosecuting societies had been to send agents to Carlile's shop with orders to purchase copies of works on which they proposed to found charges; and it was part of the shopman's duty to spot these informers and refuse sales—except on occasions when a particular prosecution was being actually courted. At one critical stage of the struggle in 1822 Carlile's shopmen resorted to the device of selling dangerous publications from behind a screen, on which was a clockface bearing the names of the works and equipped with a movable hand. This hand could be pointed to the work which the purchaser wanted; and the hidden shopman thereupon poked it through a hole in the screen, and thus escaped identification.

Well before his release from jail Carlile, in May 1825, had added a fresh count to the charges levelled against him by his opponents. He had published, in the *Republican,* the full text of a handbill, which was circulating widely in the North of England, giving practical advice to women on the best method of preventing conception as a consequence of sexual intercourse. It does not appear that Carlile himself had anything to do with the issue of this or other handbills which were at that time being circulated among the working classes, though in at least one instance a parcel of such bills had passed through his shop and been forwarded to Manchester at someone else's request. The story as told at the time was that Robert Owen had made a special journey to Paris to study the methods of contraception extensively practised on the Continent, and that the origin of some at any rate of the handbills rested with him and his disciples. Francis Place, an ardent advocate of birth-control, also came into the story. The handbill reprinted by Carlile recommended the use by women who wished to avoid conception of a moistened sponge, and held out the hope that this method would be found highly effective.

After his return Carlile in 1826 followed up the article in the *Republican* by publishing *Every Woman's Book,* which sold several thousand copies during the next few months, and was referred to in the last volume of the *Republican* on more than one occasion. These activities are enough to give Carlile a niche in the early history of the birth-control movement. But he did not follow them up. He wrote as follows several years later, in the *Isis* of 7 July, 1832 :— 'With the exception of a few physiological and social ideas bearing upon the welfare of mankind, the mention of which would have only gained me ignorant and inveterate and dangerous abuse, I have concealed nothing that I have acquired as knowledge.'

Carlile came out of prison full of fight, and for a year after his release all seemed to be going well. The Joint Stock Book Company was floated in January 1826, with shares of a value of £100 each, but with a provision whereby sums of £5 and upwards could be sent to Carlile, and invested in his name. Interest on all shares and deposits was to be paid at 5 per cent. But this venture did not last long. Carlile had been much too ambitious, and had hoped for much larger sales than were actually forthcoming; and he was soon again in financial trouble. Towards the end of 1826 he was taken seriously ill, doubtless partly as the deferred result of his long imprisonment. He was practically out of action for the best part of a year, during which, he tells us, he wandered about the country, not knowing what to do in London, and in a condition near despair. From this time onwards he was liable to recurrent illness during the winters for the rest of his life. His breakdown and the too ambitious way in which he had proceeded after his release accomplished what the Government had been unable to do; and the *Republican* ceased publication at the end of 1826. His creditors were pressing him hard, and his printing presses as well as his furniture were seized under distraint. He had even to offer to give up his stock of books and pamphlets, and to attempt to sell his Fleet Street shop. But he could find no buyer for the shop; and his creditors had no wish to burden themselves with such dangerous cargo as his stock in trade. He was therefore left in possession, and presently, as his illness passed, he made up his mind to essay a fresh start. But he was still heavily weighed down with debt, and was not able to attempt a great deal. The most that can be said, at this stage, is that the shop was reopened, and that business was resumed in the writings which the Government and the Vice Society had failed to suppress.

A NEW ALLY

Well before this a new figure had entered the scene, to rival Carlile as the leader of the Freethought crusade. The Reverend Robert Taylor, an Anglican priest who had been trained as a doctor before taking orders, and had lost his faith and become a convert to Deism, came to London in 1824 and founded the Christian Evidence Society. By 1826 he was established at Founders' Hall, Lothbury, with a large following to which he delivered his 'astronomico-theological' discourses, expounding all theological beliefs as allegories derived from the works of nature, and adducing a curious mixture of learning derived from many sources in support of his views. Taylor was in effect an early protagonist of the study of comparative natural religion. He added to his offensiveness, in the eyes of the orthodox, by a habit of jesting about the Scriptures; but he possessed a personality which strongly attracted many persons, especially women, and his following soon numbered a good many well-to-do ladies.

Taylor went unmolested for some years. But in 1827, after his removal to Salters' Hall, Cannon Street, he was prosecuted for blasphemy, and in February, 1828 he was sentenced to four years' imprisonment in Oakham Gaol. Carlile, who had been in touch with him since 1825, promptly espoused his cause, and in January 1828, before his sentence, started a new periodical, the *Lion,* which was largely devoted to his support. Carlile also lectured all over the country in Taylor's interest, and enrolled his own considerable body of provincial followers in Taylor's defence. Meanwhile Taylor, in gaol, wrote two books, the *Syntagma* and the *Diegesis,* expounding his astronomico-theological views; and these works undoubtedly had a powerful influence on Carlile's mind.

The *Lion,* which was published without paying tax, was soon

threatened with trouble from the Stamp Office; but it seems to
have been the authorities' policy at this period to let Carlile
alone, and no proceedings were taken against him. Presently, in
1829, Taylor was released from prison, and Carlile at once
invited him to join forces. Together they conducted Sunday
morning Bible discussions on Carlile's premises and elsewhere;
and later in the year they left London and went on what they
called an 'Infidel Tour' of lecturing in the industrial districts.
On their return they set about finding a suitable home for their
missionary activities; and this they found in the famous Rotunda
in the Blackfriars Road, a large building which had been in
turn a theatre and a literary institution. Coleridge, Hazlitt and
other leading lights had lectured there; but the place had fallen
on evil days, and Carlile and Taylor were able to get a lease
of it on easy terms. For the next two years the Rotunda was the
great centre for all manner of Radical and Freethought activities.
It was the chief meeting place of the London Radicals during
the critical years of the struggle for Parliamentary Reform, as
well as the centre of 'infidel' propaganda; and for part of the
time it was also an important centre of Owenism.

A NEW CAUSE

Soon after opening up the Rotunda with Taylor Carlile started
a new journal, the *Prompter,* as successor to the *Lion*; and in
this journal he published the article which brought him into
fresh trouble with the law. By this time the Whig Government
under Lord Grey was in power, and the struggle for Parliamentary Reform had entered upon its final and decisive phase. It
was at this point that the agricultural labourers, driven to
desperation by the repeated cuts in the standard of living allowed
under the Speenhamland poor law system and bitter in their
resentment at the tithes which farmers advanced as a reason for
their inability to improve wage-rates, broke into sporadic revolt
all over the Southern and Eastern Counties. The Whigs, anxious
to prove themselves no less devoted to the interests of property
than the Tories and actually frightened by the spontaneous up-
rising of a class hitherto regarded as free from Radical taint,
resorted to measures of drastic repression. Special Commissions
were sent round from county to county to administer condign
punishment; and savage sentences were passed upon hundreds

of labourers, despite the essentially unviolent character of the movement. The full story of the labourers' revolt has been told by the Hammonds in their *Village Labourer*; and there is no space to repeat it here. We can concern ourselves only with Carlile's part in the affair.

The offending article in the *Prompter,* while affirming that it was wrong to proceed to acts of destruction such as the attacks on agricultural machinery which had occurred in the course of the movement, defended the labourers on the plea that they had been driven to action by an intolerable oppression. They had been reduced to starvation in the midst of plenty and made virtually the slaves of the ruling class which had shown no disposition to hearken to any appeal to reason. Only by taking matters into their own hands could they hope to make any impression upon their masters. Destruction of property was generally regarded as legitimate in war; and the labourers, he maintained, were engaged in a righteous war against despicable oppression.

The prosecution now launched against Carlile was based not exclusively on this passage but also on others published in early issues of the *Prompter,* including one in which he had attacked constitutional monarchy. The indictment as a whole charged him with inciting to violence and seeking to bring the Constitution into contempt.

Carlile, in his defence, argued in favour of the right of rebellion against tyranny, and adduced proof that this right had been recognised by leading constitutional authorities, including Locke and Blackstone. He spoke of Hampden's resistance to Ship Money and Wilkes's to General Warrants, and defended his justification of the labourers' conduct by bringing forward proofs of the unbearable condition to which they had been reduced. The jury at first disagreed; but the Recorder, by keeping them locked up most of the night without refreshment in a fireless room, at length induced them to bring in an adverse verdict on the count of Carlile's upholding the actions of the agricultural labourers. The Recorder thereupon sentenced him to two years' imprisonment, to pay a fine of £200 and to give £1,000 security to be of good behaviour for a period of 10 years —his imprisonment to last after the two years until the fine had been paid and the security deposited.

Thus, early in 1831, Carlile found himself once more in jail, with a prospect of long incarceration in front of him. Later in the year, Taylor was again convicted of blasphemy, and their joint activities at the Rotunda were thus brought to an end. Their followers, however, remained active, and by the beginning of the following year Carlile had found a new and valuable ally.

THE LADY OF THE ROTUNDA

This ally was a woman from Lancashire, by name Eliza Sharples, who had listened to Carlile during his 'Infidel Tour' of 1829, and had become an enthusiastic convert to his views. Late in 1831 she opened up a correspondence with him in jail; and in January 1832 she left her home and family and came to London to offer her services as a missionary to the cause. Eliza Sharples was an educated woman, the daughter of a Bolton manufacturer; and her relatives were entirely out of sympathy with her attitude. Carlile, at her own suggestion, immediately turned her devotion to propagandist use. The Rotunda was reopened; and Eliza Sharples, under the name of 'Isis', began delivering there lectures which were mostly written for her by Carlile, combining with his Freethought doctrines the theme of women's emancipation. In February, in place of the *Prompter,* began the *Isis,* edited by the 'Lady of the Rotunda', the first journal produced by a woman in support of sex equality and political and religious freedom. Doubtless, Carlile in fact wrote most of her lectures; for Eliza Sharples was at this stage not much more than a devout disciple. But the effect was considerable; and for a time audiences flocked to the Rotunda to gaze and to listen to the new prophet, who is said to have been a remarkably stately and good-looking woman as well as an impressive speaker.

CONVERSION

Meanwhile, the cholera had come to London, and there was a good deal of panic. Carlile found his jail visitors seriously restricted, none being allowed except relatives or persons who came on important business. Much to Carlile's indignation, 'Isis' was excluded from the Giltspur Street Compter, the jailer refusing to recognise her lecturing and editing as a business entitling

her to admission. In February, we find him offering the Rotunda
to the Government as a cholera hospital, and also his premises
in Fleet Street, with a broad hint that he should be released to
take charge of them. Already he was in serious financial difficulties over the Rotunda. Although his friends Julian Hibbert
and John Gale Jones, in addition to 'Isis', lectured there
regularly, it was impossible to cover the costs of so large a building with both Carlile and Robert Taylor out of action. Accordingly in March the Rotunda was closed down and leased as a
theatre, and 'Isis' transferred her lectures to the Burton Street
Theatre, near King's Cross, which had just been vacated by the
Owenites on their removal to larger premises near at hand. But
this removal was a failure. It involved attracting a quite new
audience and doing so in direct competition with Robert Owen,
whose influence was then at its height. In April 'Isis' moved to
the lecture room attached to Carlile's shop in Bouverie Street,
where she began to deliver a course in Bible Lectures, plainly
written very much under Taylor's influence.

Indeed, what was happening to Carlile in his new imprisonment was a rapid conversion to Taylor's allegorical interpretation of Christianity. Early in May we find in the *Isis* the startling
announcement of his conversion. 'I declare myself a convert to
the truth as it is in the Gospel of Jesus Christ. I declare myself a
believer in the truth of the Christian religion. . . . I declare for
the spirit, the allegory, and the principle, and challenge the
idolatrous pretenders to Christianity to the field of discussion.'

What Carlile meant by this conversion we shall try to see
later. In the meantime, what concerns us is that it set his little
band of followers by the ears. Julian Hibbert was soon expressing strong dissent from 'Isis's' Bible Lectures, which were no
doubt in fact Carlile's. By July, though the *Isis* continued to
appear, with some interruptions, the lectures seem to have been
given up, to be renewed for a while in August in fresh quarters,
under the auspices of a Society of Ladies, formed to give support
to the victims of the 'unstamped' agitation. But soon these lectures too ceased, and the *Isis* struggled on more and more inter-
mittently to its end in December 1832. There was in its columns
much controversy between Carlile and 'Isis' and the Owenites.
Carlile expressed strong sympathy for Owen's Rational Religion,
but was an entire sceptic about the Owenite Labour Exchanges,

which were then beginning to be active, and about Cooperation generally. He did not question Owen's good intentions; but he regarded him as an impracticable visionary who based his schemes on an essentially wrong view of human nature, and was therefore bound to fail. In economic matters Carlile was a strong individualist. He did not deny that Cooperation might come to be the right system when mankind had become fully emancipated and enlightened by the spread of knowledge; but he had no use for Utopian schemes that seemed likely to interfere with the concentration of the Reformers' efforts on the struggle for religious and educational freedom.

CARLILE AND POLITICS

The year of the great Reform Act was naturally one in which Carlile felt called upon to state afresh his attitude to the political Reformers. He had been steadily hostile, as we have seen, to Political Unions, holding that the only useful Unions or Societies were those devoted to the cause of enlightenment and religious liberty. But this did not prevent him from offering himself as Radical candidate for Ashton-under-Lyne, the moment the Reform Act became law. Ashton was one of the places where his following was strongest; but Joshua Hobson, the leader of the Radicals there, wrote at once to say that they were already provided with a candidate, and that there would be no chance at all of the electors returning 'so sweeping a reformer' as Carlile. Therefore, Carlile got no further than a declaration of the programme on which he proposed to stand. It included the repeal of all laws dealing with matters of religion, the abolition of customs, excise and stamp duties, the levying of all necessary public revenue in the form of a property tax, an 'accommodation' of the question of the National Debt (much on Cobbett's lines), and the abolition of the new police system.

SECOND FAMILY

In the meantime, Carlile's relations with Eliza Sharples had been developing fast. From the very first, her attitude to him had been one of adoring veneration. She wrote, two years later, 'My spirit was wedded to the spirit of my husband before I had spoken to him'; and it is beyond doubt that she came to London to offer herself as a personal sacrifice to Carlile as well as to his cause. Their association took on, from the very beginning, the character of a love-affair as well as a propagandist crusade. Her letters to him, which have been preserved, are couched in terms of high romantic adoration; and Carlile's answers, adjuring her to a more philosophic mood of intellectual comradeship, are also those of a lover. For many years past, there had been no love between Carlile and his wife. At the time when Eliza Sharples first came to London, he had not seen Jane for nearly a year; he wrote a few years later that they had been in effect divorced since May 1830—the time at which he had opened the Rotunda jointly with Taylor. I do not know what precisely caused their parting at this date; but it is clear that all was finished between them some time before Eliza appeared on the scene. Carlile spoke later of having endured 20 years' unhappiness with his first wife; and, though this was by no means the tone in which he had spoken of her when she was faced with prosecution on his behalf for managing his shop, there seems no doubt that by the end of their joint imprisonment at Dorchester their estrangement had begun, or that during this joint incarceration in the same cell they had agreed to separate as soon as Carlile found himself able to make financial provision for her and their three children. The children, as they grew up, seem to have taken the mother's side; and Carlile, without ever breaking with her or them, makes complaint in his letters of their attitude towards him.

Not until 1832 was Carlile able to make the promised financial provision for his wife. Then, thanks to a legacy from a fervent admirer, which he made over to her entire, a formal separation was arranged; and at some later date Jane Carlile appears to have acquiesced in his relations with Eliza. At all events, sometime early in 1832 Carlile and Eliza agreed to live together as man and wife as soon as he could procure his release from jail without compromising his principles. Release came late in 1833, after he had served two years and eight months; and thereafter he and 'Isis' regarded themselves as married. In May 1834, in a preface to a collected edition of the *Isis,* she announced and justified their union to the world. 'Nothing,' she wrote, 'could have been more pure in moral, more free from sensuality'; and Carlile himself wrote of their union more than once in very much the same terms. In due course, she bore him four children, of whom one died in infancy. The survivors appear to have been devoted to both their parents. Carlile's letters, and his younger daughter's biography of him, bear ample witness to his affection for his second family.

Well before this, Carlile had started yet another journal, the *Gauntlet*, replacing the *Isis*, which had served its turn. In the *Gauntlet* he returned to politics. While he had been in jail the Reform Act had become law, and he came out to find the country in a ferment. In Parliament, the Government's measures of coercion in Ireland occupied the centre of the stage; and in the country attention was divided between the Irish question and the Trade Unions, which were developing at a prodigious pace. The National Union of the Working Classes, the political body which had rallied the working-class forces during the Reform struggle, was everywhere denouncing the Whigs as the betrayers of the people, and making common cause with the Irish; and the Owenites, busy creating the Grand National Consolidated Trades Union and endeavouring to bring the Trades Union movement over to Owenite Socialism, were for the moment keeping their 'Rational Religion' in the background, and concentrating on their economic schemes.

Carlile, in the *Gauntlet,* gave much space to Irish affairs, and full support to the Irish claims. But he did not give up his opposition to political unions, or his belief in individual resistance as the only effective instrument. From jail he began calling for volunteers, who would pledge themselves to take whatever action might be necessary in the cause of freedom. He proposed to drop all Unions except those formed for purely educational purposes; and when he was asked for what purpose his volunteers, whose names appeared week by week in the *Gauntlet,* were being enrolled, he replied that they were to be ready to fight for liberty with arms in their hands when the moment for action arrived. Of the Owenites and their Labour Exchanges he wrote with praise and some sympathy, though not with agreement; but he would have nothing to do with the Political Unions, which he regarded as mere talking places. Instead of them, he favoured, in opposition to Lord Brougham's Society for the Diffusion of Useful Knowledge, then at the height of its activity, the rival Societies for the Diffusion of Really Useful Knowledge, which were being set up under the leadership of William Hassell,

formerly one of his convicted shopmen. He also wrote the leading
articles for a second paper, the *Cosmopolite,* and in this stressed
the need for an educational campaign designed to bring the
soldiers over to sympathy with the cause of the people. Presently,
the *Cosmopolite* changed its name to the *Political Soldier*; and
Alexander Somerville, best known under his pseudonym 'One
Who Has Whistled at the Plough', became the editor. Somerville
had served in the Scots Greys; and at this time he and Carlile
were political allies. Carlile was advising the people to 'arm
silently and quietly', instead of talking about revolution in political meetings, and was openly telling his readers that they must
expect to have to fight for their rights. But the Government, at
this period of general excitement, was walking warily; and
Carlile was left alone until he plunged of his own accord into
a further struggle by deciding to resist payment of Church rates
due upon his Fleet Street shop.

CHRISTIAN—NEW STYLE
Soon after his release from prison he hired the Rotunda for a
big public meeting to celebrate his renewed victory over the
forces of law and order; and he announced that he was planning
for a new Rotunda as the centre of his propagandist activities.
But funds were low with him, though he had by this time
escaped from the debts which had embarrassed him as a result
of his ambitious proceedings during the period of his collaboration with Taylor. Taylor, after his second imprisonment, had
married one of his rich disciples and had retired to Jersey; and
when Carlile went on a provincial lecturing tour Eliza Sharples
replaced 'the Devil's Chaplain', as Henry Hunt had called
Taylor, as his companion and fellow-orator.

Carlile's struggle over Church rates came to a head in 1834.
His refusal to pay led to repeated distraints upon the property
exposed for sale in his shop; and he retaliated in a fresh newspaper, the *Scourge,* which replaced the *Gauntlet,* and in more
spectacular fashion, by setting up in his shop window two effigies,
of a bishop and a distraining officer, subsequently adding a
third, of a devil, arm-in-arm with the bishop. Crowds gathered
outside the shop, and Carlile was prosecuted for obstruction and
nuisance, and called upon to give security for his good behaviour.
This he refused to do; and he accordingly went back to prison,

under a liability to serve for three years unless he agreed to
give the required security. But after serving only four months
he was released unconditionally, after repeated attempts to
persuade him to arrive at a compromise had been scornfully
rejected.

This was the last time Carlile was jailed. He improved the
occasion by writing, from prison, a long pamphlet on *Church
Reform,* in the guise of an open letter addressed to Sir Robert
Peel. In this work, in addition to arguing in favour of civil
marriage and easier divorce, he put forward his changed views
about religion—or rather his changed method of expressing
views which were fundamentally at one with those of his 'blasphemous' period. For some years before this, his attitude to
religion had been gradually altering. He had become convinced
that the methods of direct attack which he had practised up to
the time of his association with Taylor were doomed to ineffec-
tiveness, and that the correct method of reaching the minds of
the people was to accept the language of Christianity and to use
that language for an attack on superstitious belief. He had taken
over from Taylor the view that all theological doctrines were to
be interpreted in allegorical terms, as attempts by man to understand and explain the forces of nature. By this route his attack
on religious dogmas passed by stages into a scientific-allegorical
interpretation of them; and his language often appeared to be
that of mysticism, when he sought to express his rationalist
notions in theological terms. He went through a parallel evolution in his attitude to Freemasonry, which he began by exposing
in the *Republican,* only to offer later to tell the Freemasons
what their ceremonies really meant, and to convert the exposure
of Freemasonry, which he had published first serially in the
Republican, and thereafter in book form in 1831, into a curious
Manual of Freemasonry, which had a wide circulation long after
his death.

In *Church Reform,* Carlile put himself forward, no longer as
the enemy of the Church, but as its regenerator. His desire, he
said, was to save the Church and its property and to 'annihilate
the Dissenters', not by prosecuting them, but by giving them
no argument for standing out against reconciliation with a
reformed and rationalised Establishment. Faithful to his idea
of the overmastering importance of knowledge, Carlile declared

that the Church should be 'a School of Moral Science'. 'Man,' he
asserted, 'is the inventor of the Spiritual Deity,' and the Bible
should be read not in a literal but in a purely spiritual sense.
He proceeded to interpret the doctrine of the Trinity in his own
terms. 'God the Father personates all science, under the attribute
of omniscience.' God the Son personates the human mind. The
Holy Ghost personates the spirit of truth—of that free communication of knowledge which should be found in the Church. The
property of the Church should not be alienated for secular uses:
it should be employed in the promotion of knowledge, and the
Church should become a Catholic Church from which there
could be no dissent. 'Real knowledge,' Carlile wrote, 'is the
water-cup of sobriety for a people'; and summing up his case,
he said that 'in my lecturings and discussions both in town
and country I find this revelation has a great charm among all
classes who have good temper and good manners to hear
patiently'.

EVANGELIST

This tract on Church Reform is the most complete record of
Carlile's transformation from a professing 'blasphemer' into an
evangelist of a new allegorical Christianity which brought him
into strange company. Before his last imprisonment he had been
on a joint lecture tour with Eliza; but he was then still in a
transitional stage in his thinking, and it was only during his
period in jail that his change of attitude became complete. After
his release he set up house with her at Enfield Highway, well in
the country. His health was impaired; and he suffered badly
from asthma, especially during the winter months. Thereafter,
during the spring, summer and autumn he went about the
country lecturing, sometimes moving quickly from place to place,
and sometimes settling down for a time in some town where he
had attracted a following of disciples. In 1838, for example, he
settled for some time in Manchester, where he set up his own
'Hall of Science', published a series of 'Religious Tracts' which
included a vigorous attack on the Owenites and a proclamation
that 'Christ is the only Radical Reformer', and lectured regularly
to his disciples in the neighbouring Lancashire towns. But generally as the weather grew cold he came back from these missionary
journeys to Enfield and kept his room with a good fire for much

of the winter. Long spells of prison had left him exceptionally sensitive to exposure; and he was half an invalid for part of the year.

As long, however, as the weather was favourable he was active; and in his new guise he lectured not only to unbelievers but also to Christian audiences which but imperfectly understood what he was saying. Unorthodox ministers received him gladly in their chapels, and he spoke to mixed audiences in the open air. Frequently he fell foul of Rationalists who regarded him as an apostate; and he had many acrimonious passages with the Owenites, who, after the collapse of the Grand National Consolidated Trades Union in 1834, became more and more a sect of 'Rational Religionists', but were mostly quite out of sympathy with Carlile's attempt to clothe his rationalism in the terms of religious orthodoxy. Presently, like the Owenite missionaries, Carlile took out a licence to preach, without which he would not have been able lawfully to carry on his religious services. This licence entitled him to style himself 'Reverend', equally with the Nonconformist preachers; and he did this, with a touch of sardonic amusement at the scandal created in orthodox quarters by the metamorphosis of the arch-infidel into a sort of priest. From 1836 to 1839 he engaged regularly in these missionary tours; and the titles of the new journals which he started during this phase of his career show how far he had travelled from his earlier attitude. The *Church* was one of them; a second, his series of Religious Tracts published in Manchester in the days of feverish speculation in railway shares, included an issue entitled *Carlile's Railroad to Heaven*; and the last of his periodical ventures, begun shortly before his death, was the *Christian Warrior*.

Failing health presently compelled him to give up his extensive tours; and he began, under various names or anonymously, to write articles for all manner of papers, suiting his style to his audience and ready to adopt any terminology he regarded as suitable for getting his ideas into people's heads. He would write in Whiggish terms for the Whigs, in terms of Toryism for the Tories, and would use any kind of religious terminology that he thought likely to appeal to some class of readers. Through all these permutations, he denied absolutely that he had changed any of his fundamental ideas. His God remained a man-made

God, having no existence outside the minds of men. But allegory had taken complete hold of him; and, more and more, those who had followed him in his anti-God days regarded him as an apostate. It appears that even the devoted 'Isis' did not travel all the way with him on his railroad to heaven. He wrote to her when he was away on one of his tours, half in fun, 'I salute you with a holy kiss; but you are not quite a Christian yet'. What he was preaching in these latter days was not unlike modern Theosophy : it reconciled all religions by regarding them as repositories of allegorical truth.

Through all these latter years Carlile was very poor. Money had been forthcoming in reasonable plenty to sustain his long crusade against authority; but it was much less plentiful after the Government had decided to let him alone, and especially after the death of his principal benefactor, Julian Hibbert, in 1834. He had much ado to keep his home together during his years at Enfield; and Isis had a hard time of it.

Carlile's alienation from the political Radicals had been complete for a long time; and he was wholly out of sympathy with the rising Chartist movement. One of his sons by his first wife, Thomas Paine Carlile, became an active Chartist, and ran a Chartist newspaper, first in Manchester, and later in London, where he had a shop in Fleet Street, and carried on in imitation of his father's earlier proceedings. Carlile offered himself as a contributor to his son's paper, only to find his articles rejected— not unnaturally, for his line was to set up the need for personal regeneration as a prior condition for all political activity. Another son, Richard, also set up as a bookseller, and published some of his father's later work.

The final episode came in 1843. The lease of his Enfield cottage ran out. 'Isis' was away, recovering from an illness, on a visit to relatives in Torquay. Carlile, despite the fact that he had been for years unable to endure the London climate in winter, decided to move back to Fleet Street in January, in order to carry on his *Christian Warrior*. He moved to his son's shop at the corner of Bouverie Street, only to be taken ill and to die. His first wife, Jane, and Eliza Sharples were both with him when he died.

Carlile had six children who grew up to manhood, three by Jane and three by Eliza, besides his first child by Jane and his first by Eliza, both boys, who died in infancy. With Jane's children, as they grew up, he was not on the best of terms, though there seems to have been a reconciliation in his latter days; but his second family appears to have been very fond of him, and the youngest, Theophila, wrote his life after she had settled down and married in the United States. George Jacob Holyoake, the Secularist, is also among Carlile's admiring biographers, and was befriended by him when he was imprisoned under the Blasphemy Laws in 1842. Carlile went down to Gloucester on this occasion and remained with Holyoake for ten days, including the whole period of his trial. For Carlile, in his latest phase, did not cease to regard himself as the friend and ally of the 'blasphemers', or modify in the smallest degree his faith in the virtues of untrammelled freedom of speech and discussion. The mode changed; but his essential ideas about such matters remained the same to the end.

EPITAPH FOR A REBEL

In passing judgment on Carlile, it is fairest to take him as he was at the height of his powers, before he had entered on the sophistical phase in which he veiled his atheism under the frame of an allegorical Christianity. In his prime, he was above all else the apostle of Republicanism; and this word had for him at once a politico-social and theological meaning. In common with not a few of his contemporaries, he saw Church and State, God and King, as equally the enemies of his faith in republican equality and in a reason which could endure no trammeling by any pretensions of divine or human authority. God and King were equally out of place in Carlile's Republic; and he saw in both the enemies of the free spirit of inquiry on which he rested his hopes for the future of mankind. This attitude was common in his day, when the corruptions of Church and State hung closely together, and prosecutions for blasphemous and seditious libel were promoted in a single Act of Parliament and the Church of England was treated as a part of the British Constitution by law established. Those were the days of absentee parsons drawing as pluralists several fat stipends while they paid out miserable pittances to the curates who did their duty for them; of bishops who regarded it as incumbent upon them to live on the scale of great temporal landowners; and, above all, of a persecution which drew no fine distinctions between treasonable conspirators and blasphemers and rational seekers after political or religious truth.

Carlile was, no doubt, the kind of man who would have been a rebel in any society. His entire attitude was individualistic, and he had a deep disbelief in all forms of associative action, from Owenite Cooperative Societies and Trade Unions to political clubs. He held that each man ought to take his personal stand by his own convictions, regardless of the consequences to himself; and he acted up to this principle through nearly ten years of imprisonment. This experience impaired, I think, his mental as well as his physical health; and the allegorical Christianity of his latter days degenerated into a disingenuous ranting in which he half-deliberately deceived his audiences into mistaking what he meant. But a man is to be judged by his best days, and not by the doings of his decline; and no one can take from Carlile the credit of having made the greatest stand of any man in the nineteenth century for freedom of speech and writing, or of having done more than any other to bring the more flagrant forms of press persecution to an end. The battle for the freedom of the unstamped press had indeed to be renewed, after his initial victory, by Henry Hetherington and his helpers, who were jailed in dozens well after Carlile had proclaimed, on his release in 1825, that he, and he alone, had beaten the Government and set the written word free. Carlile's claim was exaggerated; but it was not invalid. Some freedom he had won for the journalists, though by no means all. 'Blasphemy' was still to be prosecuted, but not with the same violence as before; the printers and vendors of the 'unstamped' newspapers were still to be imprisoned, but for shorter periods; and the prosecuting societies, the Vice Society and the Constitutional Association, he did rout decisively. These were great achievements, which only an indomitable spirit could have won; and Carlile deserves to be remembered for them. He was always a 'lone wolf'; but in the fight for human progress the 'lone wolf' has at times an indispensable part to play.

APPENDIX

CARLILE'S PERIODICALS

The Republican was started in 1817 by W. T. Sherwin, and
Carlile acted as agent for its sale. Its name was changed after
a few issues to *Sherwin's Political Register,* and under that name
it continued to appear until 1819, when Carlile took it over, and
re-named it *The Republican.* It continued until the end of 1820,
and was then dropped for a year. Resumed at the beginning of
1822, it lasted until the end of 1826.

During this period Carlile also issued *The Deist* (1819-20),
and *The Moralist* (1823). *The Newgate Monthly Magazine,*
edited by his shopmen imprisoned in Newgate, was also issued
from his shop in 1824-25.

In 1827, Carlile was without a journal; but in the following
year he started *The Lion* (1828-29). This was followed by *The
Prompter* (1830-31). In 1832 Eliza Sharples edited for him *The
Isis,* which contains many articles by him. This was succeeded
by *The Gauntlet* (1833); and during this period Carlile was
also writing regularly for *The Cosmopolite* (1832-33), which was
edited during the latter part of its existence by Alexander Somerville, better known as 'The Whistler at the Plough'. I have never
seen copies of Carlile's later periodicals, which were short-lived;
but he appears to have conducted *The Scourge* in 1834, and *The
Church* about 1838. At the very end of his life he started *The
Christian Warrior* (?1842-3).

CARLILE'S BOOKS AND PAMPHLETS

The Bullet Te Deum (1817); *The Canticle of the Stone* (1817);
The Order for the Administration of the Loaves and Fishes
(1817); *A Letter to the Society for the Suppression of Vice*
(1819); *Life of Thomas Paine* (1820); *A New Year's Address to
the Reformers* (1821); and five further *Addresses to the Reformers*
(1821); *An Address to the Men of Science* (1821); *An Effort to
Set at Rest some Little Disputes and Misunderstandings between
the Reformers of Leeds* (1821); *Observations on Dr. Gregory's
Letters to a Friend* (1821); *Reports of the Proceedings of the
Court of King's Bench . . . being the Mock Trials of Richard*

Carlile for Alleged Blasphemous Libels (1822); *Every Man's Book, or, What is God?* (1826); *Every Woman's Book* (1826); *Richard Carlile's First Sermon on the Mount* (1827); *The Gospel according to Richard Carlile* (1827); *Freemasonry Exposed* (later rewritten and reissued as *A Manual of Freemasonry*) (1831); *A Form of Prayer on Account of the Troubled State of certain parts of the United Kingdom* (1831); *A New View of Insanity, in which is set forth the Mismanagement of Public and Private Madhouses, with some Suggestions towards a New Remedy for that Almost Universal Disorder of the Human Race* (1831); *A Letter to Charles Larkin of the Newcastle Press* (1834); *Church Reform: the Only Means to that End, stated in a Letter to Sir Robert Peel* (1835); *The Letters of Richard Carlile to the Inhabitants of Brighton, with a Syllabus of his Course of Seven Lectures* (1836); *Carlile's Railroad to Heaven* (1838); *Jesus Christ the Only Radical Reformer* (1838); *A View and Review of Robert Owen's Projects* (1838).

[The above list is certainly incomplete; but it is the best I have been able to make. There were in addition a considerable number of bound-up offprints from series of articles in *The Republican* and other journals, as well as a number of handbills, etc.]

TRIALS

In addition to Carlile's own *Mock Trials,* mentioned above, of which parts were issued in 1819-20, though the full Report did not appear until 1822, attention should be drawn to the published Reports of the Trials of Jane Carlile (1821), Mary Anne Carlile (1822), Susannah Wright (1822), William Campion, Thomas Jefferies and others (1824), and to other Reports of similar trials; also to the pamphlets *Suppressed Defence: the Defence of Mary Anne Carlile to the Vice Society's Indictment* (1825), and *Bridge Street Banditti versus the Press, with the Speech of Mr. Cooper in Defence* (1825).

Julius West

5 JOHN STUART MILL 1806–1873

ACROSS THE BLEAK desert of intellect which coincides with the first 50 years of the reign of Queen Victoria there run numerous uncertain pathways, all starting from the Temple of Mammon. These pathways meet and mingle in all sorts of unexpected, complicated fashions, and the majority of them lead nowhere. One, known as Carlyle, for example, appears ever to be getting more distant from the Temple, but in the end goes no farther than Chelsea. Another, called Ruskin, leaves the Temple of Mammon with a grand blazing of trumpets, but, going a little way, stops before a Gothic Temple, and the call of the trumpet is converted to the dronings of an organ. Of all the pathways, Mill is perhaps the clearest. It sets out from the front parlour of a man, Bentham, of whom more will be said; it leads down a steep precipice called the Wages Fund Theory (where danger notices have been but lately erected); it traverses a bit of boggy ground which is marked on the maps as the Law of Population; it turns a few curious corners, when, lo, the Promised Land is in sight.

Now, as to this man Bentham. About 1800 there was in existence a body of philosophers who believed that the purpose of all human effort should be the increase of the sum total of human happiness; with real, perfervid energy and emotion they sought, in their own words, 'the greatest good of the greatest number'. Of these Bentham was the founder, and when he died, in 1832, he left a particularly unpleasant prison at Westminster (the Millbank Penitentiary) as a monument to his endeavours to increase human happiness. In 1808, when Bentham was 60 years of age, he made the acquaintance of a rigid and logical Scotsman named James Mill. Mill sat at Bentham's feet, assimilated his doctrines, made them a shade more rigid, and finally became Bentham's lieutenant. And Mill dedicated his (at that time) only son, John Stuart, that the youngster, who was only born in 1806, should be a worthy successor to the two friends, and should continue to proclaim the truths of Utilitarianism to all the world. The history of the intellectual life of J. S. Mill is contained in his efforts to escape from the narrow individualistic creed of his progenitors, real and spiritual, and his gradual approach towards Socialism.

We need not close our eyes to the fact that Bentham was a power, that he profoundly influenced the evolution of the law and of public administration, to be nevertheless extremely critical of his influence upon J. S. Mill. At this distance from the Benthamites it is difficult to realise how starkly intense was their individualism. 'Laissez faire' with them was more than a theory; it was a faith. Bentham, who wrote on almost everything, produced a small 'Manual of Political Economy', from whose dark, unfathomed depths the following gem has been extracted : 'With the view of causing an increase to take place in the mass of national wealth, or with a view to increase of the means either of subsistence or enjoyment, without some special reason, the general rule is that nothing ought to be done or attempted by government. The motto or watchword of government on these occasions ought to be—*Be quiet*'.[1] He died in 1832, at the age of 84, leaving behind him 140 boxes of manuscript. For many years his life had been that of a tabulating machine with a mania for neologising. He invented, for example, seven classes of 'Offences against the positive increase of the National Felicity.'[2] These include the heinous crimes of offending against epistemo-threptic, antembletic and hedomonarchic trusts. He is at present probably tabulating and renaming the numerous varieties of asbestos.

THE MISFORTUNES OF MILL : HIS FATHER

But long before his death James Mill, observing that the mantle of Bentham was in danger of being soiled by continual dragging through the muddy waters of the elder's verbiage, took it from his shoulders and placed it upon his own. (This is no mere figure of speech; for the unpruned language of Bentham's later days

[1]Works, Ed. Bowring, 1843.
[2]'Principles of Morals and Legislation,' Chap. XVI.

was incomprehensible to the public, and so his notes had to be edited and his books written by his disciples.) With James Mill there is little need for us to tarry. He is best remembered by his character and his eldest son.

James Mill came to London from Scotland, and having for some years earned a precarious living by journalism, proceeded to write a History of India. It appeared in 1817, the result of nine years' hard work. That he had no first hand knowledge of his subject was, he considered, all to the good. It permitted full play to the objective attitude. But the three substantial resultant volumes of conscientious drought brought him a reward. Established as an authority on the country he had never seen, he succeeded in obtaining a post in the office of the East India Company. In 1836, the year of his death, he was drawing a salary of £2,000.

THE MISFORTUNES OF MILL : HIS UPBRINGING

In the intervals of his journalistic work, and, later, in the leisure accorded by his official duties, James Mill educated his son. The course of instruction prescribed and administered by this, the most ruthless of all parents, was encyclopaedic in its scope and devastating in its character. John Stuart Mill, while yet infant and amorphous, was destined by his father for leadership and educated accordingly. In his 'Autobiography' (p. 3) he says, 'I have no recollection of the time when I began to learn Greek; I have been told it was when I was three years old'. At the age of seven he had read the first six dialogues of Plato, and subsequently acted as teacher to his younger brothers and sisters. Such inexorability as his father's in teaching young minds to shoot would lead many to suicide. There is little need to detail. The practice of long walks with his father, in which instruction was combined with exercise, was perhaps the principal reason for J. S. Mill's physical survival. Intellectually, his persistence to years of discretion must be credited to his heredity. Of boyhood he had none. Says Mill : 'He was earnestly bent upon my escaping not only the corrupting influence which boys exercise over boys, but the contagion of vulgar modes of thought and feeling; and for this he was willing that I should pay the price of inferiority in the accomplishments which schoolboys in all

countries chiefly cultivate'.[3] It is astonishing that this system
did not convert his brain into a sort of *pâté de foie gras.* But
he survived. The worst efforts of his father failed to affect the
stability of his marvellous brain. Having left his childhood with
his cradle, he proceeded to absorb all that there was to be absorbed of Greek and Latin, mathematics, history, both ancient
and modern, and the remaining subjects prescribed by convention and his father's views. At the age when, nowadays, he
might be qualifying for a Boy Scout, Mill took to philosophy,
psychology and logic. In 1823 (age 17) his father obtained
him a clerkship in the India House, where he remained until
1858. About this time he began to write for the *Edinburgh* and
Westminster Reviews. In 1825 he 'edited' in manner aforesaid,
Bentham's 'Rationale of Judicial Evidence', much to his own
edification.

THE STRENUOUS LIFE

Of this period of his life, when the rigidity of parental control
had been somewhat relaxed, it would have been not unreason-
able to expect that Mill, like Richard Feverel, might have
rebelled against the 'system'. Far from it; the process had been
too thorough. Mill never sowed any wild oats of any species
whatsoever; he did not even cut down the familial apple-tree.
At the age of 20 he virtually founded the 'London Debating
Society', which seems to have been something like the Fabian
Society would have been if it had no Basis and no external
objects. To this belonged, amongst others, Macaulay, Edward
Bulwer Lytton, a large number of incipient reputations, and the
élite of the Oxford and Cambridge Unions. Concurrently with
the existence of this society, Mill and Grote, the future historian,
formed a study circle which met twice a week at the latter's
house for the discussion of Economics. When this subject contained no more unexplored regions, the circle took up Logic
and Analytical Psychology. In all the meetings extended over
five years, giving Mill an additional stratum upon which to base
his subsequent work. As one result of these meetings, we should
note the 'Essays on Unsettled Questions in Political Economy',
which was written about 1830-31, but not published until 1844.

[3]'Autobiography,' p. 20.

Throughout this whole period Mill was a frequent contributor to the Reviews. His literary output previous to 1843 was
voluminous, but consisted almost entirely of criticism. In that
year he published his first classic, 'A System of Logic, Ratio-
cinative and Inductive; being a connected view of the principles
of evidence and the methods of scientific investigation'. To this
portentous work belonged all the characteristics enumerated above
of his father's 'India'; it was perhaps the most important book
of its time, and its merits were such that eight editions were
exhausted in the author's lifetime. Having completed this, Mill
shortly turned his attention to his next classic work, which
appeared in 1848. Of this, the 'Principles of Political Economy',
more will be said later, when some of its points will be examined.
These two books are Mill's most substantial contributions to
human thought. Of those of his smaller works with which we
shall be concerned the most important are the 'Representative
Government' and the 'Subjection of Women'. These each
contain, roughly, the full development of a single idea, and,
although by no means trivial, are scarcely entitled to rank with
his 'classic' works. Before allowing his books to speak for themselves, the outstanding features of the remainder of his life must
be stated.

HIS MARRIAGE

In the first place, as to Mill's marriage. At the age of 23 Mill
became acquainted with a Mrs. Taylor, wife of a City drysalter.
He sat at her feet some 16 years when she became a widow, and
two years afterwards Mill and she were married. He continued to
sit at her feet for seven more years, until 1858, when she died.
Of her he writes throughout in terms of extreme admiration,
which, coming from a man of Mill's dispassionate temperament,
approach rhapsody. For example, in dedicating his 'Liberty' to
her, the year following her death, he concludes with these words:
'Were I but capable of interpreting to the world one half the
great thoughts and noble feelings which are buried in her grave
I should be the medium of a greater benefit to it than is ever
likely to arise from anything that I can write, unprompted and
unassisted by her all but unrivalled wisdom.' Mill's biographers,
Leslie Stephen and Bain, are somewhat sceptical. Bain writes,
'Grote used to say "only John Mill's reputation could survive

such displays." [4] There is no point in endeavouring to estimate the accuracy of such declarations; we must take Mill's word and leave it at that, perhaps with the added comment that a woman capable of inspiring such depths of feeling would also be capable of affecting the quality of Mill's work; of improving it without necessarily herself touching it.

In the year of her death the East India Company ceased to exist. The Indian Mutiny had convinced the Government that it was, on the whole, inadvisable to run an empire by private enterprise, and the business of administering India was nationalised. The Company, of course, was unwilling, and resisted the divestment of its interests. It fell to Mill, by this time virtually in command at India House, to draft the Company's petition for reprieve, in a document which was pronounced by Earl Grey 'the ablest State paper he had ever read.' [5] But all in vain; the India Office superseded the India House and Mill was retired on a pension of £1,500.

M.P. FOR WESTMINSTER

Then Mill went into Parliament. The story of his election, which took place in 1865, is strikingly characteristic of Mill's tenacity of opinion and undeviating pursuit of whatever path of conduct he held to be right. In these days the term 'principle' is in danger of obliteration, save only in so far as it enters into the adjective 'unprincipled', and Mill's own account of the election has a distinctly humorous touch. Westminster was the favoured constituency. He writes, for example, 'I was convinced that no numerous or influential portion of any electoral body really wished to be represented by a person of my opinions. . . . It was, and is, my fixed conviction that a candidate ought not to incur one farthing of expense for undertaking a public duty. . . . I felt, therefore, that I ought not to seek election to Parliament, much less to expend any money in procuring it.' [6] Authors are not generally gifted with such a degree of self-effacement, not to mention politicians. However, a body of electors came and asked Mill to stand, and he, having 'put their disposition to the proof by one of the frankest explanations ever tendered, I should

[4]Bain, 'J. S. Mill: a Criticism,' p. 167.
[5]Bain, p. 96.
[6]'Autobiography,' p. 160.

think, to an electoral body by a candidate,'[7] consented. A well
known 'literary man was heard to say that the Almighty himself
would have no chance of being elected on such a programme.'[8]
The result of this amazing election was that Mill secured a
majority of 700 over W. H. Smith, his Conservative competitor.
He attached himself to Gladstone, but in fact retained his independence, and not infrequently opposed his own party. He remained in Parliament for three years, during which he took a
prominent part in the troublous passage of the Reform Bill
of '67, and otherwise. It was on an occasion connected with this
Reform agitation that the Hyde Park railings were pushed down.
Mill appears to have mediated between the demonstrators and
the Government with the result that serious collisions were prevented. It was not to be expected that the miracle would happen
twice; Mill was not re-elected. He himself does not seem to have
greatly regretted losing his seat.

THE LAST YEARS

So he went back to his books and to Avignon, to pass the remaining years of his life near his wife's grave. He there wrote the
'Subjection of Women', and planned a book on Socialism, which
was left unfinished. These and voluminous replies to correspond-
ents appear to have been the principal occupations of the years
1868-73. In the latter year he died, at Avignon, as a result of
a local epidemic disease.

This is but the briefest sketch of Mill's life. The four aspects
of his work most likely to interest Socialists will be studied
separately. Until his work has been discussed it is useless to
attempt framing an estimate of his influence. Moreover, we
shall not be dealing at all with some of perhaps his most important aspects. As a Rationalist and as a Philosopher he takes a
high place amongst the world's thinkers, but we need only study
him in his relation to society.

In 1865, the year Mill went into Parliament, he published his
substantial 'Examination of Sir William Hamilton's Philosophy',
a work from which most Englishmen drew their philosophy for
the subsequent decade. He had already (1863) published 'Utili-

[7]'Autobiography,' p. 161.
[8]Ibid, p. 162.

tarianism', wherein the opinions of Bentham and his father were rendered with more qualification than sympathy. 'On Liberty' (1859), in which he and his wife collaborated, is a fine piece of writing, but curiously inconsequent, and does not advocate anything more exciting than non-interference, and not always that.

Mill was an honourable, upright man, capable of commanding firm friendships and the greatest respect. 'Saint of Rationalism' was the title bestowed on him by Gladstone. Herbert Spencer gives many instances of Mill's generosity, and wrote an almost emotional obituary notice.[9] His was a noble, unselfish life, and with it passed perhaps the greatest purifying force of the last century.

ECONOMIST

ECONOMICS IN 1836

Roughly speaking, Mill's work as an economist may be summed up by saying that he found economics a body of doctrines and left it a body of doctrine. For the first time the mass of theories evolved by and since Adam Smith were integrated into a coherent and, on the whole, a moderately consistent statement. Adam Smith popularised economics; that is to say, for all practical purposes he founded it. A little later Malthus added the theory of population with considerations arising therefrom. Sir Edward West introduced the notion of the margin of cultivation. Ricardo stated the idea of economic rent. Nassau Senior evolved the quaint 'abstinence' theory—abstinence being 'a term by which we express the conduct of a person who either abstains from the unproductive use of what he can command, or designedly prefers the production of remote to that of immediate results.'[10] They took this sort of thing very seriously in 1836. It will be readily understood therefore that the 70 years following the publication of the 'Wealth of Nations' (1776) had literally made a hash of economics. It had appeared with certain pretensions to be a science; it had degenerated into a gallimaufry. Hence the importance of Mill's work.

[9]See Appendix G. Spencer, 'Autobiography,' Vol. II.
[10]Senior, 'Political Economy,' p. 58.

THE PERILS OF POPULATION

Yet the result was not altogether satisfactory. Mill's unfortunate education was to blame. He had started life upon a Ricardian diet, and absorbed Malthus with depressing avidity. Hence he was incapable of seeing facts for himself : he could squeeze out the full content of other writers' syllogisms, but himself refrained from stating new premises. To the end of his days he was haunted by the bogey of population; he despaired of ever achieving a state where the distribution of wealth should be equitable; multiplication would hinder division. It is seldom that philoprogenitiveness was dealt with as severely as by this son of a philoprogenitive father. Sinking for a moment his accustomed humanitarianism, he descends to the level of a hardened official of the Charity Organisation Society. 'Poverty,' he declares, 'like most social evils, exists because men follow their brute instincts without due consideration.' In a footnote he adds : 'Little improvement can be expected in morality until the producing of large families is regarded with the same feelings as drunkenness or any other physical excess.'[11] His whole attitude towards social reforms is tempered by the fear that, perhaps, they would only increase man's unfortunate liability to be born; that generosity would merely induce generation.

Hence Mill's condemnation of a minimum wage, legal or moral. 'If nothing more were necessary than a compulsory accumulation (i.e., of money to be available for wages), sufficient to provide employment at ample wages for the existing numbers of the people, such a proposition would have no more strenuous supporter than myself. Society mainly consists of those who live by bodily labour; and if society, that is, if the labourers lend their physical force to protect individuals in the enjoyment of superfluities, they are entitled to do so, and have always done so, with the reservation of a power to tax those superfluities for purposes of public utility, amongst which purposes the subsistence of the people is the foremost. Since no one is responsible for having been born, no pecuniary sacrifice is too great to be made by those who have more than enough for the purpose of securing enough to all persons already in existence.'[12] All of

[11]'Principles,' Book II., Chap. XIII.
[12]'Principles,' Book II., Chap. XII.

which shows how Mill's progress towards Socialism was turned aside by an optical illusion. He could not realise, as Sadler had already realised, that comfort was a very potent preventive check, and that Malthus, whose anxieties were justifiable at the time he wrote, would be disproved by the lapse of time.

WAGES AND WELFARE

Of Trade Unions and their future development Mill does not seem to have had much idea. On the first occasion when he refers in his published works to unions, in a pleasantly amusing letter to Carlyle, written from Paris, he slightly jests at their expense. On the authority of an 'impartial' person, he states of French Unions, that 'their object is not so much more money as to elevate their rank in society, since at present the gentlemen will not keep company with them, and they will not keep company with the common labourers.'[13] That was in 1833. In later years his views were softened. He could never recognise that trade unions were of much positive utility, even though he would not admit they were actually harmful. But Mill's keen sense of justice made him actually befriend the unions, without admitting their efficiency. Wages, he believed, were settled for the individual by competition between masters and workers. So long as the masters could do as they pleased in order to lower wages, so long was it unjust to forbid workers to combine in order to raise wages. He inveighs against combination laws, 'laws enacted and maintained for the declared purpose of keeping wages low', because 'such laws exhibiting the infernal spirit of the slave master, who, to retain the working classes in avowed slavery, has ceased to be practicable.'[14] He goes even further: 'The best interests of the human race imperatively require that all economical experiments, voluntarily undertaken, should have the fullest licence, and that force and fraud should be the only means of attempting to benefit themselves which are interdicted to the less fortunate classes of the community.' This last passage was added in the third edition of the 'Principles' four years after the original appearance of the book, and illustrates Mill's advancing views.

[13]'Letters,' p. 74.
[14]'Principles,' Book V., Chap. X., S 5.

Holding, as he did, the Malthusian theory of population, it would have been illogical on Mill's part to have definitely gone over to the support of trade unionism. For this theory held a corollary, the wages fund theory, and the two were inseparable: vicious doctrines have extraordinary powers of cohesion. We need not excite ourselves over the esoteric aspects of this particular dogma. Briefly and exoterically they are as follows. Malthus and his followers believed that overpopulation was the cause of most misery, as a quotation made above has illustrated. From this it was permissible to deduce, subalternately, that overpopulation was the cause of low wages. Hence there was supposed to be a connection between population and wages, and the more there was of one, the less there would be of the other. A step further, and we have the idea stated, to quote Senior, 'that wages depend' on 'the extent of the fund for the maintenance of labourers, compared with the number of labourers to be maintained'. This is the celebrated Wages Fund theory, to which Mill was a subscriber. In these enlightened days, when everybody disbelieves in Malthus's theory, but is hyper-Malthusian in his practice, the sister doctrine of the Wages Fund is no longer with us. Moreover, it has been pointed out that wages are not paid out of a fund earmarked, as it were, for that purpose. Wages are paid out of the produce of labour, which can be increased indefinitely until the point is reached when all human wants are satiated and machinery can do no more to stimulate desires, either by producing things cheaper or by producing anything at all that man has not got, but would like to have if he saw it.

Holding this theory, Mill could not but believe (1) that if any body of workers succeeded, by means of a trade union or otherwise, in raising their wages, it could only be at the expense of other workers; (2) that any permanent improvement in the wage position of all the workers must await the time when their rate of multiplication would be considerably decreased.[15]

It was a distinctly uncomfortable theory and so plausible

---

[15]For full discussion of the Wages Fund Theory see Cannan, 'A History of the Theories of Production and Distribution in English Political Economy from 1776 to 1848,' *passim*; Marshall, 'Principles of Economics,' Appendix J; Taussig, 'Wages and Capital, an Examination of the Wages Fund Doctrine'; and Webb, "Industrial Democracy,' Part III., Chapter I.

that it was universally believed. Lassalle's 'Iron Law of Wages', emanating from a fervent Socialist, is a restatement of the theory, before which Socialists, as well as the orthodox, were forced, in default of an alternative theory, to prostrate themselves. Mill's is the glory of upsetting the care of Juggernaut, although Frederic Harrison had already noted the fallacy. In a review of a work of Thornton, a fellow economist, in the *Fortnightly Review* in May, 1869, the theory was solemnly stated, examined, and disproved. Economics was never the same after this inroad into its hitherto unquestioned sanctities. Mill himself died shortly afterwards, and it was left to others, notably to Jevons, to collect the tattered fragments of political economy; and by the publication of the 'Theory of Political Economy' in 1871, with an exposition of his theory of marginal utility, once more to give the science an appearance of respectability, not to say probability.[16]

THE FUTURE OF LABOUR

There are discrepancies between the first and second halves of the 'Principles'. Mill began as an individualist advocate of peasant proprietorship, converted himself as he went on, and ended almost as a Socialist. But, as nobody held out to the end of the book, and very few got beyond the first half, its influence was in favour of peasant proprietorship.

No essay upon the economic principles of Mill is exempted from referring to Book IV, Chapter VII, of his 'Principles'. For that bears the title 'On the Probable Futurity of the Labouring Classes'. In 1817 the House of Commons appointed a 'Select Committee on the Education of the Lower Orders'. In 1848, in his chapter on the 'labouring classes' (the term itself shows an advance), Mill says he uses the term in the conventional sense, as 'I do not regard as either just or salutary a state of society in which there is any class which is not labouring, any human beings exempt from bearing their share of the necessary labours of human life, except those unable to labour, or who have fairly earnest rest by previous toil'(¶1). The interest of this passage lies in the change of attitude indicated, not the change which

[16]See Mill's 'Principles of Political Economy,' edition Ashley, Appendix O, Longmans, 1910.

had taken place between 1817 and 1848, but the expressed possibility of social transformation. And this possibility is presented in a description which, if it suffers somewhat from Malthusian squint, yet also contains something of a prophet's vision. The relation between rich and poor is to vanish. Just as feudalism is now dead, so must the poor of to-day emerge from their tutelage. Independence is the key to the future of the workers. 'Whatever advice, exhortation, or guidance is held out to the labouring classes must henceforth be tendered to them as equals, and accepted by them with their eyes open.' Then he proceeds briefly to survey profit sharing. The results have sometimes been favourable, but the capitalist is not eliminated; in fact his hold is strengthened over his employees. 'The form of association, however, which, if mankind continue to improve, must be expected in the end to predominate, is not that which can exist between a capitalist as chief, but in . . .' (¶ 6), and Mill proceeds to narrate the history and the results of cooperative production. Here the prophet's voice was speaking. The future of co-operation is hidden from us, but who knows how far it will evolve? Once the great mass of the people begin to produce the necessaries of life for themselves without the needlessly insinuated mediation of predatory capital, the future state will evolve with a swiftness and a certainty unprecedented in the annals of civilisation. With the displacement of the capitalist will come, not the millenium, but at the least a society whose basis is not that of our own, capital needlessly deviated from production to advertisement, advertisement, and ever more advertisement. Mill's great position as an economist does not rest, as he considered it to rest, upon a discovery of his concerning distribution, nor, as other persons have considered, upon his treatment of value. It rests upon his humanity and the introduction of the element of humanity into economics. He attempted to apply to what others had regarded as an art, to be treated entirely for art's sake, the saving grace of human fellowship.

FEMINIST

The abuse of power and the detrimental effects of involuntary subordination are themes which recur more frequently in Mill's work than any other. It is because he objects to the dominance of capital that he becomes so nearly a Socialist. It is because government by the few is a system too apt to ally itself with tyranny that he is so strong a democrat. It is because he realises the peculiar evils which arise from the subjection of women that he is a feminist.

There are two species of prophets. One is the man who utilises the historical method, the inductive method, or what not, and foretells a fragment of the events of the coming year, or perhaps of the next few years—he sees, but has no vision. The other species has no use for the inductive method, and regards a telescope as an anachronism. He sees far ahead and is emphatic. Isaiah belonged to this class, Marx to the former, Mill we may class with Marx in this respect, save only in a single direction. Where the future of women is concerned he ceases to rely on the creaking machinery of the syllogism, and with no thought of inconsistency, speaks the truth that is in him. Although 'The Subjection of Women', his most extended statement on the subject, was the last work to be published in his lifetime, yet in every one of his earlier works he had dwelt on the subject, wherever opportunity arose, with insistence, with indomitable iteration. He wished to see the status, legal, political and social, of women raised to that of men, but concentrated on endeavouring to obtain for women the vote on the same terms as men had it, claiming throughout that as men had no abstract right to decide for women, women should be put into a position to decide for themselves. In a letter to Florence Nightingale, written in 1867, he says: 'I will confess to you that I have often stood amazed at what has seemed to me the presumption with which persons who think themselves humble set bounds to the capacities of improvement of their fellow creatures, think themselves qualified to define how much or how little of the divine light of truth can be borne by the world in general, assume that none but the very élite can see what is perfectly clear to themselves, and think themselves permitted to dole out in infinite doses that daily bread of truth upon which they themselves live and without which the world must come to an end.'[17]

[17]'Letters,' Vol. II., p. 104.

THE TRUTH ABOUT WOMEN

His 'Liberty' bears as its text a quotation from Humboldt's 'Sphere and Duties of Government', concluding with 'the absolute and essential importance of human development in its richest diversity'. The whole case against the present position of women was just that this diversity of development was prohibited, and that even undiversified development was stunted. In a diary he kept for a few months in 1854, wherein Mill inscribed a curious mixture of platitude and epigram, he states his 'deliberate opinion that any great improvement in human life is not to be looked for so long as the animal instinct of sex occupies the absurdly disproportionate place it does therein,' and that firstly, in order to attain any improvement, 'that women should cease to be set aside for this function, and should be admitted to all other duties and occupations on a par with men.'[18] He develops in this place, in fact, an epigram he had put to paper three weeks before, that 'What is called morality in these times is a regulated sensuality.'[19] Sex is an accident, and should not be a determinant. In the drama of life it is illogical that women should never enact more than a secondary rôle—especially to Mill, who believed that they are usually 'of far greater versatility than men'.[20] Sex is considered 'as entirely irrelevant to political rights as difference in height or in the colour of the hair.'[21] Again, 'The ideas and institutions by which the accident of sex is made the groundwork of an inequality of legal rights, and a forced dissimilarity of social functions, must ere long be recognised as the greatest hindrance to moral, social, and even intellectual development.[22] To the objection (how tenacious are these barnacles!) that women are as a matter of fact unequal to men in the character of their achievements, that history, novels, art, etc., proceed from men alone, for all practical purposes, Mill had the reply that women are going along the same paths as men; they have not yet left their leading strings. They have always had men's works set before them; when they cease to copy them, your objections will fall to the ground and you will see that, after all, sex *is*

[18]'Letters,' Vol. II., p. 382.
[19]Ibid, Vol. II., p. 376.
[20]'Principles,' Book I., Chap. VIII., Sec. 5.
[21]'Representative Government,' Chap. VIII.
[22]'Principles,' Book IV., Chapter VII., Sec. 4.

an accident. Besides, 'how many of the most original thoughts of male writers came to them from the suggestion and prompting of some woman.'[23] The same case is stated in great detail in 'The Subjection of Women'. In brief, it may be summarised: 'Women's work is not, at present, equal to men's work. But women have never been allowed to be original. Release them from their subjection, and the consequences will prove whether or not women are essentially inferior. But don't punish them for their inferiority before they have had a chance to demonstrate their relative worth. And, my dear sir, if I may be permitted to express a personal opinion, I should not be at all surprised if your own morals did not benefit somewhat by such a demonstration.'

So much for Mill's attitude. Now as to his acts.

THE INVASION OF WESTMINSTER

In 1866 Gladstone introduced a Reform Bill, was defeated on it, and resigned. Lord Derby formed a Conservative Government, and Disraeli became the Leader of the House of Commons. In due course he, too, introduced a Reform Bill to enfranchise the small town householder and the lodger. Long and tiresome were the debates, and countless amendments marked the tortuous, serpentine progress of the Bill to the Statute Book. Here Mill had his opportunity. Woman Suffrage was no longer to be a thing unuttered in Parliament. On 20 May, 1867, he moved an amendment to omit 'man' and insert 'person' in place thereof, and so to make the Bill apply to both sexes. Mill made a long and eloquent speech, which, perhaps, suffered from lack of precedent. He was not to be contented with the mere verbal substitution, but proceeded to dilate on the position of women, economic and legal, to describe the educational disadvantages under which they lived, in short, to give a lecture on the Woman Question. The following is an example; it illustrates his somewhat ponderous style no less than his matter: 'The notion of a hard and fast line of separation between women's occupations and men's—of forbidding women to take interest in the things which interest men—belong to a bygone state of society which is receding further and further into the past. We talk of political

[23]'Letters,' Vol. II., p. 381.

revolutions, but we do not sufficiently attend to the fact that there has taken place amongst us a silent domestic revolution—women and men are, for the first time in history, really each other's companions.'[24] The result was the usual one. There were the immemorial asseverations adduced in opposition, that the amendment, if carried into law, would set a premium upon spinsterhood, that the law was not really unjust to women on the whole ['If an hon. gentleman married a widow with ten children, he had to support every one of them,' said one of the hon. gentlemen], that God never intended women to vote, and so on. A 'great man who flourished about 500 years before Christ' and the court of Dahomey were brought up and used in evidence against Mill. Gladstone was asked to express an opinion. He said nothing, but voted against the amendment. Seventy-three voted in favour and 196 against. True to posterity, a Lord something Hamilton voted against the proposal. But, including pairs and tellers, at least 80 members of Parliament 45 years ago found themselves in favour of Woman Suffrage. It was not a triumph, but a highly successful initiation. The London Woman's Suffrage Society was started, and Mill's motion developed into a movement.

A SUMMARY

It is no easy task to collect and integrate all Mill's scattered dicta on women. Nor indeed would much interest be attached to the performance, for many of the evils, against which he stormed with his greatest energy, have been lessened, if not eradicated. Property rights have been granted, and the law has generally receded from its former implicit tenet that women form a criminal class. Custom (call it convention, if you will) no longer holds women in thraldom to the extent of forbidding any voluntarily undertaken remedy for economic dependence. It is permitted to women to become educated. Previously, curious as it may appear, women had only been permitted to educate. The self-supporting woman of the middle class is no longer the mid-Victorian governess, anaemic and, perhaps excusably, ready to descend upon the marriageable younger sons of her employers, pictured in many novels of the period. To what extent these

[24]'Hansard,' 30 Vict., 1867, Vol. III., p. 821.

changes may be attributed to Mill is only conjecturable. Whatever may be said to minimise his work, it cannot be disputed that he has been the inspirer of progressive women in every country where there are such women to a degree untouched by any predecessor.[25]

Generally speaking, Mill's attitude was a very simple one. The well-worn metaphor of the ivy twined lovingly about the sturdy oak was no doubt picturesque and the rights of publication were enjoyed by a thousand minor poets. But the ivy is a parasite, and nobody but a decadent sentimentalist can extract much pleasure from the contemplation of parasitism practised upon a national scale. Let the law treat men and women as equals, and all the rest will follow. Writing on divorce, for example, he says, 'I do not think that the conditions of the dissolubility of marriage can be properly determined until women have an equal voice in determining them, nor until there has been experience of the marriage relation as it would exist between equals. Until then I should not like to commit myself to more than the general principle of relief from the contract in extreme cases.'[26] Let women be admitted to qualifying examinations for occupations on the same basis as men, then it will be seen whether women are capable of practising as doctors, lawyers, and the like. If they are found incapable, not much harm has been done; presumably there would be few women anxious to enter a profession, knowing that their predecessors in that profession had been unsuccessful by reason of their inherent and ineradicable sexual qualities. But, on the other hand, if they are successful, then the sources are doubled of the supply of skill, of knowledge, of energy to produce necessary services, to alleviate sufferings, and to add to the positive goods of life. They are more than doubled, for the introduction of fresh skill will be accompanied with a new and keener competition waged between equals and beneficial in its outcome. With the improvement in the position of women, men too would gain. Then and then only will it be possible to imagine an ideal liberty, a state where the vague aspirations of to-day would be translated into achievements and facts enduring and powerful.

[25]See Dr. Stanton Coit's introduction to the 1909 edition of the 'Subjection of Women.'
[26]'Letters,' Vol. II., p. 212.

DEMOCRAT

There are persons to whose mental eyes democracy best presents itself as a great quasi-religious service. Such are Whitman, Carpenter and their followers. The conception lends itself to criticism because to attain good government it is highly undesirable that all the governed should worship at the same shrine; dissent is the very life-blood of harmony in things political. There are other persons, such as Mr. Asquith, for whom democracy is a limited liability affair, with an undistinguished coat of arms, bearing for its device a registration official, couchant, except in the first fortnight of July. Both these conceptions are sincerely held by a large number of excellent people, who firmly believe that the sovereign power resides in the people, and that it is desirable that it should continue to reside there.

It is, however, possible for a man to be a staunch democrat and yet to have the greatest possible detestation for the numerical majority—the 'compact majority' at which Ibsen jibes so vigorously. England is, from a numerical point of view, governed to-day by the working classes. The working classes allow government to be conducted along lines which, frequently enough, are detrimental to their own interests, and, as we all believe at times, to the country's interests.

The distinction between the general idea of democracy and Mill's lies in this: by democracy is generally meant one active and combined majority, while Mill preferred to regard it as an agglomeration of minorities.[27] The problem of democracy was to him, how to provide for the adequate expression of the different minorities. The greatest minority of all was, and still is, the women. The next greatest minorities were, then more than now, the several sections of the manual workers; and, after that, there were the numerous political minorities for whom the exigencies of parliamentary government prohibited representation in Westminster. For, to Mill, the free and unrestricted discussion of ideas was all-important. A person might hold any opinions under the sun—he might conceivably be a mad eugenist favouring unnatural selection in the form of mating by *ad hoc* state

[27]See Chap. VII., 'Representative Government.'

officials—but it was not for any man or any institution to forbid the discussion of such ideas.

LABOUR REPRESENTATION

It has just been mentioned that Mill held views on Labour Representation. Indeed, they circumstanced the genesis of the Labour Party. Mill had always maintained the friendliest relations with the trade union leaders of his time, especially with George Odger. In 1857 we find that he was encouraging and aiding Holyoake to put up one of the first parliamentary candidatures of a working man.[28] John Bright was of opinion that Parliament was above classes and represented all; that the introduction of a labour element would add a class spirit of an unfortunate description. It was all very well to have extreme Radicals, who preached revolution, republicanism, etc., and were at times even punished for treasonable behaviour. But Bright knew very well that Horne Tooke, John Wilkes, and the rest were middle-class men (and Charles James Fox was an aristocrat!), whose sentiments, even in their most vehement moments, were not those of the multitude, and at times shared equally with Burke a certain academicism. Holyoake stood for the Tower Hamlets, but withdrew before the polling took place.

Mill realised, too, that government would not remain as it then was, a hobby of the wealthier class. 'We are now, I think, standing on the very boundary line between this new statesmanship and the old, and the next generation will be accustomed to a very different set of political arguments and topics from those of the present and past.'[29] The representation of the unrepresented was all-important. The presence of working men in the House of Commons seemed to him 'indispensable to a sufficient discussion of public interests from the particular point of view of the working classes'.[30] The policy he favoured was one of 'keeping the Liberal out'. In a letter written to Odger in 1871, when the latter was standing for Southwark, Mill says: 'The working men are quite right in allowing Tories to get into the House to defeat this exclusive feeling of the Whigs (then in office),

[28]See A. W. Humphrey, 'A History of Labour Representation,' and Holyoake's Biography (McCabe) and Autobiography.
[29]'Letters,' Vol. II., p. 56.
[30]Ibid, p. 268.

and may do it without sacrificing any principle. The working
men's policy is to insist upon their own representation, and, in
default of success, to permit Tories to be sent into the House
until the Whig majority is seriously threatened, when, of course,
the Whigs will be happy to compromise and allow a few working
men representatives in the House.'[31] Well has experience justified
this advice.

THE HERITAGE OF HARE

As to smaller minorities, for them he strongly supported a plan
of proportional representation invented by Thomas Hare, in
which Mill found the salvation of 'independent opinion'. 'I saw
in this great practical and philosophical idea the greatest
improvement of which the system of representative government
is susceptible, an improvement which, in the most felicitous
manner, exactly meets and cures the grand, and what before
seemed the inherent, defect of the representative system. . . . This
great discovery, for it is no less, in the political art, inspired me,
as I believe it has inspired all thoughtful persons who have
adopted it, with new and more sanguine hopes respecting the
prospects of human society; by freeing the form of political
institutions towards which the whole civilised world is manifestly
and irresistibly tending, from the chief part of what seemed to
qualify or render doubtful its ultimate benefits. Minorities, so
long as they remain minorities, are, and ought to be, outvoted;
but under arrangements which enable any assemblage of voters,
amounting to a certain number, to place in the legislature a
representative of its own choice, minorities cannot be suppressed.
. . . The legislature, instead of being weeded of individual
peculiarities and entirely made up of men who simply represent
the creed of great political or religious parties, will comprise a
large proportion of the most eminent individual minds in the
country, placed there, without reference to party, by voters who
appreciate their individual eminence.'[32] This much-belauded
plan was a simple variant of the proportional representation
idea : to secure election only a quota of votes are necessary, the
remainder polled by a successful candidate are transferable to

[31]Webb's 'History of Trade Unionism,' p. 272.
[32]'Autobiography,' p. 148.

another candidate whose name the voter might himself put on the ballot-paper. Any elector is at liberty to vote for any candidate in any part of the country. These are the main provisions of the scheme. Mill's conversions to new ideas were always of the thoroughgoing nature. He appears to have preached the new invention in season and out of season, and, no doubt, made himself unpopular thereby.

PROPOSED IMPROVEMENTS

Mill subjected the entire Parliamentary system to a fairly searching analysis, both in his 'Representative Government' and in a pamphlet 'Thoughts on Parliamentary Reform'. It must be confessed that he placed rather too high an estimate on the values of various points in the electoral machine. He believes that voting should be public and opposes the ballot. 'The *spirit* of an institution,' he comments, 'the impression it makes on the mind of the citizen, is one of the most important parts of its operation.'[33] Money payments of any sort should not be required of the candidate; they should be borne by his constituents. Members of Parliament should not be paid. If a Member is poor and requires pecuniary aid, his constituents should subscribe for the purpose. Perhaps the most curious of his efforts to tinker with the legislative machine is his recommendation that plurality of votes should be given, 'not to property, but to proved superiority of education'. This recommendation, however, he pathetically admits, did not meet with widespread approval. 'As far as I have been able to observe, it has found favour with nobody.'[34] Possibly even Mill had his doubts about it, for he says it was a suggestion 'which I had never discussed with my almost infallible counsellor, and I have no evidence that she would have concurred in it.' Another suggestion was that Parliament should not be burdened with the details of law making. 'Any government fit for a high state of civilization would have as one of its fundamental elements a small body, not exceeding in number the members of a Cabinet, who should act as a Commission of legislation, having for its appointed office to make the laws. . . . The Commission would only embody the element of intelligence in their construction; Parliament would represent that

[33]'Representative Government,' Chap. X.
[34]'Autobiography,' p. 148.

of will.'[35] Parliament was to issue instructions (presumably in the form of general resolutions), the Commission was to draft a Bill accordingly, which Parliament could either accept, reject, or refer back for amendment. Similarly Mill wished to separate the executive and administrative functions. 'Instead of the function of governing, for which it is radically unfit, the proper office of a representative assembly is to watch and control the government.'[36]

These suggestions—or, at any rate, some of them—may be considered as of nugatory importance and hardly worth discussing. But although their intrinsic worth may be nominal, they afford an excellent insight into the spirit inherent in all Mill's theories. The mental attitude of the bulk of mankind, so far as it has any, on the subject of democracy is, granted amiability and the absence of political discord, 'There are wonderful things latent in democracy. May they remain so'. Experimentation in democracy is now inextricably connected with the name Pankhurst. Pressed on the subject, the Bulk of Mankind develops distrust and party views. Mill is different. Believing, too, that there are wonderful things latent in democracy, he wishes them to be made patent. To secure this object no possible method is too minute, too circuitous. To develop every personality to its utmost was his ideal, and democracy was the most obvious of the many means by which that ideal was to be attained. The rights of the individual soul arose with Bentham; Mill adapted the patriarch's ideas to the requirements of his age.

SOCIALIST

In the course of its century-old career, the word Socialism has continually been changing its connotation. But, whatever might be its precise meaning about the time when Mill wrote his 'Principles of Political Economy', there can be no possible doubt that the revolutions of 1848 gave the word a popular meaning synonymous with the terms applied to political behaviour of the most abominable character. And the sister-term Communism

[35]'Representative Government,' Chap. V.
[36]Ibid, loc. cit.

shared the approbrium. Yet Mill, who always sought the truth, gave the schemes of Fourier, Saint-Simon and Louis Blanc careful attention in his 'Principles of Political Economy'; and when the 1852 edition appeared the following extraordinary expression of opinion was included in his study of Communism: 'If, therefore, the choice were to be made between Communism with all its chances, and the present state of society with all its sufferings and injustices; if the institution of private property necessarily carried with it as a consequence that the produce of labour should be apportioned as we now see it, almost in an inverse ratio to the labour—the largest portions to those who have never worked at all, the next largest to those whose work is almost nominal, and so in a descending scale, the remuneration dwindling as the work grows harder and more disagreeable, until the most fatiguing and exhausting bodily labour cannot count with certainty on being able to earn even the necessaries of life; if this or Communism were the alternative, all the difficulties, great or small, of Communism would be but as dust in the balance.'[37] It is almost necessary to remind oneself that the writer was the son of James Mill, and the spiritual heir of the individualists.

On the subject of State enterprise he maintains silence, although, generally speaking, he is opposed to any extension of government interference, on the grounds that a multiplicity of functions must lead to inefficiency. Yet he is always anxious to learn by experiment; on no account will he have an experiment hindered because it does not fit in with his views. Writing to Edwin Chadwick in 1877 he says: 'I think there is a chance that Ireland may be tried as a *corpus vile* for experimentation on Government management of railways.'[38] In 1898 the Fabian Society published Tract No. 98, 'State Railways for Ireland'. In 1910 the Vice-Regal Commission on Irish Railways declared by a bare majority in favour of nationalisation. The mills of God grind slowly.

THE INDIVIDUAL AND THE STATE

Mill was for ever insisting upon the necessity for a moral as well as an economic improvement. Writing to Auberon Herbert the

[37]'Principles,' Book II., Chap. I., Sec. 3.
[38]'Letters,' Vol. II., p. 194.

year before his death, Mill said : 'My idea is (but I am open to
correction) that, for some time to come, politics and social and
economic questions will be the absorbing subjects to most of
those working men who have the aspirations and the mental
activity to which the appeal would have to be made. . . . You
wish to make them feel the importance of the higher virtues.
I think this can be most effectually done by pointing out to
them how much those virtues are needed to enable a democracy,
and above all any approach to Socialism, to work in any satisfactory manner.'[39]

It is not unfair to suggest that, before the last few years of his
life, when Mill made a special study of Socialism, he was by no
means clear as to what Socialists wanted, and whether or not he
was one of them. The following passage, for example, while it
teems with the utmost philanthropy, at the same time reveals a
curious indecision. It refers to Mrs. Mill and himself : 'While
we repudiated with the greatest energy that tyranny of society
over the individual which most Socialistic systems are supposed
to involve, we yet looked forward to a time when society will no
longer be divided into the idle and the industrious; when the rule
that they who do not work shall not eat will be applied not to
paupers only, but impartially to all; when the division of the
produce of labour, instead of depending, as in so great a degree
it now does, on the accident of birth, will be made by concert
on an acknowledged principle of justice; and when it will no
longer either be, or be thought to be, impossible for human
beings to exert themselves strenuously in procuring benefits which
are not to be exclusively their own, but to be shared with the
society they belong to. The social problem of the future we considered to be how to unite the greatest individual liberty of
action with a common ownership in the raw material of the
globe, and an equal participation of all in the benefits of combined labour.'[40] He consistently affirmed what he denied, and it
is difficult to place him with absolute accuracy.

Reference has already been made to a work on Socialism
planned by Mill in his last years. Of this only four chapters
came to be actually written, and were first published in 1879

[39]'Letters,' Vol. II., p. 328.
[40]'Autobiography,' p. 133.

in the pages of the *Fortnightly Review*. Mill begins by showing that the gradual arrival of manhood suffrage in all countries would lead sooner or later to the thorough discussion of the subject of property. In fact, the Labour Congresses and the 'International Society' (probably the International Working Men's Association) were already discussing the subject, and so formulating the future courses of action of the working classes of the different countries of Europe. He then proceeds to study the Socialist indictment. It is curious that he makes neither here nor elsewhere any mention of Marx or the Communist Manifesto.

THE SOCIALIST INDICTMENT

The Socialist indictment constitutes, he admits, 'a frightful case, either against the existing order of society or against the position of man himself in this world'. He believes that Socialists generally placed too much emphasis on the evils of competition, without noticing its beneficial consequences. Nevertheless, on this subject 'Socialists have really made out the existence not only of a great evil, but of one which grows and tends to grow with the growth of population and wealth'. He then himself gives at some length some of the less obvious evils of fraud, bankruptcy, etc., but thinks that in production fraud could be largely 'overcome by the institution of co-operative stores'. Yet, having examined the expressions of Socialists, and convicted them of exaggeration, he admits that that by no means settles the whole matter, and concludes a chapter with the words. '. . . the intellectual and moral grounds of Socialism deserve the most attentive study, as affording in many cases the guiding principles of the improvements necessary to give the present economic system of society its best chance'. It is instructive to make an analysis, paragraph by paragraph, of his final summing-up. It is then seen that the favourable and unfavourable dicta alternate in an uninterrupted sequence throughout. The conclusion is as follows : 'The result of our review of the various difficulties of Socialism has led us to the conclusion that the various schemes for managing the productive resources of the country by public instead of private agency have a case for a trial, and some of them may eventually establish their claims to preference over the existing order of things, but that they are at present workable only by

the *élite* of mankind, and have yet to prove their power of training mankind at large to the state of improvement which they
presuppose.' As to taking over the whole land and capital of the
country and centralising its administration, that is 'obviously
chimerical'. The revolutionary plan of taking over everything by
one blow meets with no grace whatever.

But this does not conclude Mill's survey. He realises that the
root of the matter is the conception of property. He agrees that
the right of holding property, and to a still larger extent of trans-
mitting it, is conferred and maintained by the State. Hence this
conclusion : 'A proposed reform in laws or customs is not necessarily objectionable because its adoption would imply, not the
adaptation of all human affairs to the existing idea of property,
but the adaptation of existing ideas of property to the growth
and improvement of human affairs. . . . Society is fully entitled
to abrogate or alter any particular right of property which, on
sufficient consideration, it judges to stand in the way of the
public good. And assuredly the terrible case which, as we saw
in a former chapter, Socialists are able to make out against
the present economic order of society, demands a full consideration of all means by which the institution may have a chance of
being made to work in a manner more beneficial to that large
portion of society which at present enjoys the least share of its
direct benefits.'

What does all this come to? It may at first sight appear
feeble, tentative, undirected. But before pronouncing a final
judgment, a glance at Mill's material will be instructive. This
consists mainly—almost exclusively—of the visions of Owen, the
far-fetched schemes of Fourier, and the aspiration of Louis
Blanc.

Yet, in all this amorphous and inchoate matter, Mill was able
to discern many of the stable elements. He exclaims against centralisation just as he had doubted the possibility of any great
growth of joint stock enterprise merely because he could not fore-
see the extent of its future development. But he sees behind all
the cloudinesses of the Socialists of 1848 something substantial,
something real. He is able to sketch something very near the
actual line of the future evolution of Socialist thought. Had he
lived another 10 years he would almost certainly have been
amongst the founders of the Fabian Society.

BACK TO MILL

The Socialist movement to-day, or rather, the evolutionary
section, stands far from the field of combat selected by its progenitors. To-day many ideas are regarded as of secondary
importance, or nugatory or actually wrong, which a generation
ago were held as dogma, beyond criticism or attack. And the
evolutionary Socialist of to-day may find himself opposed to land
nationalisation, or even to any accepted *ad hoc* nationalisation.
He may be opposed to the multiplication of State officials; he
may support or he may, on the whole, oppose the Labour Party,
preferring to throw in his lot for the attainment of his ideals with
a party until recently unanimously denounced as bourgeois
capitalist. And even then he will, and does, sincerely believe himself to be a Socialist. The idea of what constitutes Socialism and
a Socialist is changing. What is the direction of the change? It
appears well within the bounds of probability that the attitude
of the evolutionary Socialist upon matters connected with society
(granted some few exceptions) is approximating to that of Mill.
To the present writer it seems probable that the history of the
next few years of the Socialist movement will accentuate the
changing attitude. It is almost safe to predict the development
of the movement. The next few years of its history will be marked
by the augmented value attached to the 'moral factor', which
will be used by Socialists as a touchstone in matters of legislation.
The co-operative movement will meet with support from
Socialists, and will probably extend its scope. The Socialist programme will shrink to the dimensions of a single session's poss-
ibilities, and will refuse to discuss the nationalisation of any
services not already, as it were, upon the list. A larger share of
attention will be given to problems specially affecting women.
These are but a few of the salient probabilities: their derivation
is obvious. And long before they emerge as things accomplished
Mill will have received his rightful share of recognition as one
of the moulders of modern Socialism and the future State.

CONCLUSION

Perhaps the most important point about Mill is his attitude. He
was the son of his father in more senses than one. There is an
extraordinary parallelism between their works. The father wrote
an 'Elements of Political Economy', the son wrote the 'Principles

of Political Economy, with Some of their Applications to Social Philosophy'. The father wrote an essay on 'Government', the son an 'Essay on Representative Government'. The father wrote 'An Analysis of the Problems of the Human Mind', the son wrote his 'Logic' as a sort of introduction and the 'Examination of Hamilton' as a sort of supplement. As we have seen, both hereditary and environmental influences were applied in the most thorough manner possible. The mental attitude of J. S. Mill therefore is indivdual only so far as it differs from his father's. Very largely the broadness of his views, even when they appear opposed to his father's, is simply to be ascribed to the gradual exploitation of the elder's theories. But to whatever degree his work is put down to paternal influence, there can be no doubt that J. S. Mill exerted a wonderfully broadening effect over English political thought. Mill translated the notion of police, as held by Bentham, into the notion of a polity. The study of the affairs of the State was held to be the study of the means of attaining the greatest cheapness. Mill changed the idea of economy into the idea of economics. In Mill's childhood the greatest importance was attached to the study of the humanities; he made the greatest importance attach to the study of humanity. It is as a broadening influence that he is most important, infusing the doctrines of Liberalism with something more approaching liberality, and directing, for the first time, to the claims of labour a substantial portion of public attention.

Another point is worth briefly discussing. There are two lines along which changes in the body politic may arrive : by gradual evolution and by cataclysmic revolution. The method of evolution is slow, sure, and unattractive. The other method is attractive because of its pyrotechnic qualities, and windy philosophies will ever sway the imagination of the politically uninstructed. Mill is noteworthy principally as an excellent doubter. He had no originality; he hesitates always. But out of his hesitations come great things. If his direction be zigzag, nevertheless he marks a path; and in his case, at any rate, his end was worth more than his conclusions.

Edith J. Morley

6 JOHN RUSKIN AND SOCIAL ETHICS

INTRODUCTORY

RUSKIN NOT ONLY denied that he was a Socialist: he asserted that the Socialist ideal of human equality was unattainable and undesirable. He even wrote of 'liberty and equality', that he detested the one, and denied the possibility of the other ('Time and Tide', chap. xxii, § 141). He proclaimed himself a 'violent Tory of the old school', and an 'Illiberal', and it is certain that, for a clear exposition of Socialistic doctrine, we must look elsewhere than in the volumes of Ruskin.[1] Moreover, economists tell us that many of his theories are unsound, and that his attempts to work them out in detail are as unpractical as the ill-starred Guild of St. George.

It is probably true that any movement to remodel society precisely on the lines he laid down would be foredoomed to failure. It is at least equally true that to ignore his teaching becomes every day more impossible and disastrous. For Ruskin, who is accepted neither by Socialist nor by practical political economist, nevertheless strikes at the very root-disease of modern 'civilisation' when he condemns commercialism and the struggle for more material possessions, showing that life is the only true wealth, and that the richest man is he whose existence is the most useful, many-sided and helpful.

Ruskin himself says 'that in a science dealing with so subtle elements as those of human nature, it is only possible to answer for the final truth of principles, not for the direct success of plans;

[1]See, on the other hand, Collingwood's 'Life of Ruskin,' Book III., Chap. IV., 'For when, long after "Fors" had been written, Ruskin found other writers advocating the same principles and calling themselves Socialists, he said he too was a Socialist' (and *ante*, p. 242. 1/- edition).

129

130 WRITERS AND REBELS

and that in the best of these last, what can be immediately accomplished is always questionable, and what can be finally accomplished inconceivable'. ('Unto this Last', Preface.) Though we may frequently refuse to accept the special application of Ruskin's principles; though in a good many instances we are forced to regret that those applications were ever made, yet concerning the principles themselves there can be but one opinion. They may be summed up in his own statement that 'Life without Industry is Guilt; Industry without Art is Brutality' ('Lectures on Art', III).

Whatever the particular phase of human activity which he might be considering, Ruskin revealed its relation to the ultimate truth and meaning of life. He showed, and in no narrow didactic spirit, the necessary connection between art and ethics; he traced the links between morals and sociology, and pointed out that scientific economics are inevitably bound up with the reform of the individual. Above all, he proved incontrovertibly that increased prosperity, whether national or individual, industrial or social, must go hand in hand with increased capacity and with a desire for a prosperity and advance which are above and beyond all these. 'It is open, I repeat, to serious question . . . whether, among national manufactures, that of Souls of good quality may not at last turn out a quite leadingly lucrative one.' In all the many forms of teaching which he undertook, this manufacture of souls, this awakening of the spiritual in the material, was John Ruskin's chief end and aim. In art and in economics he applied the same touchstone, for it was his distinction to see life always as a whole and to refuse to divide it into the watertight compartments beloved of specialists.

CHILDHOOD AND EARLY LIFE

Ruskin was of opinion that the study of a man's work should begin with an attempt to become familiar with his life and character, more especially as these were shaped and developed in his childhood. Thus, in his autobiography, 'Præterita', he dwells in great and loving detail on his early life and upbringing, but discontinues the story soon after the completion of 'Stones of Venice', and before the beginning of his campaign of social reform. A similar disproportion may, therefore, be excused in a tract which essays only to give a brief account of his aims in

that campaign. But these cannot justly be appraised unless we
understand something of the man who devoted the best of himself to their achievement, and realise something of his passionate
concentration, his intense emotional nature, and of his 'unusual
moral principle and self-command'.

John Ruskin was born, of Scottish parentage, at 54, Hunter
Street, Brunswick Square, W.C., on February 8th, 1819. His
father was a well-to-do wine-merchant, hard-working, energetic
and successful in business, and 'entirely honest', as his son later
on described him, in words of praise which meant much coming
from that source. He was also cultured and intelligent, with a
real appreciation of scenery and travel, and a lover of art and
literature. His wife, who was some years older than her
husband, held a more puritanical view of life, and it was she
who took the lead in the early upbringing of the precocious and
not very robust little son. Her methods were as stern as they were
affectionate and careful; he was allowed no toys but a cart and
a ball and two boxes of well-cut wooden bricks; he had few or
no playmates, and he was taught to rely on himself for amusement and occupation. 'I . . . could pass my days contentedly in
tracing the squares and comparing the colours of my carpet. . .
The carpet, and what patterns I could find in bed-covers,
dresses, or wall-papers to be examined, were my chief resources.'
It sounds a lonely and self-centred life for a small boy, though
doubtless it resulted in the powers of concentration and accurate
observation which were to distinguish him later on.

Ruskin, in his own summary of the 'blessings' of his childhood,
puts first the fact that he had never heard his parents' voices
raised in anger, nor seen any disorder in any household matter.
Thus, he early learned 'the perfect meaning of Peace, in thought,
act and word'. On the other hand, he complains that he had
no one to love or assist or thank, and nothing to endure. 'My
strength was never exercised, my patience never tried, and my
courage never fortified.'

In 1823 his parents moved to Herne Hill, and, from this time
onwards, his outdoor recollections were of the garden where he
played and of the surrounding country in which he delighted.
It is tempting to linger over these early days, and to trace in the
child the father of the man. Narrow and conventional as was his
home in many ways, it was in other respects unusually cultured

and intellectual. From his babyhood, long before he was supposed to care to listen, he heard great books read aloud by his
parents for their own amusement—the eighteenth-century
novelists and Byron, as well as the authors usually considered
more suited to the family circle. Above all, his imagination was
awakened by the yearly journeys all over Great Britain, and,
later, on the Continent, which gave him his first introduction
to the beauties of nature. His father 'travelled' for his own orders,
and wife and child accompanied him on the pilgrimages, which
combined pleasure and sight-seeing with business. The happy
weeks spent on these driving tours gave Ruskin just the education he needed. Old buildings stirred his interest in the past;
beautiful scenery and, above all, mountains, stimulated the love
of nature which, at the age of three and a half, already led him
to ask for a background of 'blue hills' when his portrait was
painted by Northcote. A little later he was enquiring of what the
mountains were made, and soon he was poring over minerals,
beginning his study of geology, and pulling to pieces every
flower he could pluck, until he knew 'all that could be seen of
it with child's eyes'.

Very early in life he learned, after his own fashion, to read
and write, and he soon began to imitate his father by keeping
a journal, in which every detail of his travels was set down.
Thus, naturally, the habit of descriptive writing was acquired.
Doubtless, Ruskin was right in supposing that his extraordinary
command of rhythm and language was largely due to his
mother's training. From the time he could read, until he was
14, and about to start on his first continental journey (1833),
morning after morning, year by year, they read together two
or three chapters of the Bible, completing the whole, from the
first verse of Genesis to the last verse of the Apocalypse, only
to begin once more at the beginning. Every day, too, the child
committed to memory some verses of the Bible and of the Scottish paraphrases, and was compelled to repeat them over and
over again until not a syllable was missed or misplaced, not a
sentence wrongly accented. To his daily discipline, he rightly
attributed 'the best part of his taste in literature', his appreciation of the music of words, and also his capacity for taking
pains.

Pope's Homer, Walter Scott's poems and novels, 'Robinson

Crusoe', 'Don Quixote' and 'Pilgrim's Progress', were his other 'text-books' of literature, but these from choice, not compulsion.

Human companions he had few : his Scotch cousins, one of whom became his adopted sister, his cousins at Croydon and a boy friend at Herne Hill, are all that he mentions, and we know that he was not allowed out except under supervision, that he was not sent to school until he was 14 and then only to a small private class to which every day he was personally conducted by his father, and where he remained less than two years. There is no doubt that he suffered from this mode of upbringing in so self-contained a household. He was over-fostered and over-cared for, 'safe against ridicule in his conceit', his 'father and mother in their hearts caring for nobody in the world but me.' He developed prematurely in many directions; he wrote too much, both of prose and verse; he exerted his mind more than was wholesome, and he became too self-opinionated.

The first disturbance in his sheltered life came when, somewhere about the age of 17, he fell in love with the young daughter of his father's French partner; M. Domecq. The passion was not requited, and four years later, in 1840, the girl married Baron Duquesne. The effect of the disappointment on a lad of Ruskin's temperament was great : 'Men capable of the highest imaginative passion are always tossed on fiery waves by it,' he writes; and again, in referring to the evil consequences of his isolated childhood, 'when affection did come, it came with violence utterly rampant and unmanageable, at least by me, who never before had anything to manage.' We know that the young man broke down in health and spirit as a result of this unfortunate experience, which darkened several years of his life.

Meanwhile he had been prepared for Oxford at King's College, London, and, in 1836, he matriculated as a gentleman-commoner at Christ Church, going into residence in the following January. Already he had made his appearance as the defender of Turner in *Blackwood's Magazine* (1836), and earlier than this he had seen his verses in print in *Friendship's Offering*. But his regular academic studies were less advanced, and his lack of accurate scholarship was a drawback to him at college, and a hindrance all his life. Yet he did well at Oxford, not only taking the Newdigate Prize for English Verse, as he had intended, but winning a reputation as a writer and student, and

raising hopes that he would secure a first class. Then at the
critical point, when all seemed going well, and in spite of the
care of his mother, who had followed him up to Oxford in order
to watch over him, the crash came and his health broke down.
For two years he was more or less an invalid, threatened with
permanent lung trouble. Foreign travel restored his health, but
all idea of an honours degree had to be abandoned. In 1841 he
went up for the pass examination and did so well that he was
granted the highest distinction possible—an honorary double
fourth class in honours—always a most unusual, and nowadays
an impossible, reward of merit.

RUSKIN AS ART CRITIC

By this time (1841-42) his ill health, combined with his interest
in art, changed his plans for the future, and Ruskin finally
abandoned the idea of taking Holy Orders. He settled down
to serious art study, and it was in this same year that an
attempt to sketch a tree-stem with ivy upon it, forced upon him
the consciousness of his vocation. Suddenly he realised that
it was his mission to preach the gospel of sincerity in art, 'to
tell the world', in the words of Mr. Collingwood's 'Life', 'that
Art, no less than other spheres of life, had its Heroes; that the
mainspring of their energy was Sincerity, and the burden of
their utterance, Truth.'

It was many years before Ruskin passed from the rôle of
art-critic to that of social reformer and preacher, and there is
no room in the limits of this tract to trace in detail the process
of the evolution. But a cursory investigation is enough to show
that it was by a natural course of development, and not by any
sudden change of idea, that the author of the first volume of
'Modern Painters' (1843) became the inspired prophet of 'Unto
this Last' (1860) and 'Munera Pulveris' (1862). Because, not
in spite of, his study of art, Ruskin was bound to grow into a
student of sociology. The underlying principles of his teaching
develop, but fundamentally they remain the same. The foundations of his creed, whether in art, in thought, in morals, or in
sociology, may be expressed in his own words: 'Nothing can
be beautiful which is not true.' Sincerity is the foundation of all
true art; honesty of purpose in the artist, truth and beauty in
the thing portrayed; and to Ruskin, art, religion and morality

are different only in so far as they reveal different aspects of the same thing. Hence 'all great art is praise', that is to say, it is the result of the artist's instinctive reverence and delight in the beauty, which it is given him to see more truly and accurately than other men, and which it is his supreme mission to reveal to others. He sees more truly and must make others see too; he must be faithful to nature, representing with exactitude that which he perceives. But there is a spiritual as well as a physical perception—the insight which pierces through externals to the essential truth that is beyond, and is the result of intuition, inspiration, enthusiasm and of all that is implied by the word 'imagination'. To Ruskin, as to other great critics of the nineteenth century, imagination is the interpreter, the power which transforms or transfigures reality, but without destroying the basis of ordinary perception. It does not change facts, but, by rendering them imaginatively, it forces them to yield something beyond themselves. It is this 'putting the infinite within the finite' that differentiates art from 'imitation', which can be only of the material.

Essential truth is, then for ever inconsistent with imitation. 'Ideas of truth are the foundation, and ideas of imitation the destruction of all art'; for, in the words of Goethe, 'The *spirit* of the real is the true ideal'. This being so, it is not difficult to understand how Ruskin came to connect morality with art : he shows us the links between the two when he writes that art is an inspiration, 'not a teachable or gainable thing, but the expression of the mind of a God-made great man'; and again, from a somewhat different angle, art 'declares the perfectness and eternal beauty of the work of God, and tests all work of men by concurrence with or subjection to that'. Art unites the real, the ideal, the moral and spiritual, and by this union it is serviceable to man. 'All art which involves no reference to man is inferior or nugatory. And all art which involves misconception of man, or base thought of him, is in that degree false and base.' In other words, art must be brought to the test of life, and is worthy, as all other work is worthy, when it is of use, though the kind of usefulness is of course quite different from that of the things which as Ruskin says disdainfully, 'only help us to exist'. It is by presenting noble ideas nobly that art fulfils its function of service.

By criticism on these lines he justly claims that the distinctive character of his 'essays on art is their bringing everything to a root in human passion and human hope.' He holds that art exists for the service of man, and is greatest when its service is greatest; without this motive no true art can come into being.

A study of 'Modern Painters', shows that Ruskin was early led to the belief that the nature of the work of art depends primarily on the character of the artist. Later, he came to the conviction that a nation's art is the expression of its life and character, the individual artist being moulded by his surroundings and by the age in which he lives, so that, if these be unclean, the resulting art will be, like Renaissance architecture, decadent and unpure. Thus, he writes in 'On the Old Road' (§ 276): 'Let a nation be healthy, happy, pure in its enjoyments, brave in its acts and broad in its affections, and its art will spring round and within it as freely as the foam from a fountain; but let the springs of its life be impure and its course polluted, and you will not get the bright spray by treatises on the mathematical structure of bubbles.' And again, in 'Lectures on Art' (§ 27): 'The art of any country *is the exponent of its social and political virtues.* . . . The art or general productive and formative energy of any country is an exact exponent of its ethical life.' From this position there was no very startling transition to the famous chapter 'On the Nature of Gothic' in 'Stones of Venice' (1851-3), which contains in embryo all his later sociological and economic teaching. From teaching art and from the promotion of culture, both ethical and intellectual, Ruskin passed to the final phase of his life-work, and that which he considered by far the most vital.

RUSKIN'S LATER LIFE AND WORK AS PRACTICAL REFORMER

In the years which had elapsed since his graduation as M.A., and his subsequent settlement with his parents at Denmark Hill in 1843, Ruskin had succeeded, in spite of violent opposition, in establishing himself as the leading critic and exponent of painting and architecture. A series of provocative and brilliant volumes[2] had gained him this position; his defence

[2]Of these, the chief are: 'Modern Painters,' five vols., 1843–1860; 'Seven Lamps of Architecture,' 1848–9; 'Notes on the Construction of Sheepfolds,' 1851; 'Stones of Venice,' 1851–3; 'Lectures on Architec-

of the Pre-Raphaelites had won for him the affection of Rossetti
(whom he helped in a characteristically quixotic fashion),
Millais, and their circle, while of the older men, Turner, Carlyle, and Browning were among his friends. Lastly, he had
secured devoted adherents among his pupils and fellow-teachers
at the Working Men's College; while his own old College had
recognised his achievements by the award of an honorary stu-
dentship of Christ Church in 1858. Thus, though his marriage
had been brief and unhappy (1848-1854), and his private disappointments many; though his violent assertion of his opinions
had aroused enmity and detraction, it nevertheless seemed by
this time that he had outlived the period of storm and stress,
and might look forward to a future of happy and successful
work as an art-critic. But from 1860 onwards, that is, from the
time when the last volume of 'Modern Painters' was published,
he no longer made art his main theme. Art he believed to be
the outcome of a true and elevated national life, and he had
been forced to realise that English national life was neither
pure nor elevated. Social evils went too deep for philanthropic
tinkering, and he therefore set himself to plan a complete
scheme for social reorganisation. This scheme, unfortunately,
never systematically developed, has as its leading feature the
banishment of utilitarianism and materialism, for which it
substitutes the beauty which is also justice and truth. It insists
that there is no necessary antagonism between industry and
art; that on the contrary, both are indispensable elements of
the social organism, though they can be combined in various
ways in order to fulfil various functions. But unless work is
beautiful, it is not true work, and unless the life, even of the
humblest worker, is beautiful, it is not a true life.

It is difficult to speak quite dispassionately and temperately
about this last development of Ruskin's teaching; difficult, too,
to realise what was entailed by his change of plan. For years, he
had struggled single-handed, against enormous odds, in his
endeavour to revivify English thought about art, and to overcome its insincerity and conventionality. Now, when any success he could desire seemed within his grasp, he came to realise

---

ture and Painting,' 1853-4; 'The Political Economy of Art,' 1857;
'The Two Paths,' 1859.

that his most important work was still before him, and the
battle still to wage. Never for a moment did he flinch or hesi-
tate. He allowed his books on art to run out of print, that
attention might be concentrated on the new message he had
to deliver; while he withdrew into the solitude of the seer and
prophet, upon whom are laid the burden and the consciousness
of a great mission. 'The loneliness is very great,' he cried; 'I
am . . . tormented between the longing for rest and lovely life,
and the sense of this terrific call of human crime for resistance
and of human misery for help, though it seems to me as the
voice of a river of blood which can but sweep me down in the
midst of its black clots, helpless.'

It is not necessary to dwell in much detail on the outward
circumstances of the remaining years of Ruskin's life. His father,
who had loyally endeavoured to understand his vagaries in art,
was bitterly distressed by his heresy in economics, while his
mother was wholly out of sympathy with his falling away from
religious orthodoxy. At home, as abroad, he had to submit to
misunderstanding.

From his parents, Ruskin inherited £157,000 in money, as
well as houses and land. The whole of this property he expended
during his life-time upon the promotion of reforms in which he
was interested, while he lived for many years solely upon the
proceeds of his books. Much of his money went to the foundation of the St. George's Guild, which was intended to prove the
possibility of uncommercial prosperity in a society contented
to get its 'food . . . out of the ground and happiness out of
honesty.' (See 'Fors,' Letter LVIII., for the creed of the Guild).
What it did prove was Ruskin's lack of success in the management of men and of detailed and complicated business affairs.

Again, he gave liberally to many individuals, educating pro-
mising young artists, or subsidising craftsmen and their crafts;
he founded and arranged a model museum at Sheffield; gave
pictures to the Universities of Oxford and Cambridge; established a drawing-school at Oxford; and bestowed collections of
drawings and of minerals on museums, colleges and schools.

His belief that all children should be taught to draw, as a
means of training eye and hand and mind; his pioneer work in
founding the Art for Schools Association; and his sympathy
with the education of women, are other instances of his practical

wisdom. Similarly, his suggested reforms in education, which are founded on the assumption that every child has the right to be properly housed, clothed, fed, trained, and taught until it reaches years of discretion, are for the most part now generally accepted, at any rate in theory. Ruskin was, for example, the pioneer of technical education in England; and even his road-making experiment with the Oxford undergraduates, which brought him so much ridicule, was the result of a sound educational ideal.

Ruskin also spent much time and money on sociological innovations, which have since been generally approved and imitated. For instance, he gave Miss Octavia Hill the means to manage house-property by a system of helping the tenants to help themselves. In pursuit of this aim he himself became a slum-landlord. Moreover, he never ceased his demand for the provision of decent accommodation for the working classes, though his agitation for housing reform made him many enemies. Another of his enterprises was the establishment of a model tea-shop; yet another, a scheme for the organised relief of unemployment and for the training of the unemployable.

Indeed, it is scarcely an exaggeration to say that almost every modern measure of social improvement may, either directly or indirectly, trace its origin to the precepts and example of John Ruskin.[3] Thus, nothing can be more fallacious than to regard him as merely capricious and fanciful in matters of practice, or to forget his proposals for definite schemes of social regeneration, because he blinds us with the lightening of his zeal, or deafens us with his moral fulminations.

'He was like the living conscience of the modern world,' says Sir E. T. Cook, his editor; and his health, never robust, was eventually undermined by the strain of his exertions and disappointments. The last 25 years of his life were clouded by frequently recurring attacks of illness, which sapped his powers

[3]'National Education, National Hygiene, National Dealing with the Housing of the Poor, even National Succour for those who fall by the way in the toilsome march of the Army of Labour, National Dealing with Land, National Dealing with Trade, with colonisation, with all the real National Interests—all these measures, so long denounced without distinction by the old sham political economy of the past, be advocated, and now they are within or at our doors.'—YORK POWELL.

and added to the misery of private grief and mental overstrain.
The first grave collapse occurred in 1878, and soon afterwards
he resigned his Oxford professorship (1870-1879) and retired
to the peace of Brantwood on Lake Coniston. The retirement
was not absolute : he wrote much and gave many lectures during
the ensuing ten years, and from 1883-1884, he was even well
enough to return to Oxford; while as late as 1888 he went once
more abroad—his farewell journey to France and Switzerland
and Italy. But from that date onwards until the end he was in
a state of mental decay, when 'his best hours were hours of
feebleness and depression.' Death released him on 22 January,
1900, and he lies buried, as he wished, in Coniston churchyard.

When, in 1860, Ruskin ceased to devote himself to pure art,
and turned instead to the problems of sociology, when he abandoned the search for abstract beauty, in order that a little more
beauty might be brought into unlovely human lives, then by that
sacrifice of inclination and of popularity he enrolled himself
among the lonely thinkers whose message is not accepted by
their own generation, and whose lot in this world is aching
disappointment. Ruskin had tasted the joys of popularity and
friendship; he had known the smoothness of a life of wealth and
ease; above all, he possessed the artistic and poetic gifts which
made the strife or the arena particularly hateful to him, and
rendered him peculiarly sensitive to harsh criticism. These facts
give the measure of his sacrifice and of his faith. They explain,
too, the emotional strength of his social criticism, and of his
demand for social regeneration. It was no Utopian dreamer, no
armchair-philosopher, who proclaimed insistently the old truth
that whosoever will save his life shall lose it. This man had made
the supreme offering, and he spoke from the certainty of his
experience.

THE MEANING OF 'WEALTH'

The warmth of Ruskin's pleading misled the so-called practical
men of his generation, who accused him of unlawfully confusing
sentiment with business. But passionate earnestness is not necessarily fanaticism, nor does burning hatred of wrong inevitably
lead to distortion or even exaggeration of fact. To apply everywhere and always the test of humanity and of life, rather than
the test of money-gain, may, even from the commercial stand-

point, in the long run be the most profitable course. Certainly, if Ruskin's standard be the right one, if 'the essence of wealth is in its power over man, and the grandeur of wealth is to make men better and happier,' then it may reasonably be accepted 'that the final outcome and consummation of all wealth is in the producing as many as possible full-breathed, bright-eyed and happy-hearted human creatures.' The most hard-headed business-man cannot, at any rate, controvert the next statement: 'Our modern wealth, I think, has rather a tendency the other way; most political economists appearing to consider multitudes of human creatures not conducive to wealth, or at least conducive to it only by remaining in a dim-eyed and narrow-chested state of being.'

It is not easy to formulate a systematic body of sociological teaching from Ruskin's writings, for he never arranged his doctrines with scientific clearness and logical consistency. Yet the underlying principles are, as we have seen, laid down with perfect simplicity. His political economy is founded on the conviction that 'there is no wealth but life—life including all its powers of love, of joy and of admiration. That country is the richest which nourishes the greatest number of noble and happy human beings.' Those who deal with the science of mere getting and spending, who conceive of 'wealth' as mere material possession, have no just claim to be called political economists. At best, they are interested only in a science of avarice, a mercantile economy, which ignores human welfare and has no right to arrogate to itself the title 'political', i.e., belonging to the citizens who form the State. At worst, their teaching is wrong, even in so far as it deals with buying and selling, since it deliberately starts from the false premise that men are moved, permanently and essentially, by nothing but their desire for material gain.

Now Ruskin interprets life always in terms of humanity, and is consequently impervious to arguments which postulate an 'economic man,' 'a covetous machine,' in whom 'the social affections are accidental and disturbing elements.' On the contrary, he proclaims, in the words of Wordsworth, that 'We live by admiration, hope and love,' and that it is for ever unsound and unscientific to ignore these permanent attributes of human nature. The individual cannot separate his work from his human feelings on the one hand, or from his physical capacities and

desires on the other. What is true of the individual is true also
of society, which is made up of individuals and cannot, therefore,
satisfactorily be regarded as an abstract theoretical entity. Any
competition or money-grabbing that injures the individual, at the
same time reacts against the State and is opposed to civic and
social welfare.

Again, things which cannot be bought and sold in the market-
place—e.g., love, friendship, self-sacrifice, capacity, truth—do
nevertheless, and must inevitably, have a very real influence even
on supply and demand. Ruskin shows, for instance, in an un-
forgettable paragraph in the first chapter of 'Unto this Last',
that 'all right relations between master and operative and all
their best interests ultimately depend' on the 'balances of justice,
meaning in the term justice to include affection—such affection
as one man *owes* another.' Since a workman is not a machine
who is moved by steam 'or any other agent of calculable force',
but 'an engine whose motive power is a Soul,' it is obviously
impossible to deal with him as if the so-called economic man
were separable from the emotional man. Even from the lowest
point of view, the greatest material result of his work will be
obtained if he serves his master gladly, i.e., if his 'soul' enters
into his work. To treat him as a machine, as something less
than a man, is to lower the economic worth of his work, which
is best done when, valued and valuable for its own sake, a blessing and not a curse, it calls into activity all the noblest human
energies and emotions. (This argument does not apply to purely
mechanical operations. But these, Ruskin would, precisely on
this ground, reduce to a minimum, as tending to the destruction
of real wealth, which is life and has no relation to market-value.)
It must be admitted that, if this be sentiment, it is sentiment of a
very practical, reasonable kind. Similarly, it is illogical and misleading to make a science of industrial wealth and to ignore
'real wealth', i.e., human welfare in the widest and deepest
interpretation. Thus the statement that 'There is no wealth but
life' is again a literal statement of fact, a common-sense doctrine which is intended for the plain business-man and not for the
idealist. Wealth, according to Ruskin, does not depend on
market-value; the worth of any object cannot be determined by
the price that may be obtained for it; and on the other hand, as
we have seen, many inestimably valuable things can neither be

bought nor sold. 'A thing is worth precisely what it can do for you, not what you can choose to pay for it. . . . The thing is worth what it *can* do for you, not what you think it can.' ('Queen of the Air', § 125.) Thus a miser, with hoards of money and jewels, is not really wealthy in any accurate sense of the term. His store benefits no one, himself least of all. Again, there is all the difference in the world between the value of a field of corn, and of a factory full of costly and death-dealing implements of war, or between a cheap edition of Shakespeare's works and an edition de luxe of the latest fashionable small poet: the corn is worth its weight in gold, Shakespeare's plays are priceless wealth—and the other things are not really valuable at all. For 'there is no wealth but life'; wealth-giving things are those which 'avail towards life'. Whether we do or do not desire them, whether there is 'demand' for them, does not affect their worth. A picture by Whistler is no more valuable now, when it fetches thousands in the auction-room, than when it first left the un-known artist's brush to be reviled by Ruskin. The worth, as distinct from the exchange-value, is not to be estimated by passing whims on the subject, nor by the price paid, but by the intrinsic power to be of service if rightly used. So that the wealthy man is he who possesses useful things and also the power and capacity to use them: wealth is the 'possession of the valu-able by the valiant': 'usefulness is value in the hands of the valiant' (or availing). Things which are desired for the base pur-poses and which pander only to the lower nature, are 'illth', not wealth, 'causing devastation and trouble around them in all direction', having no *use* at all, since they avail not for life, but for death. Wealth promotes life and all the life-giving, whole-some desires which are natural to healthy men and women. 'Perhaps it may even appear after some consideration that the persons themselves *are* the wealth.'

The above argument of Ruskin is open to certain objections which have tended to obscure the essential truth of his conten-tion. In the first place, as he says himself, though he does not always remember it, the potentiality for good, i.e., the 'value' of anything depends invariably on the owner's capacity to use it. Certain things have no life-giving power, except under certain conditions of culture. For instance, the beads given to savages by travellers are, both actually and potentially, valueless; but

Shakespeare's plays or Whistler's pictures would not give so much pleasure or produce equal effect. The *actual* worth does not vary, but the *effective* worth does. To that extent it is untrue that 'evil and good are fixed . . . inherent, not dependent on opinion or choice.' ('Modern Painters', § 33.) Ruskin states the case better when he writes that 'a horse is no wealth to us if we cannot ride, nor a picture if we cannot see, nor can any noble thing be wealth, except to a noble person' ('Modern Painters', § 14, and *cf.* 'Munera Pulveris', § 35). Secondly, though Ruskin ignores the fact, even the potential value of things varies in inverse ratio to their quantity. Thus, in spite of its intrinsic, life-giving quality, corn becomes potentially useless if there is a glut of it, and already more bread available than can be consumed.

Even more misleading, though this is not altogether the fault of Ruskin, is the fact that, as we have seen, he refuses to use the term 'value' in any current economic sense. Thus he implies by it, neither market-value, nor worth to an individual, but, almost invariably, 'life-giving quality'. Now the ordinary science of political economy is concerned very little with 'wealth' as measured by any life-giving properties. It deals simply with demand and supply, that is, with what men actually want at any given moment, and the means of satisfying their desires. Ruskin, on the contrary, insists that every demand for commodities is, of necessity, a demand for life or for death—a demand, that is, for things both in themselves and in the nature of their production, either good or evil, promoting human welfare or human misery. Thus it makes a very real difference whether money is exchanged for shoddy cloth or for hand-woven material; for penny-dreadfuls or for the romances of Scott.

THE MEANING OF 'POLITICAL ECONOMY'

Thus, Ruskin substitutes a human life-standard for a money-standard. Political economy, since it has to do with living men and women, must treat them as such, and not as money-producing and money-spending and calculating machines. Here, as everywhere else, he bases his deductions on an ethical foundation —refusing to discuss theories which leave out of sight the fundamental factors of right human nature. What *is*, cannot be made a satisfactory starting-point for the determination of what ought to be : men do not always want what is best and most desirable, but a true scientific political economy must raise them up to worthy desires, not pander to their most degraded instincts and the brute desire to over-reach one another. It must, therefore, insist that 'In true commerce, as in true preaching or true fighting, it is necessary to admit the idea of occasional loss . . . sixpences have to be lost as well as lives, under a sense of duty . . . the market may have its martyrdoms as well as the pulpit, and trade its heroisms as well as war.' The merchant's business is to provide for life, and, if necessary, like the members of the other great intellectual professions, to *die* for it; his function is to provide for the nation, not merely to get profit for himself. 'This stipend is a due and necessary adjunct, but not the object of his life,' if he be a true merchant. That object is, to produce the best commodity at the lowest possible price compatible with making himself responsible for the kind of life led by the numerous agents who necessarily work under his direction. For cheapness must not be obtained at the fatal cost of human lives or human character : the work required must be beneficial to the worker as to the consumer. In any commercial crisis, the merchant like the captain of a ship, is bound to share the suffering with his men. Thus must he prove that he cares most for the state or commonwealth, and that he understands the real meaning of political economy, the economy of the 'polis', which, if it be true to its name, is a social and not an individual science.

THE COST OF PRODUCTION AND OF CONSUMPTION
Such being the case, Ruskin is careful to point out that 'production does not consist in things laboriously made, but in things serviceably consumable : and the question for the nation is not how much labour it employs, but how much life it produces'— and life includes more than meat; it includes wisdom, virtue, salvation, the right and opportunity to be 'holy, perfect, and pure'. 'The presence of a wise population implies the search for felicity as well as for food.' Hence the authoritative command : 'In all buying, consider, first, what condition of existence you cause in the producers of what you buy; secondly, whether the sum you have paid is just to the producer, and in due proportion, lodged in his hands; thirdly, to how much clear use, for food, knowledge, or joy, this that you have bought can be put; and

fourthly, to whom and in what way it can be most speedily and serviceably distributed.'

If production consists in things serviceably consumable—tending to obtain and employ means of life—then, naturally, the use of the things produced is at least as important as their actual production. This leads Ruskin to a statement which is startlingly unlike that of most political economists, viz., that 'consumption is a far more difficult art than wise production. Twenty people can gain money for one who can use it; and the vital question, for individual and for nation, is never "how much do they make? but to what purpose do they spend?" ' What has been done with the potential wealth that has been produced? If it has been hoarded up, not used, it has been wasted, and has never really become wealth at all. 'The true home-question to every capitalist and to every nation is not, "How many ploughs have you?" but "Where are your furrows?" ' Thus, 'to use everything and to use it nobly' is the final object of political economy. 'The essential work of the political economist is to determine what are in reality useful or life-giving things, and by what degrees and kinds of labour they are attainable and distributable.' Wealth can be estimated only by discovering the remaining amount of utility and enjoyment—the life-giving properties—after the cost of production has been deducted. 'Cost' is 'the quantity of labour required' for production, and in so far as this implies loss of life to the worker, the worth of the work is diminished. When the cost includes the physical or spiritual degradation of the worker, then it can never be worth while to produce such goods, for no function of use or enjoyment which they fulfil suffices as a set-off to the harm committed in their manufacture. To produce such goods can never be 'profitable'. 'Labour is the *suffering* in effort. . . . It is that quantity of our toil which we die in.'

If, in such production, suffering outweighs the desirableness of the thing produced, then such labour is death-bringing—and 'there is no wealth but life'. It is wholly and eternally different from work and effort, the application of power (opera); that, in its noblest form, whether in physical action or mental, intellectual striving, is pleasurable and recreative. 'It does not matter how much *work* a thing needs to produce it; it matters only how much distress. Generally, the more the power it requires, the less the distress; so that the noblest works of man cost less than the meanest.' Thus interpreted, work, as distinct from labour and suffering, is salutary and beneficial to the worker. Ruskin realises the impossibility of doing away with all unpleasurable labour, but at the same time he points out that its amount may be decreased in various ways.

THE MECHANISATION AND DIVISION OF LABOUR

For instance, he shows that in manufacture the interest is diminished and the monotony, i.e., suffering, increased, when the worker continually carries out the same process without seeing any visible result of his labour. It is true that division of labour lowers the money-cost of many manufactured articles, but it is often soul-destroying to the producer. Less wages are obtained by the tailor who spends his life in stitching buttonholes, than by the skilled workman who is capable of making the whole garment or any part of it. But to counterbalance the reduction of wages, it is necessary to remember the lowered standard of workmanship, and also the lessening of power, efficiency, and well-being of the workman. It does not really 'pay', even in the lowest sense, to degrade human skill and taste, and to decrease healthy interest in the work done. This fact, almost unrealised either by economists or employers when Ruskin first stated it, led him to condemn both machine-made goods and also that over-specialisation which is the tendency of modern life. Just as the artist's personal touch differentiates a picture from the best photograph ever taken, so, in lower kinds of creative work, the maker's individuality must be expressed if the thing made is to be, in the best sense, valuable. There is an eloquent passage in one of Ruskin's books, in which he explains that no two specimens of great Venetian glass ever were, or could be, exactly similar, though modern Venetians turn out vase after vase exactly to pattern. The moral he deduces is universally applicable—namely, that the human standard alone is the true test of efficiency. Machine-made things are inferior in quality, whatever the ease with which they can be produced; purely mechanical labour is inferior, though the wages required to command it be never so low.

Hence, Ruskin's re-introduction of hand-loom weaving and handicrafts of every kind; hence, too, his tirades against steam

power and steam engines. He hated them, because they necessi-
tate all sorts of degrading labour in mines and in factories, and
because, at the same time, they destroy the beauties of nature.
For he believed 'that a nation is only worthy of the soil and the
scenes that it has inherited, when by all its acts and arts it is
making them more lovely for its children.'[4] Moreover, since
beautiful work can be produced only by people who have beautiful things about them, if the workers are surrounded by chimney-
pots and smoke, their ears deafened by steam whistles, and their
hearts saddened by a grey and dismal life of toil, they will create
nothing which contains even the elements of beauty.[5]

In spite of the common belief, Ruskin did not wish indiscriminately to destroy all railways and all factories, and very often his
complaints against them were eminently reasonable and right, as
when he objected to spoiling beautiful Swiss valleys by running
trains through them for excursionists who were too lazy or too
hurried to enjoy them wisely. He would have allowed railways
only where their presence tended definitely to broaden men's
minds and to facilitate the production of ideas; he would have
subordinated them everywhere and always to the real 'wealth'
and 'utility', which no money advantages can outweigh. Here,
as everywhere, he applied the human instead of the commercial
standard. This does not imply that he never exaggerated his
complaints or went wrong in his condemnations. Much of what
he said, for example, of hand-weaving, was the result of imper-
fect knowledge. No life could well be more brutalising than that
of an eighteenth century loom-worker; and in the same way, the
lot of an agricultural labourer was not, from any point of view,
more attractive in the days when the whole of his labour had to
be accomplished by hand. But mistakes of this kind do not in
reality detract from the truth of Ruskin's main contention, that
the mechanisation of labour and of life is an evil which needs

[4]*Cf.* 'Lectures on Art,' Sec. 123: 'Find places elsewhere than in
England, or at least in otherwise unserviceable parts of England, for the
establishment of manufactories needing the help of fire . . . reduce such
manufactures to their lowest limit.' And see 'The Two Paths,' Secs. 89,
90.

[5]Love of beauty 'is an essential part of all healthy human nature and
. . . is itself wholly good—the direct adversary of envy, avarice, mean
worldly care, and especially of cruelty.'—'Lectures on Art,' III.; and
see *infra* Secs. 25, 26.

remedy, in so far as it destroys individuality and wholesome enjoyment in men's work and in their surroundings. As long as human skill and understanding are necessary in order to guide the machine, as long as man is its master, not its servant, so long may its use be justifiable. As soon as it is possible to put in raw material at one end to come out manufactured goods at the other, without any further attention than that which is purely a matter of routine, such as stoking or turning a handle, the workman deteriorates and the kind of labour is harmful. It cannot be right, for it is degrading to press a button and let the machine do the rest.[6] The tests of wise work are, that 'it must be honest, useful and cheerful' : work that ruins the worker can be none of these things. To be occupied solely with mechanical work is necessarily and inevitably to lose in individuality and in humanity —to sacrifice soul, the development of which is the most 'leadingly lucrative' of national manufactures. When such labour is unavoidable, the hours of toil should be correspondingly short, in order that the workers may have ample time for recreation and for the development of their powers and sympathies.

THE MORALITY OF TASTE

Moreover, from another point of view, mechanical work produces mechanical results which, as Ruskin has shown in much detail and in various places, are almost, if not quite, as bad for the consumer as for the producer, since they destroy taste. This brings us to one of Ruskin's most startling assertions, which is also one of the most vital elements in his teaching. He insists upon the *morality* of taste. 'Good taste is essentially a moral

[6]*Cf.* 'Crown of Wild Olive,' Sec. 45: 'What! you perhaps think, "to waste the labour of men is not to kill them." Is it not? . . . It is the slightest way of killing to stop a man's breath. Nay, the hunger, and the cold, and the whistling bullets—our love-messengers between nation and nation— have brought pleasant messages to many a man before now: orders of sweet release. . . . At the worst, you do but shorten his life, you do not corrupt his life. But if you put him to base labour, if you bind his thoughts, if you bind his eyes, if you blunt his hopes, if you steal his joys, if you stunt his body, and blast his soul, and at last leave him not so much as strength to reap the poor fruit of his degradation, but gather that for yourself, and dismiss him to the grave, when you have done with him . . . this you think is no waste, and no sin!'

quality . . . not only a part and an index of morality; it is the *only* morality. . . . Tell me what you like and I'll tell you what you are' ('Crown of Wild Olive', § 54); and again, 'Good taste is the instantaneous preference of the noble thing to the ignoble.' Happily, it may be acquired and developed, and not least by the influence of our surroundings, natural and artificial. But since the converse is equally true, a smoke-begrimed or ugly environment has a far reaching influence for ill. For, 'what we *like*' (or endure) 'determines what we *are* and is the sign of what we are; and to teach taste is inevitably to form character.'

If Ruskin was right, it is small wonder that he protested against shoddy and machine-made goods, and against the ugliness of the modern industrial system and its productions. For to be satisfied with quantity instead of quality is a sign and precursor of worse evils which lurk behind. If we suppose, as he contended, that national taste be indeed the expression of national character, severe judgment must be passed not only on the Venetians, but on all nations who are content to exist without art or with inferior art. For they are proved incapable of delight, that is, in the true sense, uneducated, unable to be 'glad justly'. Yet enjoyment is a right which belongs to all in a well-ordered society—a right sadly curtailed for most people under present economic conditions, when they are taught neither what to like nor how to like it.

Lack of taste results, too, in the wrong use of labour and the substitution of commercialism and competition for honest work.

COMPETITION AND THE PROBLEM OF RIGHT PAYMENT

It is not too much to say that for commercial competition of all kinds Ruskin had an utter loathing. Thus his treatment of the wages-problem is unusually enlightened. At the beginning of 'Unto this Last', he insists that the question of supply and demand ought not to affect the wages paid in one sort of work more than another. A doctor's fees, quite rightly, do not vary in accordance with the amount of illness at a given time. A cabman is not allowed to ask higher fares because it is raining and his services are much in demand. Nor, in a dry season, is he expected to accept less. All work is worth a certain wage and should, in Ruskin's opinion, be paid at a fixed rate, irrespective of other factors. Bad and good workmen, who are entrusted

with the same task, should receive equal pay : in this respect
Ruskin is entirely in accord with modern trade-unionism. A bad
workman should not be allowed to undercut prices 'and either
take the place of the good, or force him by his competition to
work for an inadequate sum'. 'The natural and right system
respecting all labour is that it should be paid at a fixed rate,
but the good workman employed and the bad workman unem-
ployed.' We do not choose our doctor because he is cheap—
provided, that is, that we have money—but because we think
him efficient. The same principle should be applied in choosing
a bricklayer or any other worker. No other form of wage-com-
petition is justifiable.

Again, it is infamous that a man's necessities should determine the amount he is paid for his work : he should be paid
what it is worth—that amount, neither more nor less, he ought
to have. Moreover, to cheapen labour is in every sense bad
economy, since it results in bad workmanship and inferior
workers. From the lowest point of view, it does not pay to keep
men down to a barely living wage; it is wise policy, even from
a selfish standpoint, to let good workmen benefit from the
increased goodness of their work.

When Ruskin advanced this theory it was laughed at, like so
much else which he stated almost for the first time. Nowadays
practical business-men are coming more and more to adopt what
their predecessors termed a 'sentimental' doctrine, which after
all amounts to little more than that it is in the long-run more
profitable to pay a higher wage to an efficient, than a lower
wage to an inefficient, workman. In this instance, as in many
others, Ruskin's prophetic insight helps him to the vision of a
very practical and far-reaching reform.

In spite of this, Ruskin later, in 'Arrows of the Chase', II, 97,
makes a claim which might lead to dangerous results. He is
far ahead of his time in his demand that salaries shall be determined by a standard of life instead of by competition. He asks
for a definitely prescribed, uniform income or wage for each type
of worker, that is, as he defines it, 'the quantity and kind of food
and space of lodging . . . approximately necessary for the healthy
life of a labourer in any given manufacture'. Doubtless this is a
better method of payment than that resulting from blind
obedience to 'supply and demand', since at least it secures a

minimum of comfort to all workers, irrespective of competition. But Ruskin does not appear to recognise that this definitely prescribed, uniform wage might be a maximum as well as a minimum. It is not enough, as he himself implies in 'Unto this Last', 'Munera Pulveris' and elsewhere, that the workman shall be paid at a fixed wage. He has the right to raise his standard of life as the average product of his community increases in value; and he, as well as the capitalist-employer, ought to profit by industrial improvements.[7]

Competitive industry is not merely bad policy in so far as the workers are concerned. Its ill effects are felt in every direction, and perhaps chiefly in that it lays the main stress on 'profit' rather than on utility and good workmanship. For it is simply untrue that rivalry promotes excellence of manufacture. On the contrary, it causes that mechanisation of labour which results in the evils to which we have already referred—the deterioration of the worker and the degradation of work by the production of cheap and nasty goods which are palmed off on the consumer, whenever he can be deceived, as equivalent to something better. Advertisements tell their own tale, and are a sure indication of the dangers of trade competition. Ruskin may overstate his case and ignore everything that can be said in favour of modern commerce. Certainly he makes no reference to the social qualities sometimes developed in the struggle for life—enterprise, industry and self-sacrifice for example, all of which qualify a man for service as well as for the attainment of personal ends. But he is right in recognising the moral and material waste which normally results from the system of fraud upon which trade, to a lamentable extent, depends; and in anathematising the selfishness of the struggle and the loss of power which result from individualism.

RUSKIN'S VIEWS ABOUT INTEREST

He is not equally incontrovertible in his attack on interest, which, in the latter part of his life, he denounces as indefensible. In his earlier writings he is content to condemn usury: in 'Fors', and

[7]Compare his own assertion ('Time and Tide,' Sec. 8): 'It is the merest insolence of selfishness to preach contentment to a labourer who gets thirty shillings a week, while we suppose an active and plotting covetousness to be meritorious in a man who has three thousand a year.'

especially in Letter XVIII, he makes no distinction between this, which is rightly called extortion, and the interest on commercial capital. There is nothing surprising in the fact that Socialists accept his position, since they detest the capitalist system, which allows wealth to accumulate in the hands of the few and to be used for their personal advantage. For Socialists hold that all wealth should be created and expended for the common good, and that the conduct of the community's business for private profit is prejudicial to the body politic. But Ruskin never goes so far as this, though he advocates the increased ownership and control of industry by the State ('Time and Tide', § 81), and its organisation for social service. Consequently his condemnation of reasonable interest on capital cannot be substantiated. He argues that interest is a forcible taxation or exaction of usury, adding that, since money cannot produce money, there is no sense in the claim that savings ought to be increased by interest. 'Abstinence may, indeed, have its reward nevertheless; but not by increase of what we abstain from, unless there be a law of growth for it unconnected with our abstinence.' This is plausible, but unsound reasoning. It is easy enough to see the evil of usury, of profiting by the need of an individual, and losing all charity in the process. But if, as Ruskin rightly maintains, money consists merely of counters symbolising command of commodities and of labour, then the use of capital in production does result in an increase of the product, and investment of money in enterprises needing capital is a social service, for which (so long as there is not enough capital for its unlimited use) the consumer of the product may fairly be charged. So long as society relies, for obtaining capital, on its accumulation by individual owners, there is reason in this charge for its use, which is included in the price of the commodity.

Consequently there is an essential difference, in a capitalistic community, between reasonable interest on capital and the exaction of usury. A labour-basis of exchange and social service, instead of profit, are not feasible ideals until society has been reconstructed on a more satisfactory basis. And of this reconstruction, Ruskin refused to hear. He believed in a capitalistic society and did not altogether condemn the private control of industry for individual profit; as a result, his attacks on interest are unreasonably ferocious. Until industry is deliberately

organised by the State for the common good, social saving is
desirable, and, until borrowed capital is no longer needed for
commercial enterprises, interest is both permissible and inevitable.

SOCIETY IS AN ORGANIC WHOLE

While Ruskin refused to go the whole way towards the
nationalisation of capital and of the means of production, yet the
reforms he advocated tended always towards the promotion of
economic equality; and he had a real horror of the unlawful
accumulation of personal possessions. No one has ever more
clearly recognised the fact that society is an organic whole, and
that injury to an individual is therefore injury to the State. But
he believed that industry could be saved from the slough of commercialism only by reforming individual capitalists and members
of the ruling classes. He had a touching faith in the doctrine
of *noblesse oblige,* but no hope of any reform that could come
from the people and from democratic rule. In this we hold that
he was doubly mistaken. However enlightened and virtuous the
individual capitalist or manufacturer, it is, in the nature of
things, impossible for him to revolutionise commercial conditions.
Ruskin himself was forced to defend his own possession of
money and acceptance of interest, by pointing out the indubitable
fact that an individual can do no good, and probably will do
much harm, by tilting, as an isolated Don Quixote, at the
windmill of commercialism. Similarly, though Ruskin did not
recognise the truth, an individual manufacturer or merchant
would simply land himself in the bankruptcy-court, while benefiting nobody, were he, as an individual to refuse to conform with
the conventional conditions of trade. Individual efforts must be
supplemented by social cooperation and State action; similarly
the progress of all must come through all, that is, 'the State'
should be the expression of the whole of society, and not of any
one section thereof.

It is strange that Ruskin failed to recognise this fact. He was
hindered, as Carlyle had been hindered, by his acute realisation
of the natural inequalities of men, both mental and moral.
These convinced him that it was the duty of the strong man to
govern, and of the ordinary man to reverence and obey his
superiors. On the whole, it seemed to him that the existence of
a powerful aristocracy was the safest form of government, since

all social order must be built on authority. But the aristocracy he upheld was to be 'the assured measure of some kind of worth (either strength of hand, or true wisdom of conduct, or imaginative gift'). Position was in no way to be purchasable with money, but to be obtainable only by superior intellect and energy. Hence he was conscious that, if ruin were to be arrested, there must be 'repentance of that old aristocracy (hardly to be hoped), or the stern substitution of other aristocracy worthier than it'. Yet in the very next sentence comes the startling and short-sighted admission : 'Corrupt as it may be, it and its laws together, I would at this moment, if I could, fasten everyone of its institutions down with bands of iron, and trust for all progress and help against its tyranny simply to the patience and strength of private conduct.

Obedience may be, as he held, 'an inherent, natural, and eternal inheritance of a large portion of the human race', but there is no duty of obedience to the laws of primogeniture, nor to mere wealth and social advantages. It is true, and no modern Socialists will deny the fact, that men's capacities differ along with their functions, and that equality among millions of individually developing units is as inconceivable as identity. There are, as Ruskin says, 'unconquerable differences in the clay of the human creature'. But this does not warrant any individual in using his unequal powers as a means of injuring or oppressing those who are inferior to him. Nor ought the State to permit him to use his superior capacity in such a way as to build up either riches or dominion. Moreover, equality of opportunity ought to be secured for each individual, and for this no man has more earnestly pleaded than Ruskin himself, who even stated, in so many words, that 'this enormous difference in bodily and mental capacity has been mainly brought about by difference in occupation, and by direct maltreatment'. Let every child have his chance, and the right spirit of reverence for superiority will not disappear : rather will it grow and develop in those who have no cause for envy or hatred, but only for the 'admiration, hope and love' by which we live.

And indeed, in 'Time and Tide', Ruskin propounds a theory of government by cooperation and fellowship among nations, as among separate peoples, which is conceivable only in a world from which the evils of commercialism and tyranny have disappeared, and in which all men have been protected both from the unnatural inequalities born of oppression and from any misuse of the natural superiorities of others.

THE NATIONALISATION OF LAND

Ruskin's opinions about the possession of land are in some respect remarkably modern, and although not identical with the latest Socialist doctrine on this question, they come surprisingly near to the view that land held by occupying owners for agricultural purposes belongs to the category of tools, and is, therefore, quite properly in indivdual ownership.

Ruskin is clear that land and water and air, 'being the necessary sustenance of men's bodies and souls', must not be bought or sold. Yet he believes, up to a certain point, in the hereditary private possession of land by occupying owners, superintended by State overseers and paying a tax to the State as State tenants—the amount of land thus owned being strictly limited by the capacity to make good use of it. Apparently he has in mind a sort of peasant-proprietorship; in cases where larger tracts of land are granted in perpetuity to 'great old families', 'their income must in no wise be derived from the rent of it'. Land must never become a source of income to such owners; its possession is a trust and 'should be, on the whole, costly to them . . . made . . . exemplary in perfection of such agriculture as develops the happiest peasant-life'. (See e.g. 'Time and Tide'. Letter XXIII.)

THE ORGANISATION OF LABOUR

Perhaps he is most a pioneer in his demand for the complete organisation of labour and his belief in the right to work and to the best possible training and education for its accomplishment. His system of selecting the suitable worker for a particular job, and of utilising every potential labourer, is complete and satisfactory. All children are to be taught the laws of health, habits of gentleness and justice, and the calling by which they are to live. All those who are out of employment are to be received at once in government-schools or labour-colonies and set to such work as they can do, or trained for such work as they are fit. For the old and destitute, comfort and home are to be provided. 'A labourer serves his country with his spade, just as a man in the middle ranks of life serves it with sword, pen or lancet. If the service be less, and, therefore, the wages during health less, then the reward when health is broken may be less, but not less honourable; and it ought to be quite as natural and straight-forward a matter for a labourer to take his pension from his parish, because he has deserved well of his country.' (Preface to 'Unto this Last'). The case for old-age pensions has never been more trenchantly stated.

Lastly, he demands either government-workshops or trade guilds which shall set the standard of price and of workmanship for every commodity, 'interfering no whit and private enter-prise',[8] except in so far as their productions are 'authoritatively good and exemplary'. Ruskin's desire for some such guild system, self-governing in its constitution, but vocational and voluntary in its composition, brings him nearer to the aspirations of Guild Socialism than to the achievements of Collectivism, but in any case, and in spite of his denials, his ideal is definitely Socialistic in its trend.

THE RESULTS OF RUSKIN'S ECONOMIC TEACHING

Omitting, as we must, within the limits of a tract, a more detailed description of Ruskin's actual plans, and ignoring his somewhat perverse attitude on the subject of a fully democratic suffrage, we are now in a position to summarise something of what Ruskin effected by his economic teaching, and to estimate his influence on the nascent Socialist movement of the second half of the nineteenth century.

In the first place, he justifies his claim that 'honest production, just distribution, wise consumption' are the reforms that it is most necessary to enforce. For these reforms, radically insti-tuted, would go far towards the establishment of what to-day still beckons to us as a far-off Utopia.

But more important than any particular means that he advo-cates, is his whole attitude towards social problems, and, indeed, towards life itself. Above all else, he acts as a stimulating power,

[8]It is interesting to note that the establishment of such government-workshops, as a means to secure a high standard of workmanship and to prevent or reduce adulteration, is an 'original' panacea recently pro-posed by Mr. Emil Davies, who would, however, also use them as a method of obtaining additional revenue for the State.

a disturber of the vulgar modern complacency which he hated, an awakener of ideals, of higher motives and more generous resolves. Everywhere and always he applies the test of humanity; he breaks down the barriers which divide one human activity or instinct from another, and insists on the interrelation of all social and individual interests. The supreme moral and spiritual teacher of his age, he penetrates everywhere to first principles and ultimate truths; and whether his ostensible subject be art or economics, he attempts to alter men's aim and motive in life, to uproot evil however manifested, and to bring a little nearer 'the true felicity of the human race', by showing wherein nobility, wealth, and beauty consist.

Thus, while errors and extravagance are to be found in his teaching, and while he may justly be accused of lack of system in the presentation of his ideas about social reform, yet the abiding impression left by his work is not of these. It is rather a conviction of the breadth and vividness of his sympathies, and of his clear vision of essentials. His belief that no system of economics can be of permanent value, if it fails to develop 'souls of a good quality', the insight which enables him to recognise the ultimate connection between economics and morals—these are perhaps his most important contribution to social science. But greater even than the great lessons which he taught, the man's own nobility of purpose shines forth in all his writings—a beacon-light for future ages.

Colwyn E. Vulliamy

7 CHARLES KINGSLEY AND CHRISTIAN SOCIALISM

THE CHRISTIAN SOCIALISTS

'ALL GREAT POETS,' says Kingsley's Chartist hero, 'are by their office democrats.' Perhaps it may be said with equal truth that all real Christians are by their profession Socialists. The vital religions never have fought shy, and never can fight shy, of the social problem. The existence of poverty and evil is contrary to the religious ideal, and is in continual opposition to the religious doctrines. The founders of the Christian Church were very clear on this point. The poor and oppressed were in a special sense God's children, and their presence in society indicated a state of affairs which the Church was foremost in denouncing and in seeking to correct. Maurice, the originator of modern Christian Socialism, never hesitated to affirm the necessity for the co-operation of Church and State in any sound scheme of social reform, and his teaching lays stress on the 'radical affinity' between the principles of religion and the practice of Socialism. More, he believed in the direct action of the Church in politics and industrial regulation. That the Christian Socialist Move-ment has exercised considerable influence in both directions is beyond dispute.

Before considering the position of Charles Kingsley in this movement and his special influence, it will be well to give, first, some idea of the movement itself, and then a short account of the man whose teaching and personality led to its formation—Frederick Denison Maurice.

English Socialism and the Cooperative Idea may be regarded as of twin birth. The work of Robert Owen has been already dealt with in this series; it is not necessary here to describe his theories and reforms in detail. The wonderful, almost quixotic,

159

romance of the New Lanark mills, raised wages, reduced hours, free education and amusements, cheap provisions, and habitable dwellings—all this is well known, and so are Owen's magnificent schemes for the general organisation of industries and the free instruction of the whole community. Had the more reasonable of Owen's proposals been peacefully and persistently urged, it is likely that democratic advance during the first half of the last century would have been much more rapid. Unfortunately, the democratic cause fell into the hands of O'Connor and his 'physical force' Chartists, and with the fiasco of 10 April, 1848, when the Charter was trundled to its doom in a hackney cab and its heroes dispersed by the householder constables, it seemed as though the rights of the people had suffered a crushing defeat. But this was not so. Stimulated largely by the success of the Rochdale experiment, the cooperative schemes again came to the fore, and plans for industrial and social reform were both voiced by the new movement, which, a year or two later, was known as Christian Socialism. Realising the finer elements of Chartism, and deeply conscious of the suffering of the people, a group of devoted workers gathered round their leader, Maurice, and by means of an extremely vigorous propaganda, untiring personal labour, and the launching and financing of cooperative concerns, sought to 'assert God's order', and to establish a system of brotherhood and mutual help.

The Christian Socialists were by no means revolutionary. They were in some respects conservative—Kingsley always asserted the value of an aristocracy—and believed rather in a restoration than in a reformation of society. They did not seek to reconstruct society, but to avail themselves of the resources of the existing society, which they considered as a divine institution, soiled and corrupted by the evil practices of men, and above all by the spirit of competition. Their strength lay in the noble ideals which they set before the working men. Their weakness lay in the obvious limitations of their dogma, and perhaps also in their conception of the natural goodness of men and in a false theory of society. By 1850 they had already promoted 12 cooperative associations, all of them in trades which were then untransformed by the use of machinery—tailors, shoemakers, builders, piano-makers, printers, smiths, and bakers. It should be pointed out that the Christian Socialist theory of cooperation differed from the Rochdale plan in its fundamental principle. The Rochdale cooperatives adopted the Owenite 'elimination of profit' scheme, and formed an association of consumers, with benefits according to the amount purchased; the Christian Socialists advocated the association of producers, with benefits according to labour. The commercial failure of their enterprises was mainly caused by the fact that in small cooperative concerns run on these lines it was impossible to destroy the competitive element.

The idea of the movement was the application of the religious principle to economic problems, with special emphasis on *the supreme importance of individual character.* The life of the movement was short. After some four years of admirable and heroic effort, and the sacrifice in some cases of health and fortune, they were compelled to abandon their schemes for the regeneration of industry. But although they had failed as a working organisation, they had set an example which profoundly influenced the trend of English Socialism and has yielded a richer harvest than any of them could have foreseen. And it may be questioned whether, continuing their individual efforts independently, they did not accomplish more than they could have done had they remained united, and possibly restricted, in close association.

Taken from the religious standpoint, they differed from the great Anglican Revival—the Oxford Movement—in this respect : that instead of bringing the people to the Church, they were concerned rather with bringing the Church to the people.

The literature of the Christian Socialists will be dealt with in the course of this essay; it is time now to give attention to their leader and prophet.

F. D. MAURICE

Frederick Denison Maurice has been described as 'certainly the most typical theologian of the nineteenth century'. In addition to his great theological and metaphysical learning, he possessed what was then a rather unusual thing in a clergyman—a sturdy democratic spirit. His literary career began early. When a Cambridge undergraduate in 1825 he edited a paper, called the *Metropolitan Quarterly Magazine,* with his friend Whitmore. Most of the contributors were fellow undergraduates, and among them John Stuart Mill, who wrote an attack on *Blackwood's Magazine,* under the title of 'The New School for Cockneyism'. The *Metropolitan* ceased publication after four issues. After having contributed to the *Athenæum,* he became editor, in 1828 (at the age of 23), but resigned the following year. By 1830 he had completed a novel, 'Eustace Conway', which was published about four years later. It was at this period that he removed to Oxford and made the acquaintance of Gladstone, who was then an undergraduate. In 1834 he took orders, and was soon drawn into the pamphleteer controversies which characterised the theological history of that period. 'Subscription No Bondage' was written in 1835. From this period he broke away from the Oxford School. Pusey's writings contained 'everything he did not think and did not believe', and Pusey, on his part, was 'exceedingly angry' with Maurice's tract on Baptism, published in 1837. This year he married Miss Anna Barton, the daughter of General Barton, of the 2nd Life Guards.

In 1838 began a bitter warfare on the part of the religious newspapers, which continued, with little intermission, during his entire lifetime. Carlyle's influence was at this period affecting all ranks of intellectual society. Maurice attended his lectures, but his agreement with Carlyle was only partial, and he sometimes denounced his words and manner as 'wild pantheistic rant'. The inefficiency of the Church saddened him. 'The Church is in a sad state; we all know that—little light, little life.' In 1840 he edited the *Educational Magazine.* He became Professor of Theology at King's College and Chaplain of Lincoln's Inn in 1845. The following year he was visited by Ludlow, who sought his aid in a scheme 'to bear the leisure and good feeling of the Inns of Court upon the destitution and vice of the neighbourhood', a phrase which leaves one in doubt as to its exact meaning. He was active in the establishment of Queen's College, and was assisted by Kingsley, at a later stage, on the committee.

Politics for the People, the first periodical issued by the new Socialists (the term Christian Socialist was not currently employed until two years later), was first published under Maurice's direction on 6 May, 1848. It ran through three months of publication, and came to an end in July, having reached a weekly circulation of 2,000 copies. Maurice now held meetings of his friends once a week at his house in Queen Square; he also organised bible classes and night schools. Ludlow had persuaded the Chartist tailor, Walter Cooper, to hear Maurice preaching at Lincoln's Inn, and this, in April, 1849, led to his first meeting with Chartist working men at the Cranbourne tavern. These meetings were continued and were attended by several clergymen. The period of full activity was about to commence. 'The time had come in my father's life,' writes his son, 'when it was certain that a movement of which he would be the leader must begin.'

The little band of workers were formally organised as the Christian Socialists in 1850, and the first number of their organ, the *Christian Socialist,* with Ludlow as editor, was published on 1 November. Maurice's contributions were not numerous.

Both Maurice and his friends were subjected to a wild and bitterly unjust attack from the pen of one Croker in the *Quarterly* for September, 1851. In spite of its manifest exaggeration and open malignity, it did much to inflame public opinion against the Socialists. During the great Iron Trades Strike of 1852 the Christian Socialists were energetic on behalf of the men. The strike was a failure; the men were forced to return to work at the old terms and to abandon their union.

After a prolonged discussion, Maurice was expelled from King's College in 1853 (November), owing to certain opinions expressed in his 'Theological Essays'—a publication which could not fail, at such a juncture, to provoke controversy. The whole affair gained a wide publicity. The opinions of the press wavered: Maurice was condemned on the one hand and applauded on the other; to the Broad Churchmen he was a victim, to the High Churchmen a heretic. From conscientious motives he resigned his position at Queen's College the following month—a position to which he returned, in reply to the solicitation of the entire Council, three years later. The survey of his last years must be condensed. He was particularly interested in the instruction of women of the working classes and in the Working Men's College. A series of 'Tracts for Priests and People' was written by Maurice and his friends during 1861-2, and published in the latter year. At the same time, after many years of labour, his great work on 'Moral and Metaphysical Philosophy' was printed. Towards the close of his life he became

more and more absorbed in polemical and theological discussions, and in every kind of doctrinal controversy. He died in
1872, at the age of 66.

Maurice possessed a vast personal influence over the men with
whom he was brought into contact, and especially over the
leaders of the Christian Socialist Movement, who were in turn
led by his unanswerable resolution, his loyalty, and his calm
endurance. For example, he was able to suppress Lord Ripon's
pamphlet on Democracy ('The Duty of the Age') by the mere
weight of his objection, even after the pamphlet had been printed
and was ready to be distributed. He was the intellect and the
scholar of the movement; his disciple, Kingsley, humanised his
ideas and set them in a form 'understanded of the people'.[1]

CHARLES KINGSLEY—EARLY YEARS

Descended from men who had fought at Naseby and Minden,
the son of a country gentleman whose mismanaged fortune was
the cause of his entering the Church, Charles Kingsley was born
at Holne Vicarage, in Devonshire, on 12 June, 1819. His father
was a man of many talents and a keen sportsman, and it was
from him, doubtless, that Kingsley inherited that open-air
temperament which was always so characteristic. Kingsley's
child-play seems to have been divided between the Army and
the Church. He was either engaged upon fortification work or
he was preaching in his pinafore to an imaginary congregation.
His first poem, a very solemn reflection on human mortality,
was written at the age of four years and eight months. It is not
possible to give his boyhood in detail, but one episode must
certainly be dwelt upon.

When a lad of 12 he was sent to school at Clifton, and it was
here that, to use his own words, he 'received his first lesson in
social science'. The Bristol riots had begun in the autumn of
1831, and it was in the following year that Kingsley, fascinated,
as schoolboys are wont to be, by the horror and excitement of
a 'row', evaded supervision and went forth to see for himself.
It was a nauseating affair. Demos, in true Caliban mood, had
broached casks of spirit upon the paving-stones, had defied the

[1]Unlike Kingsley, Maurice was never at his ease when talking to
individuals of the manual working class. His manner on such occasions
was timid and conventional.

soldiers, who sat motionless, orderless on their horses, the blood streaming from their faces; had plundered, burned and violated in full sight of trembling and hesitating authority. The flames from a burning house ignited the spirit in a gutter; in one instant a blazing torrent of fire rushed down upon the drunken wretches and left behind it a line of blackened corpses—Demos, to the accompaniment of outrage and suicide, continuing his frenzied debauch. The scene produced the one possible effect on a questioning and intelligent mind : 'That sight,' he said, 'made me a Radical.'

COLLEGE DAYS AND CURACY

After a two-years' course as a day student at King's College (his father at that time having the living of Chelsea), he gained a scholarship—much to his own surprise—at Magdalene, Cambridge. He was extremely popular with his fellow-undergraduates of every description. Like all imaginative men, he found enjoyment in all kinds of society. His life was one of extraordinary mental and physical activity, though, in the academic sense, he never distinguished himself. In Kingsley, a young man possessed of a vehement and challenging spirit, the restlessness of his age became at times a veritable fever. The Tractarian Movement was in full force. It was a period of fierce and disquieting controversies. His sense of religion was overclouded. To escape from the strain of his own searching and wearing thoughts he 'went in for excitement of every kind'—horses, duck-shooting, fencing, boxing, boating and so forth. His acquaintance, through his writings, with Carlyle and his philosophy helped to ballast his unsteady and wavering opinions. It is probable, too, that friendship with another undergraduate, Charles Mansfield, proved a good influence.

The story of Mansfield's short life is particularly touching. He possessed an unusual brilliance of conversation, the most intense faith that right was might, and that there was indeed a God in the heavens. He was a student of chemistry, and became so distinguished in this science that men saw in him the successor of Faraday. In due time he became one of the Christian Socialists, and his death, which occurred as the result of an accident in the laboratory, was a grievous loss to the movement, and especially to Kingsley. From Mansfield Kingsley acquired that zeal for sanitary reform and for the institution of a sound national hygiene which became pronounced in his later activities.

Kingsley had at one time considered the law as a profession, but in 1841 he decided upon entering the Church. In striking and very significant words he announces his devotion to 'the religion which I have scorned', begins a course of desperately hard reading for his degree, cramming three years' work into six months of unceasing labour, emerges from the trial with a first in classics and senior optime in mathematics, reads for Holy Orders, and is ordained in the July of 1842. During this period of preparation, and, indeed, ever since the summer of 1839, when he first met her, Miss Pascoe Grenfell, the lady who was to be his wife (a *summum bonum* which he then despaired of), was the confidant of his thoughts, hopes and perplexities, and the kind admonitress of his troubled spirit. It was she who introduced him to the writings of Carlyle, Coleridge, and Maurice; it was she who consoled and strengthened him in the midst of doubt; and we may be pretty certain that it was for her sake that he worked so hard and so manfully when once the clear road lay before him. During the interval between leaving Cambridge and entering upon his curate life, he began his 'Life of St. Elizabeth of Hungary', illustrated with his own drawings. 'It was not intended for publication, but as a gift to his wife on his marriage day, if that day should ever come.' On July 17th he first ministered in Eversley Church—the church which was destined to be his for more than 30 years.

He seems to have found the parish of Eversley in a lamentable condition. The population were traditional smugglers and poachers. The squire had been a Prince Regent's man—a hard-riding, hard-drinking persons, and 'a strict game preserver'. Of Kingsley's rector I can learn little. Available records are silent. Perhaps we may form a sufficient judgment of his character from the fact that he absconded in 1844. Kingsley's manliness, his plain speaking and preaching, and his skill at fisticuffs rapidly gained him the friendship and respect of the villagers. The poacher and the poet, two democratic products, have always fraternised in spirit. Here was a parson who was some good at last : the empty church began to fill.

At the end of 1843 Kingsley took leave of his bachelor quarters at the corner of Eversley Green, having been offered the curacy of Pimperne. In January, 1844, he married Miss Grenfell, and, the living of Eversley becoming unexpectedly vacant, he received the appointment, and the newly married pair took up their abode in Eversley Rectory.

THE WORKING CLASSES IN 1844

It is by no means unimportant that we should try to form some idea of the industrial and rural conditions of this period. Chartism was rampant. The strikes of 1842, when wheat stood at 65 shillings a quarter, and sabotage and violence were general, had ended, but now (1844) a fierce dispute was in progress between the masters and men of the northern collieries. The men were beaten, but their defeat led to the enlistment of 30,000 as physical-force Chartists. The misery of the industrial workers was almost beyond belief. The treatment they received from their employers was so barbarous and so overbearingly despotic that the facts read like some black and impossible fantasy of the imagination. A remarkable young man of 23 was collecting material for his book on the working classes of England. He was a German, and his name was Frederick Engels. From his book—the saddest and most terrible record of that period—I must give one or two typical illustrations.

Of the London slums he says: 'The streets are generally unpaved, rough, dirty, filled with vegetable and animal refuse, without sewers or gutters, but supplied with foul, stagnant pools instead. . . . Scarcely a whole window-pane can be found, the walls are crumbling, doorposts and window-frames loose and broken, doors of old boards nailed together. . . . Heaps of garbage and ashes lie in all directions, and the foul liquids emptied before the doors gather in stinking pools. Here live the poorest of the poor; the worst paid workers with thieves and the victims of prostitution indiscriminately huddled together. . . .' But this is nothing compared with the state of the factory hands. The facts with regard to the employment of women are too horrible to be detailed; vice and disease, the criminal tyranny of overseers, the violation of every right of womanhood and motherhood—it is as well to pass by these things in silence. Let me quote from his indictory paragraph: 'Women made unfit for child-bearing, children deformed, men enfeebled, limbs crushed, whole generations wrecked, afflicted with disease and infirmity . . . children

seized naked in bed by the overlookers and driven with kicks
and blows to the factory, their clothing over their arms . . . their
sleepiness is driven off with blows. . . .' Turn to the country
districts: 'The labourer lays snares or shoots here and there a
piece of game. It does not injure the landlord . . . for he has a
vast superfluity. . . . But if he is caught he goes to jail, and for
a second offence receives *at the least seven years' transportation.*
From the severity of these laws arise the frequent bloody con-
flicts with gamekeepers, which lead to *a number of murders
every year.*' The general misery was greatly increased by the
influx of Irish labourers, especially to the towns, and the con-
sequent lowering of wages. It is not to be wondered at that even
the *Times* spoke with a democratic accent!

PASTOR IN PAROCHIA

Kingsley was an ideal parish priest. He came to a sorely neglected
village, and won first of all the good will, and finally the deep
affection, of his parishioners. This was due less to the admirable
series of village institutions which he founded than to his real
sympathy with the people. He could talk to them, with understanding and interest, on subjects that are seldom within the
scope of the ecclesiastical mind—the crops, the weather, the
hunting field, pike fishing, the ways of birds and animals, nature
lore, and shrewd maxims of sport. His sermons were manly and
direct. His care for the suffering was less the performance of
a duty than a free act of devotion. There was little incident outside the home circle during the first years of Eversley life. His
first child, a daughter, was born in 1846, and his eldest son in
1847. With the crash of 1848 Kingsley began his Socialist work,
and the disastrous 10 April found the Rector of Eversley in
London.

CHARTISM

Kingsley was already known to Maurice. He had attended the
meetings of bible scholars at Maurice's house in 1847, and
they had corresponded extensively. To Maurice he went therefore to see what could be done to prevent a collision between
troops and Chartists. Maurice was confined to the house with a
severe cold, but he sent Kingsley to Ludlow with a letter of
introduction. The two men set out for Kennington Common,

where the Chartists were to assemble, but at Waterloo Bridge they heard of the ignominious dispersal of the demonstrators and returned to Maurice with the news. From this moment we may trace the inception of the Christian Socialist Movement. The band of men who were to lead the movement had already met —Maurice, Hare, Ludlow, Mansfield, Scott, Parker, Hughes, Kingsley, and, later on, E. Vansittart Neale.

The day following the Chartist fiasco Kingsley wrote to his wife : 'All as quiet as a mouse as yet. The storm is blown over till tomorrow, but all are under arms—specials, police, and military. Mr. Maurice is in great excitement, and we are getting out placards for the walls, to speak a word for God with. You must let me stay up to-night, for I am helping in a glorious work. . . .' Kingsley's placard, which may be considered as an attempt to dissuade the workers from direct political action and from the belief that a political remedy would suffice for the evils of the times, was posted all over London on the 11th. 'Friends, you want more than Acts of Parliament can give. . . . Workers of England, be wise, and then you must be free, for you will be fit to be free.'

However little Maurice and his friends sympathised with physical force Chartism, they recognised that Chartism in general, as an act of insurgency against the fearful social in-iquities of that period, did actually represent the claims of an oppressed and degraded people. Kingsley, addressing a meeting of workmen some time later began : 'I am a Church of England parson'—a long pause; then, defiantly—'and a Chartist.' Accordingly the pages of their first periodical (or, rather, their first series of tracts) made a special appeal to Chartists, whilst seeking to convince them of the folly and wrong of open violence, and glorying in the success of the householder constables. The first number of this publication (consisting of 16 quarto pages, and issued weekly at one penny) came out on May 6th, and was called *Politics for the People*. The paper was jointly edited by Maurice and Ludlow, and, in addition to their contributions, papers were written by Archbishop Whateley, Archbishop Trench, Bishop Thirlwall, Dean Stanley, Professor Connington, Dr. Guy, Charles Mansfield, A. J. Scott, Lord Sydney Godolphin Osborne, Sir Edward Strachey, and Charles Kingsley. Maurice's chief contributions were : 'Dialogues in the Penny Boats';

'Liberty: a Dialogue between a French Propagandist, an English Labourer, and the Editor'; 'Equality', another dialogue; papers on historical subjects and education; and a Chartist story. Kingsley, besides 'Parson Lot's Letters to Chartists', wrote articles on the National Gallery and the British Museum. All the articles were unsigned or signed by a *nom de plume.* Although short-lived, as we have seen, *Politics for the People* had considerable influence, and did good work in consolidating the new movement, in spreading its ideas, and in gaining enthusiastic recruits.

SOCIALIST ACTIVITIES

Their activities were now chiefly directed to the work of education; classes were formed, and the friends met each week for study and discussion. Kingsley's first novel, 'Yeast', came out during the autumn in *Fraser's Magazine.* This book, which at once established his reputation as a novelist, attracted a great deal of notice, partly hostile and partly appreciative, and was the means of arousing an interest in the sporting parson of Eversley which continued and increased during his whole lifetime. This is not the place for literary comment. The book is still widely read, and, in spite of a rather outworn sentimentalism and the tiresome character of its heroine, remains a very vital piece of work, endeared for ever to sportsmen by its wonderfully observant and broadly painted descriptions. Worn out by the mental and emotional strain of the past months, Kingsley spent the early part of 1849 recovering his health in Devonshire, and did not resume work at Eversley until the summer. Before returning to his parish he visited London, attended several meetings of working men, and joined in the activities of the Christian workers. Maurice was now addressing the Chartist leaders and other working men at the Cranbourne Coffee Tavern. 'I was abashed,' he wrote, 'by the good opinion they had formed of me on no evidence.' And later, writing to Kingsley, 'They seem to think it a very wonderful thing that a clergyman should be willing to come among them—a sad proof how far we have gone from our proper position.' It must be remembered that at this time there was a lamentable want of sympathy between the Church and labouring men, and that the very fact of a man being a 'parson' was enough to drive him off the platform at a public meeting. Sometimes there were stirring scenes at the Cranbourne Tavern. On one occasion the National Anthem was hissed. Hughes, like an evangelical Desmoulins, sprang on a chair, vowed that any man who insulted the Queen would have an account to settle with him personally (he was a proficient pugilist), ordered the pianist to play on loudly, and himself led the singing of the Anthem, which was continued so vociferously that interruption was either quelled or was drowned by the mere tumult.

The idea of cooperation, which was oddly associated in the minds of the workmen *with anti-Christian views,* began to make progress, and the Socialists were occupied with schemes for the launching of the small cooperative concerns to which I have referred. Ludlow had visited Paris, and had been greatly interested in the success of the *Associations Ouvrières.* He was convinced that a similar scheme of association would go far towards solving the industrial problem in England, even if it did not offer the complete solution. The workmen were equally anxious for an effective form of cooperation : the Tailors' Association had been launched, and other organisations were speedily planned.

Towards the autumn of 1849 cholera broke out in London and in other parts of the country. What is remarkable is that, with sanitary affairs in such a deplorably neglected condition, the outbreak was not more disastrous than was actually the case. Eversley seems to have escaped, but a formidable low fever to which many of his parishioners fell victims kept Kingsley hard at work during the summer, until, worn out by the anxiety of bedside vigils—for the rector himself often undertook the duties of a sick nurse—he was obliged to seek health once more on the Devonshire coast. He returned to his parish in September, and set to work with magnificent energy. The cholera was now causing great uneasiness in London. An inquiry into the state of the metropolitan water supply revealed the most scandalous things. In the poorer quarters of London conditions still remained as Engels had described them five years previously. The people had no water fit for drinking. The common sewers were filled with stagnant horrors, in which floated the putrefying bodies of cats and dogs, dead fish, and filth unspeakable. With the cholera at its height the poor wretches dipped cans into the sewer-water

—and drank it. In Bermondsey (which Kingsley visited) the distress was terrible. Such a man as Kingsley could not witness these scenes without being stung to the heart, and his efforts for sanitary reform were redoubled. Much of the subsequent improvement in these matters was due to his persistent—one might well say impassioned—labour.

He was at this time writing reviews for *Fraser's Magazine*, and was shaping 'Alton Locke'—a book written in a white-heat of excitement and zeal. 'Yeast' had made a deep appeal to the younger minds and the universities, and Eversley Rectory was already sought out by scholars and young men with problems.

IN THE FULNESS OF POWER

The year 1850 marks the flood-tide of the Christian Socialist Movement. Individualist cooperation was risking its decisive experiment. Mainly under the guidance of E. Vansittart Neale, and the general supervision of the Society for Promoting Working Men's Associations, the 12 cooperative enterprises were organised and financed.[2] Neale was the hero and the practical director. Until his death, in 1893, he devoted life and fortune to the cause of industrial unity.

The failure, in a few years time, of the Christian Socialist experiment was due to a misconception of the real economic conditions of the time, an exaggerated belief in the spirit of brotherhood, and the absence of a thorough knowledge of the market. It was found impossible to eliminate competition. Each association was perfectly autonomous with regard to its own management. The result was that the men quarrelled with their managers, were slow to admit new members, and, finally, sought to compete with the other groups. I may as well anticipate matters, by stating that the Society of Promoters dissolved in 1854, having completely drained their financial resources.

1850 was a hard year for Kingsley and for all classes. Feeling deeply for the local farmers, who found it difficult enough to struggle against high rates and poor prices, Kingsley, by an impulse of generosity which was never forgotten (for he was himself a poor man), gave them back 10 per cent of the tithe money. At the same time he decided upon that unfailing resource

[2]The zeal of the Promoters is well illustrated by the fact that they were accustomed to hold their meetings at six o'clock in the morning.

of the country rector—a private pupil. The stress of money matters induced him to proceed apace with 'Alton Locke'— whether the last chapters of the book bear evidence of having been written in a hurry I leave for others to decide. He rose at five every morning and slaved at the MS. until breakfast time. The printer's copy was prepared by his wife, and he supervised her work in the evening. The difficulty was to find the printer. Kingsley was attracting too much attention for the more timorous and conservative publishing houses, and the publishers of 'Yeast' fought shy of the offer. To his rescue in his predicament came Thomas Carlyle with an introduction to Messrs. Chapman and Hall.

'ALTON LOCKE'

'Alton Locke', the commemorative novel of the Chartist period, and a burning comment on trade conditions, gave rise to so much discussion, and is of such importance to the subjects dealt with in this essay, that we must give it rather more attention than was accorded to 'Yeast'. In incident and style it conforms to the early Victorian heavy weight model. Few of the standard essentials are lacking. We are even treated to the classic drawing-room-piano scene, and the touches of sentiment are laid on in liberal brushfuls. None the less it is a production of great force and eloquent appeal. Professing to have been written by a working man, the crudeness mentioned by Carlyle is not out of place, and it certainly contains one splendidly drawn character—that of the old Scotch democrat, Mackaye. It was a very clear and disquieting exposure of the 'slop trade', and directed the public mind to unsuspected evils. It appealed for greater efficiency in the Church, greater respect for the workman, and a more qualified regard for the 'scented Belgravian' and the aristocrat. Above all, it enlisted the sympathies of a sentimental but potent *bourgeoisie*. It was mocked by the elegant reviewers, made light of by the High Churchmen, but was bought and read by thousands. Carlyle has summed up the book admirably when he describes it as '. . . a fervid creation still left half chaotic'.

PUBLICATION OF THE 'CHRISTIAN SOCIALIST'

Maurice's workers had now officially announced themselves as the Christian Socialists, and had renewed their literary activities.

They were publishing a series of 'Tracts on Christian Socialism' as a means of circulating their teaching, and on 15 November they issued the first number of their new periodical, the *Christian Socialist*. Kingsley had written 'Cheap Clothes and Nasty' for the tract series under the pseudonym of Parson Lot, and became a contributor to the magazine.

The *Christian Socialist* was edited by Ludlow, and was beset with difficulties from the very start. The newspapers had attacked the movement in the most violent and apparently scandalised manner. It was no easy business to obtain a circulation for the new venture. The booksellers took up a prudish and circumspect attitude, and refused to stock copies. Writing to a friend in December, Kingsley stated that the circulation had risen to 1,500, and was increasing. It is doubtful whether these figures were greatly exceeded. So little interest was at first evinced by the public that the press was almost silent with regard to the magazine, and its influence was imperceptible. Maurice, it would seem, had never looked upon its publication with much favour. He had attempted to dissuade Ludlow from the undertaking —possibly because he feared its political character would become too pronounced—though he realised the importance of possessing some medium through which the whole movement might be linked together and its scattered workers kept in touch with the central idea.

Maurice himself wrote very little for it. Beyond some letters on education, written in the form of a correspondence between himself and an M.P., and the story of 'Thomas Bradfoot, Schoolmaster', his contributions were of no great significance. He was anxious that other opinions besides his own should find expression in the paper, although when the difference was too decided, he always interfered, and his objection was sufficient to ensure the withdrawal of the offending article.

There were at this time monthly conferences between the leaders of the movement and the workmen associates for the discussion of all vital points.

THE ACT OF PARLIAMENT

In Parliament, Slaney was using every endeavour to procure an Act legalising the new cooperative and investment schemes, and securing them the protection, if not the encouragement, of the

State. He obtained a Special Committee to inquire into the 'investments for the savings of the middle and working classes'. It was natural that this Committee should turn to the Christian Socialists for information on a subject to which they were known to have given a very close attention, and on which they had ascertained the exact views of the working men. Ludlow was accordingly the first witness examined. Hughes, Neale, and other members of the Society of Promoters followed, amongst them Walter Cooper, the Chartist. Some of the most weighty and conclusive evidence was given by John Stuart Mill, who spoke in vehement terms in favour of the scheme, i.e., the investment of working men's savings in cooperative concerns. The report of this Committee had been published in July, and, along with its promoters, had drawn upon itself the fire of both great and little guns in the journalistic batteries. The history of this Parliamentary agitation is interesting.

The Home Secretary, Labouchere, requested Ludlow to draft a Bill for legalising cooperative associations. Nothing could have given him greater pleasure, but the draft demanded such an alarming legal reformation that Labouchere grew timid, expressed his admiration both for Ludlow and the Bill, but did not proceed any further with the matter.

In 1851 Mr. Slaney obtained a new Committee 'to consider the Law of Partnership and the expediency of facilitating the limitations of liability, with a view to encourage useful enterprise and the additional employment of labour'. All this sonority seems to have had little effect, for it was not until a year afterwards that Slaney finally succeeded in getting the Bill once again to the fore, and it was safely passed by both Houses (under a Conservative Ministry) on June 11th, 1852. Such, in brief, is the story of the first 'Industrial and Provident Partnerships Bill', a private measure introduced by Slaney and Tufnell, Liberals, and Sotheron, a Conservative.

EVERSLEY IN 1850

It was in the autumn or early winter of 1850 that the celebrated attack on Eversley Rectory took place. A neighbouring clergyman had been murdered by a gang of housebreakers, who were at that time terrorising the countryside, and the Rectory had scarcely been barricaded and its weapons of defence made ready before it was attacked by the same gang. In the middle of the night the marauders were heard trying to force the back door. Down the stairs rushed the male inmates, with pistols, guns, and a gaping blunderbuss; the 'coolest man among them' and the only one unarmed, being F. D. Maurice, who was then paying a visit to Kingsley. Maurice strode out into the darkness in pursuit. He was recalled by Kingsley, and the two men spent the remainder of the night over the study fire, their discourse continuing until the dawn.

Already Kingsley had to deal with a vast correspondence. Young men who could not make up their minds with regard to eternal punishment and other stumbling-blocks of dogma; good fellows in the services who wished for a word of advice or prayers for camp and shipboard; men whose hearts had been stirred by his books. Never, I suppose, was a country rector the recipient of so much appreciation and questioning. No genuine letter was left unanswered. Kingsley had the tenderest sympathy for these corresponding disciples, and his replies show the thoroughness with which he answered their doubts or satisfied their requirements. All the time he was working hard for the welfare of his parish and was much occupied with his pupil, Martineau.

A letter written from Dr. Jelf, the Principal of King's College, to Maurice, in 1851, shows the attitude of the orthodox and outraged mind with regard to Kingsley's books and essays. Archdeacon Hare had accused him of conceit and irreverence a few years before, but Dr. Jelf is even more outspoken. He cannot express too much horror and indignation. Kingsley is a dangerous and reckless writer. He is indescribably irreverent. His arguments are in a high degree inflammatory. 'In fact,' says Dr. Jelf, rising to the height of his denunciation, 'his language is *almost insurrectionary.*' And, moreover, he is associated with 'several notorious infidels', and has actually mentioned Tom Paine. It was largely on account of his friendship with Kingsley that Maurice was expelled from the College.

Towards the end of 1850 Kingsley resigned his post as Lecturer at Queen's College, in consequence of an attack in the *Record.*

'Hypatia' was begun as a serial in *Fraser's Magazine* in 1851. He contributed largely to the *Christian Socialist*—15 articles— besides a story and some ballads and sonnets. He would have written more for this paper were it not for the fact that he was obliged to earn as much as possible with his pen, and the *Christian Socialist* did not pay its contributors. He reprinted 'Yeast', which was published anonymously. The Christian Socialist Movement was hotly attacked by the press, and notably by the *Edinburgh* and *Quarterly Reviews.* Kingsley would not trust himself to read the more personal of these attacks. He was a man whose quick temper and great sensitiveness were sure to lead him into the temptation of violent retort. The *Guardian,* however, had fallen foul of 'Yeast' in no measured terms, and had brought such preposterous charges against the author that he wrote a furious denial. In May he delivered a lecture for the Society of Promoters on 'The Application of Associative Principles and Methods to Agriculture', and in the summer was invited to preach one of the special sermons to working men who had come to London for the Great Exhibition.

'THE MESSAGE OF THE CHURCH'
This sermon—'The Message of the Church to Labouring Men'— led to the most extraordinary results. It was preached to a large congregation, mainly of the working classes, and produced a powerful effect. Kingsley had concluded his sermon and was about to give the blessing, when the incumbent of the church, whose name, I believe, was Drew, approached the reading-desk and denounced the preacher before the entire congregation. He agreed with much that had been said, but it was his 'painful duty' to characterise portions of the sermon as 'dangerous and untrue'. This unheard-of scene caused a great sensation. Murmurs were heard; the workmen pressed forward to the pulpit steps and grasped Kingsley by the hand. As the sermon itself was judged to be the best defence, it was decided in the vestry that it should be printed at once without the alteration of a single word. The affair was taken up by the press; Kingsley was forbidden by the Bishop of London (Blomfield) to preach in the metropolis; large numbers of the clergy and of his admirers sent messages of sympathy to Eversley; and a meeting of workmen, held at Kennington Common, expressed their allegiance to the parson who spoke so manfully on their behalf, and invited him *'to start a free church independent of episcopal rule,* with the promise of a large following'. The sermon was now printed,

and Blomfield, when he saw the truth of the matter, not only sent for Kingsley (and apologised, we may hope), telling him that he actually approved of the discourse, but immediately withdrew his prohibition.

TRADE UNIONISM—'HYPATIA'

The Christian Socialists were naturally well known to the leaders of Trade Unionism, and it followed that, when the great strike of engineers and iron-workers took place in 1852, impetuous men like Hughes and Ludlow felt their fingers tingling for the conflict. The views of the promoters were varied : some urged one thing and some another. Maurice was fearful lest they should commit themselves to a desperate and ill-judged action. At the beginning of the year the *Christian Socialist* had boldly cast off its disguise and changed its title to the *Journal of Association,* under the editorship of Hughes. The *Journal* lost no time in appealing to the 'self-sacrifice, pluck and character' of the men of the amalgamated trades. Ludlow and Hughes sought to agitate public opinion by all possible means : they lectured, wrote to a great number of newspapers, and supported the strike by subscriptions. Although the strike ended in disaster, the hand of friendship had not been extended to the trade unionists in vain, and the sympathy thus established between the more important trade associations and the Christian Socialists led to extremely practical results when, in 1854, the Working Men's College was founded.

Fraser's Magazine for January had contained a criticism of the Socialists, which Kingsley decided to answer. He was, perhaps, somewhat annoyed that his enemies should find a means of expression in the very magazine which was publishing 'Hypatia' as a serial—it was a new aspect of journalistic etiquette. After conference with Maurice, who cooled the first transports of his resentment, Kingsley finally evolved 'Who are the Friends of Order? A reply to certain observations in a late number of *Fraser's Magazine*'. It was printed by E. Lumley and J. J. Bezer, the latter 'a man who had been set up as a publisher by the promoters, no living publisher venturing to commit himself to the risk of publishing . . . either the *Christian Socialist* or the Tracts'. Bezer was described by Hughes as Movoᵠ, or 'the one-eyed Chartist costermonger'.

The *Journal of Association* came to an end this year, and Kingsley, in a final letter by 'Parson Lot', urged his fellow-workers to 'say little and work the more'. Eversley and its democratic parson were now gaining notoriety. Kingsley seems to have been a popular man with soldiers, and officers from Sandhurst would frequently walk over to see him. His sermons were so vigorous and so powerfully delivered that he always preached to a full church, and, although a man of great rhetorical ability, his discourses were as keenly followed by the farm hand or the stableman as by the scholar. 'Hypatia' was published in book form in 1853. As a literary attainment it must rank before any of his other works. To a modern reader, fascinated by the colour and graphic detail of the story, it seems remarkable that, when published first, the book caused angry excitement among the High Churchmen, by whom it was regarded as a kind of masked attack, which, indeed, it was. Ten years later, when Kingsley's name had been suggested for the D.C.L. of Oxford, the High Church party raised the voice of protest. Dr. Pusey was scandalised to a degree. Why, good gracious! This was the fellow who had written 'Hypatia', a most vile and profligate book inciting the youth to heterodoxy, and worse, if worse were possible, an *immoral* book. Under threat of a *non-placet* the name was withdrawn. Maurice's 'Theological Essays' were published the same year (1853), and outraged the doctrines of the Puseyites even more than Kingsley had outraged their self-respect. His expulsion from King's College followed, and Kingsley was vehement in defending his 'dear master' and in scourging his enemies.

DISBANDED

With the collapse of the Society for Promoting Working Men's Associations and the failure of the co-operative businesses, the first Christian Socialist movement came to an end in 1854. The Socialists had failed in their experiment, but they had accomplished a great work. They had given an intellectual expression to the new democratic tendencies. They had striven to popularise and humanise what was then a rather unpopular and inhuman thing—the teaching of the English Church. They had shown (Kingsley in particular had shown it) that a clergyman must think more of the actual needs and nature of the people than of his embroideries and rituals. They had inaugurated a new phase of national thought. Neither were immediate practical results wanting. They had collected a vast amount of evidence on industrial questions; they had exercised an unmistakable influence on political subjects, and had been largely instrumental in gaining sanitary and other improvements. Their writings— more especially Kingsley's novels— had made an appeal to all classes of readers and had stirred the national conscience. And if further proof of their power is wanting, let it be given in the furious attentions paid them by their opponents—never has a popular movement been more violently assailed by a foe made aware of his moral insecurity.

The spirit of the movement was not in reality checked by its disorganisation, and, although there was no formal association of Church Socialists until 23 years later, the force of the present social movement in the churches is certainly a consequence of the early Christian Socialist labours. The very year which saw the disbanding of the Christian Socialists saw the founding of the Working Men's College, with Maurice as president. It is only necessary to glance at a few names on the teachers' list (taking a period of several years) to see in what direction the finest intellect of that age was tending. Here are some of the names: Ruskin, D. G. Rossetti, Huxley, Tyndall, Madox Brown, Frederick Harrison, Professor Seeley, Arthur Hughes, Val Prinsep, the Lushingtons, and C. H. Pearson.

The winter and spring of 1854 was spent by Kingsley and his family at Torquay. The clergy of this place were thrown into panic at his approach, and he was denied the courtesy of the pulpit in all their churches. It is doubtful whether this caused him much disappointment. He spent the greater part of his time on the shore, indulging his naturalist and poetic passions and greatly benefiting in health. Kingsley is so well known as a nature student and as a writer of charming and thoughtful essays in natural research that there is no need to speak in detail of these wanderings on the seashore, when each withdrawing tide left a store of things wonderful, many-coloured and new. It was here that visions of old sea romance gave him the first ideas of 'Westward Ho!'

He was busy this year agitating on behalf of sanitary reforms, and was a member of the deputation to Lord Palmerston on this subject. The condition of Eversley as regarded drainage, etc., weighed heavily upon him. He did all that was possible to secure improvements, but the parish was poor and landlords (as land-lords are) indifferent. He himself, and all England with him, was at this time profoundly stirred by the Crimean War.

THE MIDWAY OF LIFE

It is not possible for me to give more than a very condensed account of Kingsley's later activities. The purpose of this essay is the study of Kingsley as a democratic Christian and a reformer. Those who wish to read of his family life, and to form a closer acquaintance with a most lovable and virile character, must read the standard biography, 'Letters and Memories of His Life,' edited by his wife, from which I have drawn much of the infor-mation set forth in this paper. Some brief survey of character I must necessarily give before the conclusion of the present study, but only a few facts and only those which most nearly concern my subject can be selected from the years of crowded activity following 1854.

We do not find Kingsley writing much on the Crimea. The war was to him 'a dreadful nightmare,' though it awoke the soldier-spirit in him, and his enthusiasm for the heroes of Sebas-topol was intense. In a few hours' time he wrote a tract, 'Brave Words to Brave Soldiers and Sailors,' many thousands of which were distributed in the Crimea, and must have proved a whole-some alternative to the usual 'goody-goody' pamphlets which the soldiers treated as so much waste paper. Cholera was still making an appearance here and there in 1855, and in the winter an outbreak occurred at Bideford, where Kingsley had taken a house. During this visitation he took charge of a district. The outbreak does not appear to have been very serious, and we find him, the same winter, instituting an evening drawing-class for the young men of Bideford, of which he was himself the instruc-tor. The sureness and rapidity with which he drew flowers or symmetrical figures on the blackboard won the admiration of his pupils. The classes became popular, and many a young loafer was enticed from the street corner to become more and more fascinated by the kindly manner and (to him, at any rate) almost unearthly accomplishments of the strange 'parson.'

As years went by the Rector of Eversley gained a popularity

which was at times almost embarrassing. He disliked the parade
of carriages and the 'talking after church' on Sundays. But for
those who came to him privately to discuss his books or confide
in him their perplexities and sorrows he had a warm affection.
After the founding of the camp at Aldershot, the 'dear fellows'
—officers of all grades besides rank and file—paid frequent
visits to the church and the rectory. One of these became a
familiar friend of the Kingsleys. He had been out in the Crimea,
and had read 'Yeast' when lying grievously stricken in the hospital at Scutari. The hunting scene had made an especial appeal
—one can imagine the effect of such a vivid home-picture on a
wounded man in Scutari— and he resolved that if ever he got
back to England he would go and hear the parson who could
write such fine sporting descriptions. He came, still on crutches.
Such episodes show very clearly one aspect of Kingsley's appeal
to his contemporaries—the appeal of a strong man to strong
men. 'He loved men and manly pursuits,' to quote the words of
an officer who used to walk over from Aldershot, and who shall
say he was not himself a tried and battle-worn fighter? Kingsley
was a welcome guest at mess; he entered into the studies and
organisation of the Staff College with the deepest interest, and
his advice to sportsmen—'He told us the best meets of the
hounds, the nearest cut to the covers, the best trout streams,
and the home of the largest pike'—must have made him extremely popular.

But the real significance of all this soldier intercourse was this :
Charles Kingsley was the very man to present religion in a
form acceptable to the soldier temperament. To a soldier, manhood is the greatest thing in the world, and the greatest qualities
of manhood are courage, physical prowess, endurance, kindness
without weakness or wordiness, loyalty, honesty, and a sane
patriotism. All these qualities were to be found in Kingsley,
with the spirit and mind of a Christian teacher superadded. We
can picture such a man casting a net with the first apostles,
and proving himself as hard-working a fisherman as any of
them, not afraid of soiling his hands with the common labours of
common men. Kingsley, in fact, preached the *manliness* of his
creed, a sin unpardonable to the High Church exquisites of that
time. He spoke, never as a superior person to inferior sinners,
but as a man who respected and loved all men. He was thus

loved and respected by all who came within the circle of his influence. The soldier loved him for his vigor and sincerity (the soldier cannot analyse, but he can appreciate character, and knows the true from the false) and listened to him because he was no humbug, and always dealt boldly with the truth. His influence among all grades of the service at Aldershot and Sandhurst was therefore strongly marked. He taught the men what is none too much in evidence in the Church of to-day—that manliness and Christianity are not merely reconcilable, but are positively essential to each other.

Soldiers were by no means his only visitors. One is glad to notice that clergymen figure in the visitors' list—of various denominations and opinions. All sorts of men came. Beneath the fir trees on that little sloping lawn they discussed all manner of things. Kingsley was fitted for conversation with every type of man and for sympathy with every kind of nature. He loved and understood them all.

His scientific repute gained him the membership of the Linnæan Society. Literary folk were delighted with the 'Prose Idylls' and other essays.

Meanwhile the Christian Socialists, working independently or in other organisations, were assisting in the advance of democracy. Trade depression was severe in 1857, and a committee of inquiry was formed, known as the 'Association for the Promotion of Social Science.' Maurice, Hughes and Ludlow all took part in this work. Maurice was a member of the committee, and the report, which was published in 1860, contained contributions from the Christian Socialists. It must be understood that, although I still employ the original term as a matter of convenience, there was not at this time any organised group of Church Socialists, and the public no longer recognised the existence of any special doctrine or activity known as Christian Socialism.

Kingsley became more and more devoted to the cause of sanitary reform. In his opinion, physics and theology should go hand in hand, and he regarded a certain amount of scientific knowledge as a thing indispensable in a clergyman. I am convinced that this opinion foreshadows the future development of the Church, and points the way to a new meaning and efficiency.

In 1860 Kingsley was appointed to the Regius Professorship

of Modern History at Cambridge. In the autumn of the same year he and his family entered into residence. It was natural that the same qualities in Kingsley which had appealed to the soldiers should appeal to the undergraduates. He became the hero of the young men. Never has Cambridge known a more popular lecturer or one more sincerely worshipped by his disciples. He began in the smaller rooms of the Schools. They were not big enough. He had to lecture in the biggest room of all, and that was not big enough. Strange scene at professorial lectures, enthusiasm would run high. The lectures were interrupted by irrepressible cheering. Kingsley would stammer with emotion, 'Gentlemen, you must not do it.' It was no good, they *would* cheer. The men were not merely interested in the great personality of their lecturer; they were interested in his subjects. The University Librarian was asked for books which seldom left the shelves. Kingsley made them think, and he made them work, too. There was never yet, I suppose, a really great man who failed to gain the younger sympathies of the age. It is very clear that Kingsley had gained them, for all the groans and sneers of the Puseyites.

THE LAST TEN YEARS

Newman's attack on the English Church could not pass unnoticed by such a loyal Churchman as Kingsley. Newman was, no doubt, his superior in sheer intellect, in theological subtlety, and in the ponderous resources of academic style. In the controversial sense Kingsley was beaten, though we are assured that it was out of a courteous regard for Newman's health, his disinclination for argument, and other personal reasons, that he forbore to attack with vehemence. This may be partly true. It is certain, however, that he had found his match. Probably no living theologian could have gained a victory over one whose craft and scholarship were unequalled, and who was as certain to maintain his defence with vigilance and caution as he was to attack with resistless weight and infallible sagacity. Maurice, who respected the learning and character of Newman, however widely he dissented from his views, 'would have given much' to have withheld Kingsley from the dispute.

Hughes, Neale, Ludlow, and others of the Christian Socialist band were active in industrial affairs in 1866. The Cobden Mills

were founded by Neale, Greening, Ludlow, Hughes, and Mor-
rison. After some 24 years of a rather disastrous existence, the
business was disposed of, and thus ended the largest, and in
some ways most celebrated, experiment of Christian Socialism.
Kingsley does not appear to have taken an active interest in
these affairs (his former comrades were zealously fighting on
behalf of trade unionism for many years), though he was always
in favour of associative principles in trade. It is probable that
three causes were responsible for this apparent withdrawal : first,
the cooling (though only to a certain extent) of his early democratic ardour; second, the necessarily changed and enlarged
sphere of work, the result of public recognition and celebrity;
and third, a gradual decline in health which marks these last
years of his life.

Science absorbed his attention to a greater and greater degree.
He was a member both of the Linnæan and Geological Societies,
had evolved a theory of raised beaches, and was a keen Dar-
winian. The Knightsbridge Professorship falling vacant in 1866,
he wrote to Maurice, urging him to accept this appointment. It
was only with difficulty that Maurice could be persuaded. 'At
61,' he said, 'I am perhaps past such work.' The question of
election depended on the votes of the seven electors. Four of
them voted for Maurice, one for a man of his own college,
and the two others abstained, but expressed satisfaction with
the result. It must have been with huge personal delight that
Kingsley (himself an elector) sent him a telegram announcing his
triumph. He wrote later : 'Your triumph could not have been
more complete. My heart is as full as a boy's. I thought I should
have been "upset" when I saw the result.' The two friends (or
the master and the disciple, as Kingsley would have said) were
thus associated in professorial work, both honoured by the
same university, and both happy in this latter-day closening of
their friendship.

Kingsley had won recognition among all classes as a man of
honest purpose, gifts approximating to genius, a sound theology,
and the talents of a skilled author and graceful poet. He was none
the less, perhaps for this very reason, ferociously assailed by
the press. In consequence of these attacks he was on the point of
resigning the professorship, but he was advised to retain it for at
least another year. Accordingly, after nine years' experience as

a Cambridge professor—years which had seen his greatest intellectual attainments and the most fruitful expression of his
teaching—he resigned the post in 1869. His last series of lectures
made a great impression.

The close of this year is marked by the fulfilment of one of
his great ambitions, a voyage to the West Indies. It was the great
holiday of his life. This world could not have supplied such a
man as Kingsley—a poet-naturalist—with anything more perfectly enjoyable. He saw 'enough to last him his life.' He was
mad with delight. He was actually moving in the land of
romance he had dreamed and written of. He was a boy, full of
wonder and surprise. He was an adventurer in tropical forests.
He was a sea rover. The Regius Professor was buried !

Parish work, scientific work, three months' residence as Canon
of Chester, a discussion with John Stuart Mill on Woman Suffrage, and a huge correspondence with various men on various
subjects give a summary of 1870. He was a Teuton in sympathy
during the war of 1870-71. He condemned the French policy
and the French leadership : it was a righteous and even necessary war for Germany. In 1871 we find him again asserting
'he need to include physical learning in the general theologica
course. He realised that the older school of natural theology
would be compelled to abandon many of its positions, or, rather,
to develop in accordance with the great scientific revolutions of
the nineteenth century. He saw that the religion of the future
would lay stress on the scientific basis of modern thought, and
that the priest of the future would deal less with fable and more
with fact. Whether he was right in seeking to unite the functions
of preacher and sanitary inspector quite as definitely as he proposed we need not stop to consider. He was certainly right in
supposing that religion must pass from a superstitious to a
scientific phase. His lectures at this period, particularly those
on geological and natural history subjects, were very remarkable. The death of Maurice, in 1872, was a sad loss to Kingsley,
and a certain despondency—partly the result of an over-worked
and continuously active brain—seems more or less evident in
his letters and conversation. But in the autumn of this year he
achieved a great practical triumph for the cause which was so
dear to him. As President of the Midland Institute he delivered
the inaugural address (on the 'Science of Health') at Birming-

ham. One of his listeners immediately placed the sum of two and a half thousand pounds at the disposal of a scheme for classes and lectures on this subject, with a low rate of payment for artisans. The project was successful, and the impetus was thus given to a very noble and necessary work. In 1873 he accepted the Canonry of Westminster, where he preached the well-known series of sermons. 1874 was largely taken up by a tour in America, crammed full of all manner of activities, and ending with a severe illness and a slow recovery in Colorado. He returned to Eversley in August. It was a hot, dry month, there was much sickness in the village, and he was busy attending to the people at all hours, and apparently with all his energy restored. But his health was rapidly failing. After his return to Westminster in the autumn he was again ill; he was now able only to preach once a week, and, although his sermons were still powerful and forcibly delivered, men were shocked to see the change in him, the worn cheeks and the bent figure. His wife's dangerous illness caused him the greatest suffering. On Advent Sunday he preached his last Abbey sermon 'with intense fervour'. The next day he caught a chill after dining at the Deanery, probably the direct cause of his death. The return journey to Eversley proved too much for his wife, and the happiness of a Christmas home-coming, so dearly longed for, was turned to a sad ministering in what seemed then to be the chamber of death. Kingsley himself grew rapidly worse. Eventually he was unable to bear the terrible strain of carrying on a pencilled intercourse with his wife, who was supposed by all to be dying. His illness (pneumonia) was fast gaining the mastery, yet his fortitude and superb courage remained unshaken. He died on the morning of 23 January, at the age of 55. His wife recovered.

HIS CHARACTER AND TEACHING

In discussing the Socialism of Charles Kingsley, which is identical with that of the Christian Socialist group, we must bear in mind two very important facts: First, that he was remarkably constitutional in principle and method, and by no means revolutionary; and, second, that his conception of Democracy was one that accepted the existing order of society with all its grades and traditions, and believed that the healthy functioning of that society was all that was needed to ensure the communal welfare. If anything was wrong—and a great deal was wrong—then the fault lay, not with the class, but with the individual. And even if the majority of individuals composing a class were at fault, that was no argument against the class itself, or, rather, against the necessity for the existence of the class. With a majority at fault, the class was *not* performing its true functions; it was not, therefore, to be abolished, but called back to its duty; the diseased organ was to be cured, by surgical steel at the worst, but not removed. There was, as I have mentioned, a divine purpose and order in the system of classes. A landed aristocracy was not only a necessary thing, it was 'a blessing to the country.' The House of Lords represented all that was noble and permanent in the national character (observe, *permanent!*); it represented the hereditary instinct, which bound together men of the past, present, and future ages. Royalty was a thing to be revered, because it was royalty. In short, the organisation of the unproductive classes was very beautiful, useful, and necessary; many individuals who belonged to these classes might fail to observe their duties, or, worse still, undertake duties which were not their own, but the class itself was a needful prop of the social fabric; and, if the tendencies of its components had to be corrected, the thing itself must be preserved at all costs.

THE SOCIALISM OF KINGSLEY

Where then, you may say, is the Socialism in all this? Of modern Socialism there is little trace, and yet it was in this urging of the duty of classes, especially as regarded the treatment of the poor, provision for the health and security of the labouring classes, and the effective ministering of the Church, that Kingsley proved himself a powerful democratic force. His accusation was so vehement that his conservative principles were frequently drowned beneath a full tide of revolt. The organisation of trade (which in his mind was a thing apart from the organisation of classes) seemed to him to need immediate reform. If, therefore, he was a Conservative as regarded the blessing of an aristocracy, he was an extreme Radical where the working classes were concerned. It was impossible for a man of strong and observant character not to possess democratic tendencies. In Kingsley those tendencies were invigorated by the scenes and events of a revolutionary period, and became the dominant force of his career. He was deeply aware, too, of the fact that the Church was in danger of losing the sympathy of the people; that she was becoming an exclusive and mystic organisation, unduly given to the study of rituals, and not noticing the bad drains and worse morality of the 'lower orders'; for the Christian Socialist ideal for the Church was that it should work *with,* and not apart from, the secular workers. When he signed his Chartist placard as 'A Working Parson', he knew that he implied a pretty obvious distinction. Kingsley was a Conservative by birth and tradition, a Chartist through force of circumstances, and a Socialist through sheer manliness and force of character. He belonged to a period when the English gentleman, though growing rare, was not obsolete, and when the middle classes did really advocate what they understood to be progressive measures. He aimed, not at a reform of society in general (which would have struck him as a blasphemous subversion of 'God's order'), but at the reform of industrial life and of the Church, the first to be made wholesome and the latter efficient.

The views and methods of Kingsley and his friends have now been sufficiently commented on by the actual passing of time and the development of modern thought. We see the clearer for their mistakes, and are the richer for their noble examples and the fine courage of their teaching. It would be entering upon a fruitless controversy to discuss here the ethics of association, the question of the self-governing workshop, or the future position of the Church. Kingsley's power is to be found, not in the startling or original nature of his views, but in his manly and uncompromising advocacy of those views, and in the example of a most living and vigorous personality.

HIS PERSONALITY

Like all poets, he was immensely receptive. His emotions were frequently and profoundly stirred by a suggestive fact or a touching scene. He was in love with Nature—every leaf, every cloud, the storm song of winter, rain, sun, the moorland, and the seashore, everything was wonderful and loveable. He possessed the most astounding vitality. It is not recorded of any man that he was more *alive.* His life was one continual excitement. In speech his vehemence was extraordinary. He would begin with a slight stammer and hesitation, but when fairly started, his oratory was fluent and impressive. His sense of the dramatic was unusually keen. He was one of the most influential and celebrated preachers of the time, and as a lecturer his repute was equally great.

He was a man of rare humour, and dearly loved anything that was laughable or even 'broad.' He could enjoy a page of Rabelais or a sly anecdote of Sterne's as much as anyone. His letters are full of pleasantry, and serve well to illustrate his versatile nature. For instance, he is writing to Tom Hughes, and is giving him some fishing experiences, with all sorts of expert comments on brass minnows, March browns, and so forth, when all at once, and without the least pause for breath, we find him talking of a poor parishioner who is lying on his deathbed. Cant or falseness of any kind were abominable to his sincere nature. A tramp who saw fit to assume the attitude and contortions of a religious zealot was seized by the collar, soundly shaken, and hurried outside Eversley gates with no little wrath.

Two answers of his, written in one of those horrible albums so typical of the Victorian drawing-room, are interesting. 'The character you most dislike?—Myself. Your ambition?—To die.' He was not a man who cared for distinction or notoriety. He acknowledged a 'hankering after' the D.C.L. of Oxford, which was denied him; but he realised his two 'great ambitions', membership of the Linnæan and Geological Societies.

Kingsley did much to popularise the study of physics and natural science, and presented the facts of advanced scientific thought in a way calculated not to hurt religious sensitiveness. I have mentioned that he foresaw the alliance which must some day openly take place between science and religion, and that he was anxious for the education of clergymen in other matters besides those which relate solely to theology. His own religion cannot be said to come under any of the recognised categories. No party of the Church could claim him. He was opposed to the extreme mysticism of the High Church, but had little sympathy with the severe ritual of the Moderates. He was no friend to dogmatism of any sort. He was described by his curate, Harrison, as 'a freelance in the ecclesiastical field.'

The most immediate and most practical results of his activity are unquestionably to be found in the improvements in sanitary affairs and in the general education of working men. The latter is less directly due to his influence than the former (in which

he was said by a great London doctor to have 'led the way'),
but it was certainly greatly advanced by his teaching and
lectures.

The charge of inconsistency has been brought against him
with regard to his democratic faith. 'In later years,' says Martineau, 'his convictions became more in accord with *the natural
tendency of his mind*' (whatever that means), 'and he gradually
modified or abandoned his democratic opinions.' I can see no
trace of all this. The burning enthusiasm of youth may have left
him; his opinions never did. From first to last Charles Kingsley
was a democrat—and *that,* I take it, was the 'natural tendency
of his mind'—and he never proved false to his social creed. The
multiplicity of affairs and a life overcrowded with interests and
duties prevented him from devoting himself to a special and
continuous work on behalf of Socialism. None the less, the author
of 'Alton Locke' and 'The Message of the Church' was no
changed man when, in 1866, he welcomed Maurice to Cambridge.

It is not the place here to speak of his home life, of his chival-
rous devotion, his intimate sympathies, pictures of the lawn or
the fireside, scenes typical of the English rectory. His love for
animals, for all living things, with the exception of spiders, is
well known. Like Agassiz, he believed in their *post mortem*
existence. Those who wish to read a detailed, though necessarily
partial, account of his life must turn to the 'Letters and
Memories.'

THE PRESENT AND THE FUTURE

We cannot doubt that Socialism in the Churches represents a
very powerful and very necessary expression of social democracy.
Religious Socialism is gaining rapidly in numbers and efficiency,
and may quite possibly modify the whole course of religious
thought in the future. Whatever significance the movement
may have to-day, whatever power it may have in the future,
the names of its two great founders, Frederick Denison Maurice
and Charles Kingsley, their noble examples of courage, manliness and faith, will always figure large on the first pages of its
history.

Mrs. Townshend

8 WILLIAM MORRIS AND THE COMMUNIST IDEAL

BOYHOOD

WILLIAM MORRIS was born in 1834 and died in 1896. His working life therefore fell in the latter half of the nineteenth century, exactly the period when Commercialism was most rampant. It was a time of peace and prosperity. Manufacturers were raking in profits from the great discoveries of the beginning of the century, railways and steamships had given fresh impetus to trade. The long reign of a virtuous and narrow-minded sovereign favoured the growth of vulgar self-complacency. It was a smug age, an age of rapidly increasing wealth ill-distributed and ill-spent.

Morris was a member of a well-to-do middle class family. His childhood was spent in a large house on the edge of Epping Forest, looking over a great stretch of the pasture land of Essex, with the Thames winding through the marshes. He passed a happy boyhood in a peaceful, old-fashioned, essentially English home. At 14 he was sent to Marlborough. He entered but little, however, into the life of the school, took no part in school games, and is remembered by his school-fellows as a strange boy fond of mooning about by himself and of telling long stories 'full of knights and fairies.' He was 'thickset and strong-looking, with a high colour and black curly hair, good-natured and kind, but with a fearful temper.' He was fond of taking long walks and collecting birds' eggs, and he was always doing something with his hands, netting if nothing else.

Like man like boy! The strangely diverse characteristics of this remarkable man were already noticeable, a poet without a poetic temperament, patient and industrious, kindly and gentle yet hasty and choleric, a lover of solitude for all his abounding sympathy with mankind. It was not at school but at home that he found congenial surroundings. 'I am sure you must think me a great fool,' he writes to his sister, 'to be always thinking about home, but I really can't help it, I don't think it is my fault for there are such a lot of things I want to do and say.'

OXFORD LIFE AND FRIENDSHIPS. CULT OF THE MIDDLE AGES

But though it is easy in his later life to trace the influence of his peaceful home between the forest and the plain, it was at Oxford that his genius found or formed the channels it was to flow through. At his own college (Exeter) and among the undergraduates of his own year he was fortunate enough to find a man with whom he was able to share his inmost thoughts. The tie between Morris and Burne-Jones was no ordinary college friendship. It lasted till death and affected the lives of both, but though (or perhaps because) Morris was the greater of the two men the intercourse between them had more important results on his career than on that of his friend.

At 20 Morris, full of vitality and with many markedly diverse characteristics, would have been singled out as a man certain to make his mark in the world, but the kind of work that lay before him would have been hard to foretell. Like his friend, he was destined for the Church. Both alike had felt the influence of that wave of mystical theology which had swept over the dry bones of Anglican Christianity, and both alike suffered a severe disillusionment during their first year at Oxford. Their readings in theology served to extinguish gradually in both the fire of religious enthusiasm, and to kindle in its stead a devotion to ideal beauty, curiously remote and exotic. It was associated with a passion for the Middle Ages and for the particular types and forms of Art that flourished in them, and of course with a contempt and loathing for contemporary life with all its seething confusion of industrial progress. In these quiet Oxford days, spent in poring over ecclesiastical poetry, mediæval chronicles and church history, it was no wonder that these youths should look at the world through a narrow peep-hole: the wonder is that in the case of one of them the peep-hole was never widened throughout a long industrious life of artistic production. Morris was too

big a man to have his outlook on the world permanently
circumscribed in this way, but in the output of his early years,
and indeed in the artistic work—whether literary or plastic—
of his whole life, we find the narrowing influence of his first
introduction to the world of thought and emotion, and of his life-
long intercourse with Burne-Jones and the school to which he
belonged.

Morris was by nature an artist. He was full of enthusiasm and
vital energy, quick to see and feel, eager to create. The pre-
Raphaelite movement, with its worship of beauty and its atmosphere of rarity and remoteness, influenced him, not by making
him an artist, but by cutting him off from the life of his day
and generation, the true source of inspiration for living art. His
life is the story of a pilgrimage out of a world peopled by
shadows into the daylight world of his fellow-men. Unfortunately,
his dearest friends continued to live in the world of shadows,
and from time to time they drew him back into it.

POETRY

The impulse towards self-expression found vent first in poetry,
and, to the end, painter and craftsman though he was, his chief
gift was literary. The gift seems to have been a sudden discovery
during college days. Canon Dixon gives an amusing account of
how he and Price went to Exeter one night to see the two friends.
'As soon as we entered the room, Burne-Jones exclaimed wildly :
"He's a big poet!" "Who is?" asked we. "Why, Topsy"—the
name which he had given him. We sat down and heard Morris
read his first poem, the first that he had ever written in his life.
It was called "The Willow and the Red Cliff". As he read it, I
felt that it was something the like of which had never been
heard before. . . . I expressed my admiration in some way, as we
all did, and I remember his remark: "Well, if this is poetry, it
is very easy to write." From that time onward he came to my
rooms almost every day with a new poem.'[1]

He was rapid and prolific, and his poems filled many books.
The best known is, perhaps, the long series of stories in verse
called 'The Earthly Paradise'. 'In all the noble roll of our poets,'
says Swinburne, 'there has been since Chaucer no second teller

---

[1]'Life of William Morris,' by J. W. Mackail, Vol. I., pp. 51, 52.

of tales comparable to the first till the advent of this one." The stories, told sometimes in verse, sometimes, and even better, in prose, continued to pour forth from his fertile brain right on to the end of his life, with the exception, as we shall see, of seven years that were devoted to sterner work.

CHOICE OF A VOCATION

But though his strongest and most enduring impulse was towards imaginative writing, it is not as a writer that his light shines before men. If he had poured the full stream of his creative vitality into this one channel, England might have added a new name to the list of her great poets, but there are things that the English of to-day need more than poetry. They need to learn that sordid labour degrades not merely those who perform it, but those who reap the fruits of it; that to enjoy cheap machine-made luxury is as degrading as to produce it; that a brutalised labouring class is sure to have for its master an unrefined, uncivilised plutocracy. These are the things Morris made clear to those who would look and listen. He could not have learned and taught them if he had sat in studious leisure producing poetry. His activity was many-sided, and he put heart and brain into it all. The real significance of his life story is that he created a fine career, a splendid personality out of the every-day experiences that come to all of us. He saw the outside world, the works of men and God, not with half-shut eyes and sleepy indifference as we most of us see them, but with vivid curiosity and wonder. Friendship and love, the home-building impulse and the sense of universal brotherhood visited him in turn as they visit every decent human being, but he received them not sluggishly, still less with stubborn resistance, but with alert and whole-hearted enthusiasm. Each new stage of experience was marked by a new departure in activity; but, and this was the most remarkable characteristic of all, the new enterprise did not supersede the old. In a prose romance, written while he was at Oxford, he has given us some suggestive touches of autobiography. 'I could soon find out,' says the hero, 'whether a thing were possible or not to me; then, if it were not, I threw it away for ever, never thought of it again, no regret, no longing for that, it was past and over to me; but if it were possible and I made up my mind to do it, then and there I began it, and in due time finished it, turning

neither to the right hand nor the left till it was done. So I did
with all things that I set my hand to.'[2]

ARCHITECTURE

This was Morris's ideal, and this, too, was his practice. It
describes the tenor of his whole life, as well as the bent of his
character, although the bare recital of these early years might
convey a very different notion. We have seen that his intention
of taking orders did not long survive his first term of study and
discussion at Oxford, and that Art in various forms, and especially the Art of the Middle Ages, began to fill the horizon of
his mind. In the glow of enthusiasm roused by the cathedrals of
northern France, where he spent two delightful holidays, it was
natural enough that he should choose architecture to replace the
Church as his future profession, the work by which he should
earn his living. Though his apprenticeship to Street was of short
duration, and though he never became an architect, yet the
purpose that underlay this change of profession never altered.
His business through life—a business pursued with unflagging
industry which reaped a substantial worldy success—was to
make modern houses worth living in. All the crafts that he
turned his hand to—painting, furniture-making, dyeing, weaving—all were subservient, and consciously subservient, to this
end : all with the one exception of the printing of books, the
beloved Benjamin of his industries, which grew, not so much
out of his life-long love of the house beautiful as out of a passion
equally enduring for literature—the thoughts and words of men.

PAINTING

It was under the influence of Rossetti, whose strange power of
fascination altered many lives, that Morris took to painting, first
as a pastime, then, dropping architecture, as his regular profession. 'Rossetti says I ought to paint,' he writes soon after his
move from Oxford to London, in his 24th year; 'he says I shall
be able. Now, as he is a very great man, and speaks with
authority and not as the scribes, I *must* try. I don't hope much,
I must say, yet will try my best . . . not giving up the architecture, but trying if it is possible to get six hours a day for drawing

[2]'Frank's Sealed Letter.' 'Oxford and Cambridge Magazine,' I.

besides office work. One won't get much enjoyment out of life at this rate, I know well; but that don't matter : I have no right to ask for it, at all events—love and work, these two things only. . . . I can't enter into politics, social subjects, with any interest; for, on the whole, I see that things are in a muddle, and I have no power or vocation to set them right in ever so little a degree. My work is the embodiment of dreams in one form or another.'[3] In this land of dreams Morris lived for a year or two, in daily intercourse with those inveterate dreamers who were his friends; but it was not to such a world that he really belonged, and he was restless and unsatisfied. 'He has lately taken a strong fancy for the human,' says one of his companions at this time; and not long after, in his 26th year, marriage and the need of making a home brought him back into touch with the life of the world.

HOUSE DECORATION

The act of becoming a householder was for him a new departure, and the building and garnishing of his home a kind of sacrament. He could not endure base surroundings. A fair orderly garden, a house wisely planned and solidly built, and within it chairs, tables and utensils that were a pleasure to make and to use—these were to him the necessary background of a decent life. His friend Philip Webb could build the house for him, and there were others among the younger architects who were of the true faith, but where was he to turn for his furniture and his wall-hangings? The domestic arts were extinct—killed by the factory system, by machinery, by steam and by industrial enterprise. Clothes, jewellery and all kinds of household gear were made, not for use, but for profit. They gave pleasure no longer either to those who fashioned them or to those who used them, but only to the huckster who made money out of transferring them from the one to the other, and whose interests it was that they should be cheap and showy and flimsy. All this was borne in on Morris just as he was beginning to feel sure that he was not meant for a painter any more than for an architect, and it helped him to find work that he *was* suited for, work that he could earn his bread by, and that needed doing.

[3]Mackail, vol. I., p. 107.

HOW MORRIS BECAME TRADESMAN AND MANUFACTURER

'The first thing that a man has to do,' Ruskin had written 10
years earlier, 'is to find out what he is fit for. In which enquiry
he may be very safely guided by his likings, if he be not also
guided by his pride. People usually reason in some such fashion
as this: "I don't seem quite fit for a head manager in the firm
of —— & Co., therefore, in all probability, I am fit to be
Chancellor of the Exchequer"; whereas they ought, rather, to
reason thus: "I don't seem to be quite fit to be head manager
in the firm of —— & Co., but, I daresay, I might do something
in a small greengrocery business: I used to be a good judge of
pease"; that is to say, always trying lower instead of trying higher
until they find bottom. . . . I do not believe that any greater good
could be achieved for the country than the change in public
feeling on this head which might be brought about by a few
benevolent men, undeniably in the class of gentlemen, who
would, on principle, enter into some of our commonest trades
and make them honourable.' When Morris and his friends
started a firm of decorators as Morris, Marshall, Faulkner and
Co., it was not with any such benevolent motive. The undertaking was nevertheless destined to become even more important
to the cause of social progress than to that of Art. It began quite
humbly, with a ridiculously small capital, but Morris threw
himself wholeheartedly into the work, for which he was extraordinarily well fitted. 'From the first the firm turned out whatever
anyone wanted in the way of decorative material—architectural
adjuncts, furniture, tapestries, embroideries, stained glass,
wall-papers and what not. The goods were first-rate, the art
and the workmanship excellent, the prices high. . . . You could
have the things such as the firm chose that they should be,
or you could do without them. . . . There was no compromise.
Morris, as senior partner, laid down the law, and all his clients
had to bend or break.'[4] We cannot here pursue the fascinating
story of the firm through its early struggles to the financial success that crowned them, and of the long list of industries undertaken, first at Queen Square and then at Merton, in which
Morris was not merely manager but working foreman, giving

[4]'D. G. Rossetti: His Family-Letters.' With a Memoir by W. M.
Rossetti. Vol. I., p. 219.

to each in turn the insight of the artist, the skill of the craftsman, and the patience and industry which were so peculiarly his own, and which combined so strangely with his boyish vehemence. The mere amount of work he got through is amazing. We read of days spent in designing wall-papers and chintzes, and contriving how they ought to be printed, in watching over dyeing vats, and working at looms, and reinventing the lost art of tapestry weaving, while all the time, in moments of leisure, the stream of poetry flowed on, and yet his friends agree that he always had time for talk and laughter and for little feasts and holidays. Many new and delightful glimpses into his home life are to be found in Miss Morris's introduction and notes to the fine edition of his works now in course of publication. Of any little family festival he was the centre and mainspring, and to any public cause that seemed to him important he was always ready to give time and energy. His love of fun was as strong as his love of work, and his knowledge of common things and interest in them was unfailing. He was a clever cook, and enjoyed an opportunity of proving his skill. 'I always bless God,' he once said, 'for making anything so strong as an onion.'

'A MASTER ARTISAN'

If one wants to understand Morris, and especially the path that led him to Socialism, one must realise how much he identified himself with his shop, and especially with his factory. This was the work that he faced the world with—his 'bread-and-cheese work', as he called it. In an intimate letter he speaks of himself as 'a master artisan, if I may claim that dignity'. That it was no empty claim one may gather from such passages as this from his letters: 'I am trying to learn all I can about dyeing, even the handiwork of it, which is simple enough; but, like many other simple things, contains matters in it that one would not think of unless one were told. Besides my business of seeing to the cotton printing, I am working in Mr. Wardle's dye-house in sabots and blouse pretty much all day long.' And again: 'This morning I assisted at the dyeing of 20 lbs. of silk for our damask in the blue vat. It was very exciting, as the thing is quite unused now, and we ran a good chance of spoiling the silk. There were four dyers and Mr. Wardle at work, and myself as dyers' mate. The men were encouraged with beer, and to it they went, and

pretty it was to see the silk coming green out of the vat and
gradually turning blue. We succeeded very well as far as we can
tell at present. The oldest of the workmen, an old fellow of
70, remembers silk being dyed so long ago. The vat, you must
know, is a formidable-looking thing, 9 feet deep and about 6 feet
square, and is sunk into the earth right up to the top. To-morrow
I am going to Nottingham to see wool dyed blue in the woad
vat, as it is called.' His toil at the dye vat was not in vain.
There is plenty of testimony that he became an expert dyer.
'When he ceased to dye with his own hands, I soon felt the
difference,' writes a lady who embroidered very skilfully for the
firm. 'The colours themselves became perfectly level and had a
monotonous prosy look; the very lustre of the silk was less beautiful. When I complained, he said: "Yes, they have grown too
clever at it. Of course, it means they don't love colour, or they
would do it."

THE GERM OF MORRIS'S SOCIALISM

That a man should put his heart into his work, and that the
work should be of a kind that he can care about: this was a
fixed belief with Morris, and it lay at the root of his Socialism.
Of himself it was true right through every detail of his many
crafts. 'Lord bless us,' he breaks out, when he had been worried
by having to write tiresome letters, 'how nice it will be when I
can get back to my little patterns and dyeing and the dear warp
and weft at Hammersmith.' His work was done for the love of it,
but there was nothing amateurish or unpractical about it. 'I
should very much like,' he writes, 'to make the business quite a
success, and it can't be unless I work at it myself. I must say,
though I don't call myself money-greedy, a smash on that side
would be a terrible nuisance. I have so many serious troubles,
pleasures, hopes and fears that I have not time on my hands to
be ruined and get really poor: above all things, it would destroy
my freedom of work, which is a dear delight to me.' It is noticeable that the work he is thinking of here is not the 'bread-and-
cheese work', but that 'pleasure work of books' that never ceased,
for he goes on to lament that for the moment he was doing
nothing original, and to express the hope that he was not going
'to fall off in imagination and enthusiasm'[5] as he grew older.

[5]Mackail, vol. I., p. 291. Letter, dated Feb. 11th, 1873.

He need not have feared, for it was only in later life that he entered fully upon the inheritance of northern story and legend that inspired his best work. It was a curious case of discovered kinship. His hatred of modern civilisation was part cause and part result of his passion for the early sagas. He saw in them a picture —far enough, no doubt, from the actual facts at any period, near or remote—of the brotherhood of man that he longed for. He was strangely out of place in artificial modern society, and the comradeship, the adventure, the freedom of these tales were like the breath of life to him, and one cannot doubt that they served to fan the smouldering sense of revolt that flamed out later into open rebellion against the sordid slavery of the workers as he knew them.

'I had been reading the Njala in the original before I came here,' he writes from Leek, where he was busy among his dye vats. 'It is better even than I remembered; the style most solemn : all men's children in it, as always in the best of the northern stories, so venerable to each other and so venerated: and the exceeding good temper of Gunnar amidst his heroism, and the calm of Njal : and I don't know anything more consoling or grander in all literature (to use a beastly French word) than Gunnar's singing in his house under the moon and the drifting clouds. What a glorious outcome of the worship of courage these stories are.'[6]

Already in the 'Earthly Paradise' we can perceive the hold they had on his mind. There is a zest and glow in 'The Lovers of Gudrun' that are not to be found in the other tales. But it is in 'Sigurd the Volsung', his most important literary achievement, that the influence of the north finds full expression. It was in the year 1876, when he was 42, that this great epic was written. One realises the extraordinary vigour and many sidedness of the man at this middle period of his life when one remembers that it was the very time when, as we have seen, his craft work seemed to occupy every scrap of leisure. But this was not all. Great as he had proved himself as poet and craftsman, he was greater yet as man, too great to be shut in by study or workshop. Courage, energy, and patience personified, he was certain to come out into the open when the time was ripe and

[6]Mackail, Vol. I., p. 335; 1877.

take his share in shaping events. It was not until middle life that
the moment came. Two causes called him. In the one case the
response came from his profound and growing sense of human
solidarity, in the other from his reverence for the past and the
work of the great men who were dead and whose art had died
with them.

THE 'ANTI-SCRAPE'

Indignation against the ruthless tide of restoration which was
fast submerging the last traces of noble mediæval architecture
finds expression again and again in the private letters tran-
scribed by Mr. Mackail. At last, when one of the ancient parish
churches that he loved so well close to his own country home
was threatened, and just afterwards the beautiful Minster of
Tewkesbury, indignation found vent in action. He wrote a letter
to the *Athenæum,* explaining the urgency of the need, and
begged all thoughtful people to join him in trying to meet it.
'What I wish for is that an association should be set on foot to
keep a watch on old monuments, to protest against all "restoration" that means more than keeping out wind and weather, and
by all means, literary and other, to awaken a feeling that our
ancient buildings are not mere ecclesiastical toys, but sacred
monuments of the nation's growth and hope.' The appeal was
not in vain. Within a month the Society for the Protection of
Ancient Buildings (the Anti-Scrape as he nicknamed it) was
founded, with Morris for its secretary. Until his death his zeal
for the cause never waned. He wrote for it a prospectus, a model
of terse and simple English, which was translated into French,
German, Italian, and Dutch; he poured out freely both time
and money; and he gave in its interests the first of those public
lectures which, fine as they were, never became a really congenial task.

'BULGARIAN ATROCITIES'

This was in the spring of 1877, a few months before Morris had
been roused to his first political utterance by the terrible accounts
of cruelty in Bulgaria and the dread lest England might take up
arms against Russia in support of Turkey. 'I who am writing
this,' he wrote in a letter to the *Daily News,* 'am one of a large
class of men—quiet men—who usually go about their own busi-

ness, heeding public matters less than they ought, and afraid to speak in such a huge concourse as the English nation, however much they may feel, but who are now stung into bitterness by thinking how helpless they are in a public matter that touches them so closely. . . . I appeal to the working men and pray them to look to it that if this shame falls on them they will certainly remember it, and be burdened by it when their day clears for them and they attain all and more than all they are now striving for.'[7]

I have quoted from this letter because it represents, together with the Manifesto to the Working Men of England issued a few months later, when war seemed imminent, Morris's first public utterance of Socialism. It is interesting to see that it was already tinged with distrust of a central representative government. The movement into which he threw himself with so much vigour was, however, Liberal, not Socialist, in its origin. Some leading Socialists, Hyndman for one, were indeed in the opposite camp. Long afterwards he described his surprise on meeting Morris in 1879 for the first time. 'It was many years after I had enjoyed his poetry and mocked a little, as ignorant young men will, at his asthetic armchairs and wall-papers that I met the man himself. . . . I imagined him as a retired and delicate gentleman, easily overwrought by his sentiments. That was not his appearance in the flesh, as we all know. Refinement undoubtedly there was in the delicate lines of the nose and the beautiful moulding of the forehead. But his hearty voice, his jolly, vigorous frame, his easy, sailorlike dress, the whole figure, gave me a better opinion of the "atrocity mongers", as I considered them, than anything I have seen before or since.'[8]

But though the Eastern question led him to act for a time with the Liberal Party, it served also to show him that it was not an organisation to which the welfare of the workers could be trusted. 'Working men of England,' he writes in the Manifesto already mentioned, 'one word of warning yet. I doubt if you know the bitterness of hatred against freedom and progress that lies at the hearts of a certain part of the richer classes in this country. . . . These men cannot speak of your order, of its

[7]Letter to the *Daily News*, October 26th, 1876, signed William Morris, Author of 'The Earthly Paradise.'
[8]*Justice* for October 6th, 1896.

aims, of its leaders, without a sneer or an insult. These men, if they had the power (may England perish rather!) would thwart your just aspirations, would silence you, would deliver you, bound hand and foot, for ever to irresponsible capital.'

Every word of the Manifesto proves that he had become a Socialist by conviction, as he had always been one by temperament, and we shall do well to pause a moment in this brief narrative of his life in order to reckon up the debt we owe to the greatest Englishman who has passed away out of our ranks.

WHAT SOCIALISM OWES TO WILLIAM MORRIS

When our children's children recall the great names of the Victorian Age, there is not one will kindle a warmer interest than that of William Morris. They will remember him for his stories and poems and for his pioneer work in the revival of handicraft, but above all for the vigour and charm of his personality. He was the sort of man who impressed his friends so strongly that the impression survives, a man who excelled the ordinary man in almost every direction of human activity and was typical nevertheless of his race and his country. He was a man of genius, but his genius irradiated not merely his craftsmanship and his poetry, but everything he turned his hand to. He was an expert not merely in literature and manufacture, but in life. A robust power of enjoyment was his most marked characteristic. He insisted on enjoying things. The very utensils in his house must give joy in the using or he would not use them. Work that brought no joy was fit only for slaves. It is this abundant vitality, this love of life and the world; it is the fact that he had eyes to see and ears to hear and a heart to perceive; it is, in short, because he was an artist and a genius, that his contribution to Socialism is of outstanding value, although he proved himself but a shortsighted leader and never grappled closely with the problems we have to face. Economic reasoning was not in his line, nor details of administration, but he knew a great deal about the world we live in and how to use it to the utmost advantage. The sense of brotherhood was strong in him, and it was illuminated by insight and sympathy. We can learn, therefore, far more from the story of his approach to Socialism, of the way in which he was driven to adopt it as the only hope, than from any formal statement that he ever made of its doctrines.

THE PATH TO SOCIALISM

That approach can best be traced in his popular lectures on Art, which began in the year 1877. In these lectures his sympathies are with the craftsman. He recognises no essential difference between the artist and the workman. As a contrast to the modest ideal of a 20s., or even a 30s. minimum wage, there is something delightfully inspiriting in his claim that the hire of the workman should include 'Money enough to keep him from fear of want or degradation for him and his; leisure enough from bread-earning work (even though it be pleasant to him) to give him time to read and think, and connect his own life with the life of the great world; work enough of the kind aforesaid, and praise of it, and encouragement enough to make him feel good friends with his fellows; and, lastly, not least (for 'tis verily part of the bargain), his own due share of Art, the chief part of which will be a dwelling that does not lack the beauty which Nature would freely allow it if our own perversity did not turn Nature out of doors'. 'I specially wished,' he writes, in answer to a complaint that he had strayed beyond the question of 'mere art', 'to point out that the question of popular Art was a social question, involving the happiness or misery of the greater part of the community. The absence of popular Art from modern times is more disquieting and grievous to bear for this reason than for any other, that it betokens that fatal division of men into the cultivated and the degraded classes which competitive commerce has bred and fosters; popular Art has no chance of a healthy life, or indeed, of a life at all, till we are on the way to fill up this terrible gulf between riches and poverty. . . . It may well be a burden to the conscience of an honest man who lives a more manlike life to think of the innumerable lives which are spent in toil unrelieved by hope and uncheered by praise; men who might as well, for all the good they are doing their neighbours by their work, be turning a crank with nothing at the end of it . . . Over and over again have I asked myself, why should not my lot be the common lot? My work is simple work enough; much of it, nor that the least pleasant, any man of decent intelligence could do if he could but get to care about the work and its results. Indeed, I have been ashamed when I have thought of the contrast between my happy working hours and the unpraised, unrewarded, monotonous drudgery which most men are condemned to. Nothing shall convince me that such labour as this is good or necessary to civilisation.'[9] It was this 'burden on his conscience', growing heavier as experience and character ripened, that drove Morris to Socialism. That very insight into the happenings of human life, into joy and grief and desire which inspired his stories, enabled him to see society as in truth it was.

To him the vulgar luxury of the rich was even more hateful than the squalor of the poor. 'Apart from the desire to produce beautiful things,' he says, 'the leading passion of my life has been and is hatred of modern civilisation. . . . What shall I say concerning its mastery of and its waste of mechanical power, its Commonwealth so poor, its enemies of the Commonwealth so rich, its stupendous organisation—for the misery of life; its contempt of simple pleasure, which everyone could enjoy but for its folly; its eyeless vulgarity, which has destroyed Art, the one certain solace of labour?' 'The hope of the past times was gone,' he goes on, telling the story of his conversion; 'the struggle of mankind for many ages had produced nothing but this sordid, aimless, ugly confusion; the immediate future seemed to me likely to intensify all the present evils by sweeping away the last survivals of the days before the dull squalor of civilisation had settled down on the world. This was a bad lookout, indeed, and, if I may mention myself as a personality and not as a mere type, especially so to a man of my disposition, careless of metaphysics and religion, as well as of scientific analysis, but with a deep love of the earth and the life on it, and a passion for the history of the past of mankind. Think of it! Was it all to end in a counting-house on the top of a cinder-heap, with Podsnap's drawing-room in the offing, and a Whig Committee dealing out champagne to the rich and margarine to the poor in such convenient proportions as would make all men contented together, though the pleasure of the eyes was gone from the world and the place of Homer was to be taken by Huxley! Yes, believe me, in my heart, when I really forced myself to look towards the future, that is what I saw in it; and, as far as I could tell, scarce anyone seemed to think it worth while to struggle against such a consummation of civilisation. So, then, I was in for a fine

[9]Letter to the *Manchester Examiner*, March, 1883.

pessimistic end of life, if it had not somehow dawned on me that, amid all the filth of civilisation, the seeds of a great change, what we others call Social Revolution, were beginning to germinate. The whole face of things was changed to me by that discovery, and all I had to do then in order to become a Socialist was to hook myself on to the practical movement.'[10]

AVOWAL OF SOCIALISM. THE S.D.F.

This 'hooking on' took place in the autumn of 1882, when Morris, at the age of 48, joined the Democratic Federation (which became subsequently the Social Democratic Federation, and eventually took the title of the British Socialist Party). 'For my part, I used to think,' he writes to a friend who remonstrated with him at this time, 'that one might further real Socialistic progress by doing what one could on the lines of ordinary middle-class Radicalism. I have been driven of late into the conclusion that I was mistaken; that Radicalism is on the wrong line, so to say, and will never develop into anything more than Radicalism —in fact, that it is made for and by the middle classes, and will always be under the control of rich capitalists : they will have no objection to its *political* development, if they think they can stop it there; but, as to real social changes, they will not allow them if they can help it.'[11]

'The contrasts of rich and poor,' he writes, again to the same friend, a few days later, 'are unendurable and ought not to be endured by either rich or poor. Now it seems to me that, feeling this, I am bound to act for the destruction of the system which seems to me mere oppression and obstruction. Such a system can only be destroyed by the united discontent of numbers : isolated acts of a few persons of the middle and upper-classes seeming to me (as I have said before) quite powerless against it : in other words, the antagonism of classes, which the system has bred, is the natural and necessary instrument for its destruction.'[12]

There was nothing half-hearted in Morris's acceptance of Socialism. He threw all his vigour, all his enthusiasm into

[10]'How I Became a Socialist.' W. M. Reprinted from *Justice.*
[11]Letter to Mr. C. E. Maurice, June 22nd, 1883. See 'Life of William Morris,' vol. II., p. 103.
[12]Ibid.

propaganda, though it was not a kind of work that gave scope for the rarest powers of his mind and heart. It is pathetic to hear how he schooled himself to study Marx and tried to grasp economic problems, for it is only now and then, when he uses his gift as seer, that his Socialist writings spring into life and are of lasting value. His friends were grieved, naturally enough, that the poet should be lost in the lecturer, especially as he had no gift for oratory, but he made light very characteristically of any possible loss to the world. 'Poetry goes with the hand-arts, I think,' he says to an intimate friend, 'and, like them, has now become unreal. The arts have got to die, what is left of them, before they can be born again. You know my views on the matter—I apply them to myself as well as to others. This would not, I admit, prevent my writing poetry, any more than it prevents my doing my pattern work, because the mere personal pleasure of it urges one to the work; but it prevents my looking at it as a sacred duty. . . . Meantime the propaganda give me work to do which, unimportant as it seems, is part of a great whole which cannot be lost, and that ought to be enough for me.'[13]

THE SOCIALIST LEAGUE

But it was not only the toughness of economic theory that made his new duties distasteful. From the first there were dissensions in the camp. 'I find myself drifting,' he says, 'into the disgraceful position of a moderator and patcher up, which is much against my inclination.' Worse still was to follow. The patching up was unsuccessful, and Morris found himself, in the beginning of 1885, the leader of a small body of seceders who took the name of the Socialist League.

For six years he gave much time and money to the internal management of the League, as well as to the revolutionary propaganda, which was its avowed object, and which was carried on chiefly by means of the *Commonweal,* first a monthly and afterwards a weekly paper, edited[14] and to a large extent written by Morris. Surely no Socialist paper can show a record so brilliant. 'The Dream of John Ball' and 'News from Nowhere' appeared in it as serials, and a long poem, 'The Pilgrims of

[13]Letter to Mr. C. E. Maurice. See 'Life of William Morris,' vol. II., pp. 106, 107.
[14]E. Belfort Bax was joint-editor with William Morris.

Hope', of which some portions stand high among his finest work —'Mother and Son', for instance, and 'The Half of Life Gone'.

In addition to these weightier contributions, few numbers are without some paragraph from his pen, all the more arresting from its simple familiar wording, that brings us directly into touch with his views on life and events.

Take this explanation, for instance, of the revolutionary attitude of the League from the first weekly issue, May 1st, 1886 :—

'We believe that the advanced part of the capitalist class, especially in this country, is drifting, not without a feeling of fear and discomfort, towards State Socialism of the crudest kind; and a certain school of Socialists are fond of pointing out this tendency with exultation. . . . But there is another thing besides bourgeois stumbling into State Socialism which shows which way the tide is setting, and that is the instinctive revolutionary attempts which drive them into these courses. What is to be said about these? They are leaderless often and half blind. But are they fruitful of nothing but suffering to the workers? We think not; for besides the immediate gain which they force from the dominant class as above said, they are a stern education for the workers themselves. . . . The worst thing that we have to dread is that the oppressed people will learn a dull contentment with their lot. . . . The rudest and most unsuccessful attempts at revolution are better than that.' 'The real business of Socialists,' writes Morris in another number, 'is to impress on the workers the fact that they are a class, whereas they ought to be society. If we mix ourselves up with Parliament, we shall confuse and dull this fact in people's minds, instead of making it clear and intensifying it.'[15] And again, under the heading 'Unattractive Labour' : 'It is no real paradox to say that the unattractiveness of labour, which is now the curse of the world, will become the hope of the world. As long as the workman could sit at home working easily and quietly, his long hours of labour mattered little to him, and other evils could be borne. . . . But now that labour has become a mere burden, the disease of a class, that class will, by all means, try to throw it off, to lessen its weight, and in their efforts to do so they must of necessity destroy society, which is founded on the patient bearing of that burden. . . .

[15]'Socialism and Politics.' Supplement to *Commonweal*, July, 1885.

True, their masters, taught prudence by fear, will try, are trying, various means to make the workers bear their burden; but one after the other they will be found out and discredited. Philanthropy has had its day and is gone, thrift and self-help are going; participation in profits, parliamentarianism and universal suffrage, State Socialism will have to go the same road, and workers will be face to face at last with the fact that modern civilisation, with its elaborate hierarchy and iron drill, is founded on their intolerable burden, and then no shortening of the day's work which would leave profit to the employer will make their labour hours short enough. They will see that modern society can only exist as long as they bear *their* burden with some degree of patience; their patience will be worn out and to pieces will modern society go.'

After a visit to Leeds and Bradford he writes : 'The constant weight of drill in these highly organised industries has necessarily limited the intelligence of the men and deadened their individuality, while the system is so powerful and searching that they find it difficult to conceive of any system under which they could be other than human machines.'[16] Elsewhere we find the same idea condensed into an epigram : 'Individual profit makers are not a necessity for labour, but an obstruction to it.'[17]

Speaking of 'Education under Capitalism' he says : 'My heart sank under Mr. McChoakumchild and his method, and I thought how much luckier I was to have been born well enough off to be sent to a school where I was taught—nothing, but learned archæology and romance on the Wiltshire Downs.'[18]

Under the heading 'How We Live and How We Might Live' he writes : 'Often when I have been sickened by the stupidity of the mean, idiotic rabbit warrens that rich men build for themselves in Bayswater and elsewhere, I console myself with visions of the noble Communal Hall of the future, unsparing of materials, generous in worthy ornament, alive with the noblest thoughts of our time, and the past embodied in the best art which free and manly people could produce; such an abode of man as no private enterprise could come near for beauty and fitness, because only collective thought and collective life could

[16]*Commonweal*, May 8th, 1886.
[17]Ibid, July 2nd, 1887.
[18]Ibid, June, 30th, 1888.

cherish the aspirations which would give birth to its beauty or have the skill and leisure that could carry them out.'[19]

POPULAR CONTROL OF ADMINISTRATION

These cuttings from the *Commonweal* show that the views of the League were definitely revolutionary, and this is clearly stated in its Manifesto. There was to be no tinkering, no half measures; the basis of society was to be changed. 'No number of merely administrative changes, until the workers are in possession of all political power, would make any real approach to Socialism.' 'By political power,' Morris goes on to explain, 'we do not mean the exercise of the franchise or even the fullest development of the representative system, but the direct control by the people of the whole administration of the community whatever the ultimate destiny of that administration is to be.'[20]

COMMUNISM

One seeks in vain in the Manifesto for any definite suggestions as to the method in which this 'direct control' was to be exercised, but Morris's lectures throw some light on the ideal of social organisation that he had formed. 'Those who see this view of the new society,' he says, 'believe that decentralisation in it would be complete. The political unit with them would be not a nation, but a commune. The whole of reasonable society would be a great federation of such communes. . . . A nation is a body of people kept together for purposes of rivalry and war with other similar bodies, and when competition shall have given place to combination the function of the nation will be gone.' 'I will recapitulate,' he continues, 'the two views taken by Socialists as to the future of society. According to the first, the State—that is, the nation organised for unwasteful production and exchange of wealth—will be the sole possessor of the national plant and stock, the sole employer of labour, which she will so regulate in the general interest that no man will ever need to fear lack of employment and due earnings therefrom. . . . According to the other view, the centralised nation would give place to a federation of communities, who would hold all wealth

[19]*Commonweal*, July 2nd, 1887.
[20]Manifesto of the Socialist League. A new edition, annotated by W. Morris and Belfort Bax. 1885.

in common, and would use that wealth for satisfying the needs
of each member, only exacting from each that he should do his
best according to his capacity towards the production of the
common wealth. . . .

'These two views of the future of society are sometimes
opposed to each other as Socialism and Communism; but to my
mind the latter is simply the necessary development of the
former, which implies a transition period during which people
would be getting rid of the habits of mind bred by the long ages
of tyranny and commercial competition, and be learning that it
is to the interest of each that all should thrive. When men had
lost the fear of each other engendered by our system of artificial
famine, they would feel that the best way of avoiding the waste
of labour would be to allow every man to take what he needed
from the common store, since he would have no temptation or
opportunity of doing anything with a greater portion than he
really needed for his personal use. Thus would be minimised the
danger of the community falling into bureaucracy, the multiplication of boards and offices, and all the paraphernalia of
official authority, which is after all a burden, even when it is
exercised by the delegation of the whole people and in accordance with their wishes.'[21]

Any detailed scheme of State Socialism roused ire and repugnance in Morris, though one does not deny that towards the
end of his life he was brought in a chastened spirit to bow his
neck to the Fabian yoke. Still, his submission had the unreality
of a death bed repentance. The creed was, in truth, alien to his
nature. His hopes and wishes for the future were dominated by
the glorious visions of free human activity, of pride and joy in
the work of one's hands and brain, which he associated, rightly
or wrongly, with the past. It was not only capitalism which he
hated. The tameness and elaboration of modern mechanical
production would be just as odious to him if the plant were in
State ownership and the management in the hands of Government officials. His delightful rural idyll, 'News from Nowhere',
was written, Mr. Mackail tells us, as a protest against the
apotheosis of centralisation and of urban life held up as the

[21]'The Labor Question from the Socialist Standpoint.' W. Morris.
(One of a Course of Lectures on 'The Claims of Labor.') Edinburgh
Co-operative Printing Company, Limited, 1886.

social ideal by Mr. Bellamy in his 'Looking Backward'. Characteristically enough the land of Morris's prevision was a Utopia
for the worker rather than for the consumer. The production
of wealth interested him more than its enjoyment, the joy of
making more than the joy of spending.

'Mr. Bellamy worries himself unnecessarily,' he wrote in the
Commonweal for June, 1889, 'in seeking, with obvious failure,
some incentive to labour to replace the fear of starvation, which
is at present our only one; whereas it cannot be too often repeated
that the true incentive to useful and happy labour is, and must
be, pleasure in the work itself.' How to preserve, or rather how
to recover, that incentive is for Morris the problem of problems;
but it is one that the orthodox Socialist is apt to overlook,
although the man in the street, that much underrated critic, is
always ready to remind him of it. It is the old story once more
of being led astray by that mythological person, the economic
man. The social reformer constructs, or rather designs, an
organisation of industry which threatens to totter as soon as it
is built for want of just this foundation stone, the significance
of which was instantly apparent to the eye of the poet, though
to the economists it seemed a negligible detail. And here we come
upon the real mission of William Morris to his generation, his
special function in the Socialist movement. A craftsman himself, he thought of the worker not as an abstraction, but as a
comrade, with motives more or less like his own. This vital
sympathetic outlook led him, no doubt, into blunders from
time to time, especially in his dealings with individuals, but it
preserved him from some serious and common errors. His view
of the future, of the new social structure for which we are all
working, may have been one sided, but the side he saw was the
side unseen by men immersed in questions of administrative
reform or in organising the class war. Fabians and Social
Democrats were alike in this. They were apt to leave out of their
calculations the humanisation of the worker in and through
his work, of bringing home to him the realisation of his own
place in the social economy. A decent life for the workman, the
recognition on his own part of the dignity of his work, seemed
to Morris not merely the end for which we were striving, but the
only means of attaining it. 'It is necessary to point out,' he writes,
'that there are some Socialists who do not think that the problem

of the organisation of life and necessary labour can be dealt
with by a huge national centralisation, working by a kind of
magic for which no one feels himself responsible; that, on the
contrary, it will be necessary for the unit of administration to
be small enough for every citizen to feel himself responsible for
its details and be interested in them; that individual men cannot
shuffle off the business of life on to the shoulders of an abstraction called the State, but must deal with each other; that variety
of life is as much an aim of true Communism as equality of
condition, and that nothing but a union of these two will bring
about real freedom; that modern nationalities are mere artificial
devices for the commercial war that we seek to put an end to,
and will disappear with it; and, finally, that art, using the word
in its widest and due signification, is not a mere adjunct of life
which free and happy men can do without, but the necessary
expression and indispensable instrument of human happiness.'[22]

DISTRUST OF POLITICAL ACTION
In his own day Morris stood almost alone among Socialists in
his distrust of political action, of a 'huge national centralisation
working by a kind of magic'. It is true that there were in England two antagonistic types of Socialism, but their opposition
was one of method rather than of aim. Both intended to capture
the Government of the country, in the one case by revolutionary,
in the other by more insidious methods. Morris, on the other
hand, was inclined to throw the government of the country to
the winds and to scorn the notion of a democratic control of
industry exercised by means of a parliamentary vote. He never
committed himself, so far as I know, as to the actual means by
which any other kind of control by the 'useful classes' was to be
brought into being, but there seems little doubt that, if he were
alive now, we should find him in the Syndicalist camp. A deep
distrust of salvation by means of the vote would lead him there,
and a profound belief that revolutionary activity in the working
class can be more effectively evoked and fostered by bringing
home to them the sense of their social responsibility as workers
than as parliamentary constituents. In the one case interest is
focused on party politics, usually in their crudest form, and the

[22]Review of 'Looking Backward' in the *Commonweal* for June, 1889, by
W. M.

lesson learned by the worker is a lesson in docility: he is taught
to function smoothly as a wheel in the party machine. In the
other case he is brought face to face with the actual problems of
industrial production and organisation; he learns to be resourceful
and self-reliant and to take his place consciously and intelligently
in the great enterprise of providing for the needs of mankind.
I have said that Morris never committed himself as to the
method in which this direct connection between the worker and
the organisation of industry was to be effected, but a private
letter of his, written in 1888, gives a naif and vivid picture of
industrial society as he visualised it in the future and the super-
cession of government: 'Our present representative system,' he
writes, 'is the reflection of our class society. The fact of the
antagonism of classes underlies all our government, and causes
political parties. . . . The business of a statesman is to balance
the greed and fears of the proprietary class against the necessities
and demands of the working class. This is a sorry business, and
leads to all kinds of trickery and evasion, so that it is more than
doubtful whether a statesman can be a moderately honest man.
Now, the control of classes being abolished, all this would fall
to the ground. The relations of men to each other would become
personal; wealth would be looked upon as an instrument of life
and not as a reason for living, and therefore dominant over men's
lives. Whatever laws existed would be much fewer, very simple,
and easily understood by all; they would mostly concern the
protection of the person. In dealing with property, its fetish
quality having disappeared, its use only would have to be considered, e.g., shall we (the public) work this coal mine or shut it
up? Is it necessary for us to lay down this park in wheat, or can
we afford to keep it as a place of recreation? Will it be desirable
to improve this shoemaking machine, or can we go on with it as
it is? Will it be necessary to call for special volunteers to cultivate yonder fen, or will the action of the law of compensation
be inducement enough for its cultivation? And so forth. . . .

'To return to our government of the future, which would be
rather an administration of things than a government of persons.
Nations, as political entities, would cease to exist. Civilisation
would mean the federalisation of a variety of communities, great
and small, at one end of which would be the township and the
local guild, and at the other some central body whose function

would be almost entirely the guardianship of the *principles* of society. . . . Between these two poles there would be various federations, which would grow together or dissolve as convenience of place, climate, language, etc., dictated, and would dissolve peaceably when occasion prompted. Of course public intercourse between the members of the federation would have to be carried on by means of delegation, but the delegates would not pretend to represent anyone or anything but the business with which they are delegated, e.g., "We are a shoemaking community chiefly, you cotton spinners. Are we making too many shoes? Shall we turn, some of us, to gardening for a month or two, or shall we go on?" And so forth. . . . To my mind the essential thing to this view . . . is the township, or parish, or ward, or local guild, small enough to manage its own affairs directly. And I don't doubt that gradually all public business would be so much simplified that it would come to little more than a correspondence. "Such are the facts with us; compare them with the facts with you. You know how to act." So that we should tend to the abolition of all government, and even of all regulations that were not really habitual; and voluntary association would become a necessary habit and the only bond of society.'[23]

It will be noticed that Morris differs both from Kropotkin with his 'groups' and from most of the modern Syndicalists with their industrial guilds in localising the communities that are to constitute his social framework. Notwithstanding his conviction that men must be organised as producers, his home loving nature refused to conceive a society which made light of the ties of neighbourhood, of growth in a common soil. England was very dear to him as a land, though not as a nation; and still dearer was the corner of England where he was born and bred. If we understand Morris and his attitude towards the future, we shall see that his Socialism was revolutionary and uncompromising just because he was conservative at heart. The transition period, as he called it, of State Socialism was distasteful to him because it seemed to substitute a dull uniformity for the detail and variety of the past. He admitted eventually that it was bound to come, he saw that it was coming by means of humdrum legislation, but he could never feel any enthusiasm about it.

[23]Letters on Socialism by W. Morris to Rev. G. Bainton. London. Privately printed. 1894. (Only thirty-four copies).

EDUCATION TOWARDS REVOLUTION

We have seen that the split with the Social Democratic Federation, in so far as it was not due merely to personal misunderstandings, was a protest against circuitous and indirect methods of advance. His desire was to found a Socialist Party which should begin to act at once not by permeating cultivated people, nor by gaining representation in Parliament, but by raising a standard of revolt to which the oppressed could rally. His one encouragement in making a new attempt had been the signs of discontent among the masses. To focus this discontent and render it articulate was his purpose in forming the Socialist League. A passionate hatred had grown up in him of a society which seemed to him 'mere cannibalism,' 'so corrupt, so steeped in hypocrisy, that one turns from one stratum of it to another with hopeless loathing.' In one direction only did he see hope, the road to revolution; but that road, as he saw it, was gradual and arduous. To educate a strong party of workers in the aims of Socialism, so that when the seething forces of popular discontent could no longer be restrained, leaders should be forthcoming among the people to tell them what to aim at and what to ask for. An aimless revolt, leading to counter revolution, seemed to him a threatening calamity. Looking back to that period, a quarter of a century ago, we see that Morris over estimated the danger of a premature upheaval. Society was not ripe for it. Education was needed not merely to guide, but to produce that impatience of injustice and oppression which must be the motive power in such an upheaval. He believed that the new birth of society was at hand, and that the work for Socialists was to strive to help it forward, so that it might come with as little confusion and suffering as might be. 'Education towards revolution seems to me,' he said, 'to express in three words what our policy should be.' It was a policy which separated him on the one hand from Parliamentarians and Opportunists, and on the other from Anarchists ready for all risks of immediate revolution; and so it came about that the League grew but slowly, and steered with difficulty between Scylla and Charybdis. Morris held the helm as long as he could, but from the first the road to revolution that he saw had little attraction for most of his comrades. After a few years a policy of high handed robbery, of bombs and barricades, came to be openly advocated by many voluble members of the League, and in 1889 these views were so much in the ascendant that Morris was actually deposed from the control of the *Commonweal*, dependent as it still was on him both for matter and money. He continued to write for it until November, 1890, when he published in it a final statement of his views under the title 'Where Are We Now?' After reviewing the seven years that had elapsed since Socialism had 'come to life again,' he goes on to describe the two lines on which the 'methods of impatience' profess to work, the line of 'palliation' and the line of 'partial inconsequent revolt,' and then explains his own policy, which differed as much from one as from the other. 'Our business,' he concludes, 'is the making of Socialists, i.e., convincing people that Socialism is good for them and is possible. When we have enough people of that way of thinking, they will find out what action is necessary for putting their principles in practice.'

This dignified protest was ill received by the majority of the members of the League, and Morris had no choice but to sever his connection with a body whose policy he disapproved.

HAMMERSMITH SOCIALIST SOCIETY
After his withdrawal it struggled on for 18 months, and then ended dramatically with the arrest of the printer and publisher of the *Commonweal*. Meanwhile Morris and the little group who shared his views organised themselves as the Hammersmith Socialist Society, and issued a circular drafted by Morris to the provincial branches of the League explaining their action.

The membership was very small at first, and never became large. Mr. Emery Walker was secretary and Morris treasurer, and the meetings took place in Kelmscott House.

Until the end of his life Morris relaxed no whit in enthusiasm for the cause, and his opposition towards Anarchism grew stronger rather than weaker. 'It is not the dissolution of society for which we strive,' he writes in December, 1890, 'but its reintegration. The idea put forward by some who attack present society of the complete independence of every individual, that is, of freedom without society, is not merely impossible of realisation, but, when looked into, turns out to be inconceivable.'[24]

[24]Manifesto of the Hammersmith Socialist Society.

SEVEN YEARS OF PEACEFUL WORK

But though his belief in Socialism was as strong as ever, he became convinced, as time went on, that the active work immediately called for was work unsuited to his taste and to his powers.

'In all the wearisome shilly shally of parliamentary politics I should be absolutely useless, and the immediate end to be gained, the pushing things just a trifle nearer to State Socialism, which, when realised, seems to me but a dull goal, all this quite sickens me. Also I know that there are a good many other idealists (if I may use that word of myself) who are in the same position, and I don't see why they should not hold together and keep out of the vestry business, necessary as that may be. Preaching the ideal is surely always necessary. Yet, on the other hand, I sometimes vex myself by thinking that perhaps I am not doing the most I can merely for the sake of a piece of "preciousness." ' [25]

To make use of Morris for organising meetings and speaking at street corners was to dig with a damascened sword blade. He was here to show how life, even in the nineteenth century, could be full of variety and delight. The revival of the lost art of printing, the engrossing occupation of his latest years, was a return to the true work of his life. We are glad to remember that the seven years of stress and turmoil, when he fought so nobly for the ideal that lay always before him, were succeeded by seven years of serene and happy work, which has left the world richer in all the crafts that subserve the making of books.

To the last, however, he went on lecturing from time to time on Socialism. On October 30th, 1895, just a year before his death, he gave an address to inaugurate the Oxford Socialist Union. A few months later he was present at the New Year's Meeting of the Social Democratic Federation, and made there a short but noble and touching speech on behalf of unity. Two days afterwards he gave his last Sunday evening lecture at Kelmscott House, again on the same subject, the title being 'One Socialist Party.'

One more year marked by failing strength but unfailing industry was spent in seeing through the press the greatest of his printing achievements, the Kelmscott Chaucer, and in

[25]Letter to Mrs. Burne-Jones, dated July 29th, 1888, quoted in Mackail's "Life of William Morris," vol. ii, p. 206.

composing the last of his long series of stories, 'The Sundering Flood.'

He died on October 3rd, 1896, aged 62, and was buried in the little churchyard at Kelmscott. The body was borne to the grave in an open haycart, festooned with vines, alders, and bulrushes, and driven by a countryman.

BIBLIOGRAPHIES

JEREMY BENTHAM. Bentham's *Works* were edited by Sir John Bowring in eleven volumes (1838-1843). The first nine volumes contain the writings published during his lifetime (with the exception of those on religion) and a number of works not previously published in English. Bentham's *Deontology or Science of Morality* (2 Vols., 1834), edited by Sir J. Bowring, were not reprinted in the *Works*.

Selected extracts of Bentham's works are to be found in J. H. Burton (ed.), *Benthamiana* (1843) and W. Stark (ed.), *Jeremy Bentham's Economic Writings* (3 Vols., 1952-54). Bentham's manuscripts, largely unpublished, are deposited in University College London and in the British Museum.

For descriptions and criticisms of Bentham's work see: L. Stephen, *The English Utilitarians* (Vol. I, 1900); C. M. Atkinson, *Jeremy Bentham, His Life* (1905); C. K. Ogden, *Bentham's Theory of Fictions* (1932); W. R. Sorley, *Bentham and the early Utilitarians* (1914); G. Wallas, *Jeremy Bentham* (1922); C. Philipson, *Three Criminal Law Reformers* (1923); J. L. Stocks, *Jeremy Bentham* (1933); E. Halevy, *The Growth of Philosophic Radicalism* (1949); B. Parekh (ed.), *Jeremy Bentham—Ten Critical Essays* (1974).

WILLIAM COBBETT. A full bibliography of Cobbett's own writings is contained in M. L. Pearl, *William Cobbett, A Bibliographical account of his life and times* (1953, reprinted 1971). Of his best works only *Rural Rides* is easily available in Everymans Library (2 Vols.). *Cottage Economy* was reprinted in 1966 and is already scarce. A selection of Cobbett's writings was published in 1968 by the Folio Society under the title *Cobbett's England*. This volume also reproduces the set of Gillray's engravings of the life of Cobbett. An excellent selection of extracts from the *Political Register* is to be found in G. D. H. and M. Cole, *Opinions of William Cobbett* (1944). W. Reitzel (ed.),

The Autobiography of William Cobbett, the Progress of a Plough-boy to a seat in Parliament (1947) is made up of autobiographical extracts from Cobbett's writings. Many of Cobbett's manuscripts are at Nuffield College, Oxford.

Of the biographies of William Cobbett the most important is G. D. H. Cole, *The Life of William Cobbett* (3rd Edn., 1947). This also contains a useful critical bibliography. E. I. Carlyle, *William Cobbett* (1904) includes very full references to books dealing with Cobbett and his times. Lewis Melville, *The Life and Letters of William Cobbett in England and America* (2 Vols., 1913) includes the text of many private letters. Useful more recent books are W. B. Pemberton, *William Cobbett* (Penguin, 1949) and J. W. Osborne, *William Cobbett; his thought and his times* (1966). For secondary school use Asa Briggs, *William Cobbett* (1967) is recommended.

RICHARD CARLILE. Details of Carlile's own writings are to be found in the Appendix on p. 98. There are a number of books and essays about Carlile but as yet, no full-scale biography. G. J. Holyoake wrote a life of Carlile in 1849 and also wrote the article in the *Dictionary of National Biography*. G. A. Aldred, *Richard Carlile, Agitator, His Life and Times* is a lively work but is not always reliable. Other works of interest are: T. C. Campbell, *The Battle of the Press, as told in the story of the Life of Richard Carlile* (1899); T. W. Mercer, *Richard Carlile on Cooperation* (1929); W. H. Wickwar, *The Struggle for the Freedom of the Press 1819-1832* (1928); and A. Calder-Marshall, *Lewd, Blasphemous and Obscene* (1972, pp. 69-120).

JOHN STUART MILL. The principal writings of J. S. Mill are: *A System of Logic* (1843); *Essays on some unsettled questions on Political Economy* (1844); *Principles of Political Economy* (1848, ed. W. J. Ashley, 1909); *On Liberty* (1859); *Dissertations and Discussions* (4 Vols., 1859-1876); *Considerations on Representative Government* (1861); *Utilitarianism* (1863); *Examination of Sir William Hamilton's Philosophy* (1865); *Auguste Comte and Positivism* (1865); *England and Ireland* (1868); *The Subjection of Women* (1869); *Autobiography* (1873); *Three Essays on Religion* (1874); *Socialism* (Chicago, 1879). Many of Mill's letters and numerous speeches have been published. In addition Mill wrote some 500 articles for newspapers. The *Collected Works* are being published in Toronto in 25 volumes. The first volumes appeared in 1963. A *Bibliography of the Published Writings of John Stuart Mill* was published at Evanston, U.S.A. in 1945 edited by N. Macminn, J. R. Haindo and J. M. McCrimmon.

Many hundreds of biographies, studies and essays have been written about Mill. Many are listed in *The New Cambridge Bibliography of English Literature* (1969, Columns 1551-76). Among these, the following are noteworthy : G. J. Holyoake, *Mill as some of the working classes knew him* (1873); A. Bain, *John Stuart Mill: A Criticism* (1882); W. L. Courtney, *Life of J. S. Mill* (1889); L. Stephen, *English Utilitarians* (Vol. III, 1900); M. A. Hamilton, *John Stuart Mill* (1933); M. Cole, *Makers of the Labour Movement* (1948); F. A. Hayek, *John Stuart Mill and Harriet Taylor; their friendship and subsequent marriage* (1951); K. Britton, *John Stuart Mill* (Penguin, 1953).

JOHN RUSKIN. Of the many collections of Ruskin's works, the only complete edition is *The Library Edition of the Works of John Ruskin* (39 Vols., 1902-12) edited by E. T. Cook and A. D. O. Wedderburn. The dates of the first publication of the works referred to in Edith Morley's essay are : *Stones of Venice* (1851); *Unto this Last* (1862); *Munera Pulveris* (1862); *The Crown of Wild Olive* (1866); *Time and Tide* (1867) and *Fors Clavigera* (1871-84). See also J. Evans and J. H. Whitehouse (eds.), *The Diaries of John Ruskin* (3 Vols., 1956-59); J. D. Rosenberg (ed.), *The Genius of Ruskin* (1963); K. Clark, *Ruskin Today* (1964). Much of the most comprehensive and reliable bibliography is by Cook and Wedderburn in Vol. 38 of the Library edition referred to above.

The most important biographies include : W. G. Collingwood, *The Life and Works of John Ruskin* (2 Vols., 1893); J. A. Hobson, *John Ruskin, Social Reformer* (1898); E. T. Cook, *The Life of John Ruskin* (2 Vols., 1911); F. Harrison, *John Ruskin* (1902); G. B. Shaw, *Ruskin's Politics* (1921); D. Leon, *Ruskin, the Great Victorian* (1949); J. Evans, *John Ruskin* (1954); J. D. Rosenberg, *The Darkening Glass, a portrait of Ruskin's genius* (1961). A brief, well illustrated study suitable for use in schools is J. S. Dearden, *John Ruskin, an illustrated life* (1973).

CHARLES KINGSLEY. The principal works of Kingsley are: various papers contributed to the *Christian Socialist, Politics for the People* and the *Journal of Association* (1848-54); *The Saint's Tragedy* (1848); *Yeast* published as a serial in *Fraser's Magazine* (1848) and in volume form, anonymously in 1851; *Alton Locke* (1850); *Cheap Clothes and Nasty* (1850); *Hypatia* published in Fraser's Magazine (1851) and in volume form in 1853; *Westward Ho!* (1855); *Two Years Ago* (1857); *Poems* (1858); *The Waterbabies* (1862); *Hereward the Wake* (1866); *Collected Essays, Sermons and Lectures, Prose Idylls* (1873, 1880, 1889). His *Collected Works* including *Letters and Memories of his Life* (edited by his wife) were published in 19 volumes (1901-3). For a full bibliography see M. F. Thorp, *Charles Kingsley* (Princeton, 1937) or M. L. Parrish and B. K. Mann, *Charles Kingsley and Thomas Hughes; First Editions in the library at Dormy House* (1936).

The most significant books dealing with the life and work of Kingsley are: M. Kaufmann, *Charles Kingsley, Christian Socialist and Social Reformer* (1892) and *Christian Socialism* (1888); C. W. Stubbs, *Charles Kingsley and the Christian Social Movement* (1899), Conrad Noel, *Socialism in Church History* (1910); W. H. Brown, *Charles Kingsley: the work and influence of Parson Lot* (1924); G. Kendall, *Charles Kingsley and his ideas* (1947); R. B. Martin, *The Dust of Combat, a life of Charles Kingsley* (1960).

WILLIAM MORRIS. Morris's works are too numerous to list here. The *Collected Works* with introductions by May Morris were published in 24 volumes (1910-15) and were reprinted in New York in 1966. Two further volumes under the title *William Morris: artist, writer, Socialist* edited by May Morris were published in 1936. In 1934, the centenary of Morris's birth, G. D. H. Cole edited *William Morris—Stories in prose, stories in verse, shorter poems, lectures and essays.* Other worthwhile selections are: H. Jackson, *William Morris on Art and Socialism: Essays and Lectures* (1947); A. Briggs (ed.), *William Morris: Selected Writings and Designs* (Penguin, 1962). See also P. Henderson (ed.), *The Letters of William Morris to his Family and Friends* (1950). The important bibliographies are: H. B. Forman, *The Books of William Morris described, with some account of his doings in literature and in the allied crafts* (1897); T. Scott, *A Bibliography of the works of William Morris* (1897); R. C. H. Briggs, *Handlist of the public addresses of William Morris to be found in generally accessible publications* (1961).

Of the numerous biographies and studies, the following are recommended : A. Vallance, *William Morris — His art, his writings and his public life—a record* (1897); J. W. Mackail, *The Life of William Morris* (2 Vols., 1889); J. B. Glasier, *William Morris and the early days of the Socialist Movement* (1921); E. P. Thompson, *William Morris, Romantic to Revolutionary* (1955); R. P. Arnot, *William Morris, The man and the myth* (1964); P. Henderson, *William Morris, His life, work and friends* (1967); P. Thompson, *The Life and Work of William Morris* (1967); R. Watkinson, *William Morris as Designer* (1967) and a brief account, excellent for use in schools, R. Tames, *William Morris—an illustrated life—1834-1896* (1972).

NOTES ON CONTRIBUTORS

COHEN, VICTOR, author of the Fabian Tract on *Jeremy Bentham* (first published April 1927) was born in London in 1896. He was educated in England and in France. He saw active service in the first world war and broadcast to France in the second. He has been Senior History Master at Leyton County High School, lecturer in Economics in the extra-mural department of the University of London and Professor in the College of St. Charles, France.

At various times he has been chairman of the Fabian Nursery, London University Labour Party and the Chingford Labour Party. He has edited a number of works in English and French including Disraeli's *Sybil or Two Nations* (1934). Among his more important books are: *The Nineteenth Century—A biographical history* (1932); *Industry and Life—a first book of social economics* (1935); *The Life and Times of Masaryk, the President-Liberator* (1941); *The British Commonweal* (1937); *Economic Society* (1947).

COLE, GEORGE DOUGLAS HOWARD, author of the Fabian Tract on *William Cobbett* (first published in April 1927); the Fabian Tract on *Richard Carlile* (first published in February 1943) and of the Fabian Tracts on *J. Keir Hardie* and *John Burns* included in the volume *Radicals, Reformers and Socialists* (Charles Knight, 1973), was the outstanding socialist writer and thinker of his day. Throughout his life he combined important academic work with the propagation of advanced political and social views in numerous books, pamphlets, articles and speeches. At the same time he took an active part in trade union and political organisations and adult education.

G. D. H. Cole was born in Cambridge in 1889, was educated at St. Paul's School, Hammersmith and Balliol College, Oxford. In 1912 he obtained a prize fellowship at Magdalen College. In 1913 he published his first political work *The World of Labour*.

228 WRITERS AND REBELS

During World War I he became research officer of the Amalgamated Society of Engineers and Honorary secretary of the Fabian Research Department and helped to prepare the Labour case in a number of industrial disputes. After the war Cole returned to teaching and writing as his main occupations. After a period in adult education he returned to Oxford in 1925 as a fellow and tutor of University College and as university Reader in Economics. In October 1944 he was made Chichele Professor of Social and Economic Theory and Fellow of All Souls. In 1957, on retirement from the Chichele Chair, he was made Honorary Fellow of Balliol and Research Fellow of Nuffield College, Oxford.

He married Margaret Postgate in 1918 and in the same year began his regular association with the *New Statesman* which was to last until his death. In 1931 he founded the New Fabian Research Bureau, which, in 1939, amalgamated with the Fabian Society, of which Cole was Chairman (1939-46) and (1948-50). From 1952 he was its President. In the period after 1931 his most important contribution to politics was the lead he gave in research towards framing new and coherent policies for the Labour Party after the 1931 *debâcle*. G. D. H. Cole died in 1959.

Of the hundreds of books and pamphlets by G. D. H. Cole, many of them written in collaboration with Margaret Cole, the most important are : *Self-Government in Industry* (1917); *The Payment of Wages* (1918); *Workshop Organisation* (1923, reprinted 1972); *Life of William Cobbett* (1924, new Edn. 1947); *Life of Robert Owen* (1925, new Edn. 1965); *Short History of the British Working-Class Movement* (1925-7, new Edn. 1948); *Intelligent Man's Guide through World Chaos* (1932); *What Marx Really Meant* (1934, revised 1948 as *The Meaning of Marxism*); *The Condition of Britain* (1937); *Persons and Periods* (1938); *The Common People*—with Raymond Postgate (1938, revised 1946); *British Working-class Politics* (1941); *Chartist Portraits* (1941); *Opinions of William Cobett*—ed. with Margaret Cole (1944); *A Century of Cooperation* (1944); *History of the Labour Party from 1914* (1948); *History of Socialist Thought* (5 Vols., 1953-1960); *Attempts at General Union* (1953); *Case for Industrial Partnership* (1957).

The Biography by Dame Margaret Cole, *The Life of G. D. H.*

Cole (1971), gives details of many other publications, including the titles of over 20 detective novels. Cole's substantial collection of material on the history of the labour movement is now in the Library of Nuffield College, Oxford.

MORLEY, EDITH JULIA, author of the Fabian Tract on *John Ruskin* (first published June 1916) was born in 1875. She was educated privately in London and Hanover, then at King's College for Women and University College London. She lectured at King's College for Women from 1899 to 1914, becoming a Fellow in 1913. In 1901 she also began lecturing at University College, Reading becoming Professor of English Language in 1908. She was a member of the Executive Committee of the Fabian Society and of the English Association.

Among her books were: *Hurd's Letters on Chivalry and Romance* (1911); *Women workers in seven professions* (1912); *Blake, Coleridge and Wordsworth, being selections from Crabb Robinson's remains* (1922); *Correspondence of Crabb Robinson with the Wordsworth Circle* (1927); *Crabb Robinson in Germany* (1929); *The Life and Times of Henry Crabb Robinson* (1935); *Henry Crabb Robinson on Books and their Writers* (1938).

TOWNSHEND, EMILY, author of the Fabian Tract on *William Morris* (first published December 1912) was born in 1849 and educated at Laleham School and Girton College, Cambridge where she was the first student to register. She married in 1873. After her husband's death in 1897 she qualified as a Sanitary Inspector, intending to become a Factory Inspector but found she was past the statutory age. She was an active suffragette and spent two weeks in prison for her activities. As a member of the Fabian Society she was a supporter of H. G. Wells in his efforts to reform the Society and was associated with the group who founded the Fabian Research Department in 1912-13. She resigned in 1915 in sympathy with G. D. H. Cole's Guild Socialist critique of Fabian policy.

Among her printed works were: *The Case for School Nurseries* (with H. H. Slesser) a Fabian Tract (No. 145, 1909); *The Case against the Charity Organisation Society* (1911, Fabian Tract No. 158). She edited *Keeling Letters and Recollections* (1918).

In 1923 she translated from the Italian two works by Odon Por, *Fascism* and *Guilds and Cooperatives in Italy*. Her *Creative Socialism* was published in 1924. For further details of her life and career see *Emily Townshend 1849-1934, Some memoirs for her friends* (1936).

VULLIAMY, COLWYN EDWARD, author of the Fabian Tract on *Charles Kingsley* (first published January 1914) was born in 1886. He was educated privately and studied art under Stanhope A. Forbes (1910-13). He served in France, Macedonia and Turkey in World War I and was the Education Officer of 28th Division 1918-19. His wide interests included archaeology and English and French literature of the 18th century. As an author he wrote books on a wide variety of subjects, as the following selection shows.

Prehistoric Forerunners (1925); *Unknown Cornwall* (1925); *Immortal Man* (1926); *Letters of Tsar Nicholas II* (1929); *Red Archives* (1929); *Archaeology of Middlesex and London* (1930); *Voltaire* (1930); *Rousseau* (1931); *John Wesley* (1931); *James Boswell* (1932); *William Penn* (1933); *Judas Maccabeus* (1934); *Mrs. Thrale of Streatham* (1936); *Royal George (Life of George III)* (1937); *The Outlanders: Imperial Expansion in South Africa* (1938); *Crimea* (1939); *A Short History of the Montagu Puffins* (1941); *Man and the Atom* (1947); *Byron* (1948); *The Onslow Family* (1953) and a number of novels and detective stories.

WEST, JULIUS, author of the Fabian Tract on John Stuart Mill (first published in January 1913) was born in St. Petersburg in 1891 and came to London when he was two months old. He went to Haberdashers' School. On leaving, he became a clerk first at the Board of Trade, then at the Fabian Society. In 1913 he worked briefly for the *New Statesman,* then did freelance journalism, lecturing and preparing material for several books. The first to be published was *Atlantis and Other Poems* (1913).

He tried to join the Army in 1914 but was refused on the grounds that technically he was a Russian citizen. In 1914 he visited Russia as a correspondent and again in 1917 in the early months of the Bolshevik regime. Famine conditions in Russia affected his health which was never good. At the end of the war he contracted influenza which developed into pneumonia and he died at the age of 27.

His most important book was *A History of the Chartist Movement* (1920) where, for the first time, the *Francis Place* collection of documents in the British Museum were thoroughly researched. His other works include a Fabian Tract *The Russian Revolution and British Democracy* (No. 184, 1917); *Soldiers of the Tsar and other sketches and studies of the Russia of Today* (1915); several translations from the Russian and a critical study of G. K. Chesterton.

BIBLIOGRAPHICAL DETAILS OF THE FIRST PUBLICATION OF THE TRACTS INCLUDED IN THIS VOLUME

1. JEREMY BENTHAM (1748-1832) by Victor Cohen (Fabian Tract No. 221, Fabian Biographical Series No. 11). First published April 1927, pp. 19.
2. WILLIAM COBBETT (1763-1835) by G. D. H. Cole (Fabian Tract No. 215, Fabian Biographical Series, No. 9). First published June 1925, pp. 19.
3. RICHARD CARLILE (1790-1843) by G. D. H. Cole (Fabian Biographical Series, No. 13—not included in Tract series). First published February 1943, pp. 37.
4. JOHN STUART MILL (1806-1873) by Julius West (Fabian Tract No. 168, Fabian Biographical Series No. 4). First published June 1913, pp. 23.
5. JOHN RUSKIN AND SOCIAL ETHICS (1819-1900) by Edith J. Morley (Fabian Tract No. 179, Fabian Biographical Series No. 6). First published June 1916, pp. 24.
6. CHARLES KINGSLEY AND CHRISTIAN SOCIALISM (1819-1875) by Colwyn E. Vulliamy (Fabian Tract No. 174, Fabian Biographical Series No. 5). First published January 1914, pp. 27.
7. WILLIAM MORRIS AND THE COMMUNIST IDEAL (1834-1896) by Mrs. Townshend (Fabian Tract No. 167, Fabian Biographical Series No. 3). First published December 1912, pp. 23.

Not reprinted, see p. 12
ROBERT OWEN, IDEALIST (1771-1858) by C. E. M. Joad (Fabian Tract No. 182, Fabian Biographical Series No. 7). First published June 1917, pp. 32.

CHECK-LIST OF THE FABIAN
BIOGRAPHICAL SERIES

In order of publication
1. FRANCIS PLACE, THE TAILOR OF CHARING CROSS
   By St. John G. Ervine.
2. ROBERT OWEN, SOCIAL REFORMER
   By Miss B. L. Hutchins.
3. WILLIAM MORRIS AND THE COMMUNIST IDEAL
   By Mrs. Townshend.
4. JOHN STUART MILL
   By Julius West.
5. CHARLES KINGSLEY AND CHRISTIAN SOCIALISM
   By Colwyn E. Vulliamy.
6. JOHN RUSKIN AND SOCIAL ETHICS
   By Edith J. Morley.
7. ROBERT OWEN, IDEALIST
   By C. E. M. Joad.
8. WILLIAM LOVETT
   By Mrs. L. Barbara Hammond.
9. WILLIAM COBBETT
   By G. D. H. Cole.
10. THOMAS PAINE
    By Kingsley Martin.
11. JEREMY BENTHAM
    By Victor Cohen.
12. JAMES KEIR HARDIE
    By G. D. H. Cole.
13. RICHARD CARLILE
    By G. D. H. Cole.
14. JOHN BURNS
    By G. D. H. Cole.
15. BEATRICE AND SIDNEY WEBB
    By Margaret Cole.

INDEX